THE BOOK OF NEW TESTAMENT WORD STUDIES makes difficult words easily understood. Each word is illustrated with Scriptural cross references. Each word study contains modern word meanings vs. Bible time usage as well as references to the original Greek texts.

THE BOOK OF
NEW TESTAMENT
WORD STUDIES

By

ERIC PARTRIDGE

BARBOUR BOOKS
164 Mill Street
Westwood, New Jersey 07675

ISBN 1-55748-031-1

Published by: BARBOUR AND COMPANY, INC.
164 Mill Street
Westwood, New Jersey 07675

(In Canada, THE CHRISTIAN LIBRARY,
960 The Gateway, Burlington, Ontario L7L 5K7)

EVANGELICAL CHRISTIAN PUBLISHERS ASSOCIATION **ECPA** MEMBER

Printed in the United States of America

ABBREVIATIONS

A.V.: the Authorized Version (1611) of *The Bible*.
adj.: adjective.
adv.: adverb.
C.: Century; as C. 18, the 18th Century.
cf.: compare.
Cruden: *Cruden's Concordance*, revised editions, by Youngman and Irwin.
e.g.: for example.
esp.: especially.
fig.: figurative(ly).
Fr.: French.
Ger.: German.
Gr.: Greek.
Gr. Test.: *The N.T.* in Greek (Oxford University Press edition of 1881).
Hastings: J. Hastings (and others), *Encyclopædia of Religion and Ethics*, 1908–1926.
Heb.: Hebrew.
i.e.: that is.
ibid.: in the same Book of *The Bible*.
Jack and Jill: Ernest Weekley, *Jack and Jill. A Study in Our Christian Names*, 1939.
L.: Latin.
Leclercq: F. Cabrol and H. Leclercq, *Dictionnaire d'archéologie chrétienne et de liturgie*, 1903 ff.
Lewis & S.: Lewis and Short, *A Latin Dictionary*.
Liddell & Scott: Liddell and Scott, *A Greek Dictionary*.
lit.: literal(ly).
M.E.: Middle English (ca. 1100–1500; sometimes narrowed to 1150–1450).
n.: noun.
N.T.: *The New Testament* (in the A.V. unless otherwise stated).

O.E.: Old English (less accurately: Anglo-Saxon).

O.E.D.: *The Oxford English Dictionary*.

O.T.: *The Old Testament* (in the A.V. unless otherwise stated).

Partridge : Eric Partridge, *Name This Child: A Dictionary of Christian Names*, 1936.

prep.: preposition.

R.V.: the Revised Version (1881) of *The New Testament*; sometimes known as the Westminster Version.

sc.: L. *scite*, know!; i.e., please supply (such or such a word, to complete the sense).

Souter: Alexander Souter, *A Pocket Lexicon to the Greek New Testament* (1916; reprint of 1935).

Tyndale: Tyndale's version of *The N.T.*, 1526 (or 1534, if so stated).

v.: verb.

Verdunoy: Chanoine Verdunoy (and others), *Bible Latine-Française*, N.T., 1935.

Vulgate: St. Jerome's Latin version of *The Bible*; completed in 405 A.D.

Wright: W. Aldis Wright, *The Bible Word-Book*, 2nd edition, 1884.

[ ]: this indicates an editorial interpolation or gloss.

=: is (or are) equal or equivalent to; hence, (a certain word or phrase) means.

GLOSSARY

A

abide. To await.

'. . . The Holy Ghost witnesseth in every city, saying that bonds and afflictions abide me' (*Acts*, xx, 23).

From the O.E. *abídan*, 'to wait for, await; remain ready for, watch for, expect' (O.E.D.). The intransitive sense, 'to remain in expectation, wait' arose about a century later. The prevailing modern intransitive sense, 'to continue in existence, to stand firm or sure', did not arise until late in the 14th Century—some four hundred years after the primary O.E. sense appears—and it occurs in *Psalms* (cxix, 90) thus, 'Thou hast established the earth, and it abideth'. The sense, 'to bear, tolerate, put up with' ('I can't abide love-stories!') is now English so familiar as to be almost colloquial.

accomplish. 'To complete or make complete; to fulfil; almost, to comply with', applied to time or number. 'And when eight days were accomplished for the circumcising of the child, his name was called JESUS' (*Luke*, ii, 21). Cf. Shakespeare's 'And all the number of his fair demands | Shall be accomplish'd without contradiction' (*Richard II*, iii, iii, 124).

Through Old Fr. from late L. *accomplere* (*complere*, 'to fill up', hence 'to complete').

Acts. See **Apostles.**

addict oneself. '. . . Ye know the house of Stephanas, that it is the firstfruits of Achaia, and that they have addicted themselves to the ministry of the saints' (1 *Corinthians*, xvi, 15).

I.e., devoted themselves to, given themselves up to (as

servants or adherents or disciples): cf. 'True bishops should addict themselves to a particular flock', 1621; 'We sincerely addict ourselves to Almighty God' (Fuller, 1655). This reflexive use was common ca. 1575–1720. Probably formed from the adjective *addict* (bound; devoted, consecrated), which represents L. *addictus*, 'assigned by decree; bound; devoted' (O.E.D.).

Now used only as participial adj., generally with an unfavourable connotation, as in *addicted to drink*.

adjure. 'But Jesus held his peace. And the high priest answered and said unto him, I adjure thee by the living God, that thou tell us whether thou be the Christ, the Son of God' (*Matthew*, xxvi, 63), cf. *Mark*, v, 7; 'We adjure you by Jesus whom Paul preacheth' (*Acts*, xix, 13).

'To charge earnestly by word or oath' (Cruden); 'to bind by oath, solemnly entreat, conjure' (Wright); perhaps rather to charge or entreat as if under oath, cf. 'The earnest intreaty of my friends daily requesting, importuning, and as it were adjuring me' (T. Morley, 1597: O.E.D.). Deriving from the original sense, 'to put (a person) to his oath, to impose an oath upon' (as in 1 *Kings*, xviii, 10; 1 *Samuel*, xiv, 28; *Joshua*, vi, 26; but apparently not in the N.T.): from L. *adjurare*, 'to swear to (a thing)', hence in late L., 'to put (a person) to an oath'.

admiration. 'And I saw the woman drunken with the blood of the saints, and with the blood of the martyrs of Jesus: and when I saw her, I wondered with great admiration' (*Revelation*, xvi, 6).

Cf. 'Admiration is the daughter of Ignorance' (Fuller, 1642: O.E.D.).

I.e., astonishment: a sense common in C. 16–17. Via Fr. from L. *admiratio*, itself from *admirari*, 'to wonder at'.

adventure oneself. 'And certain of the chief'—i.e. the chief men—'of Asia, which were his friends, sent unto him, desiring him that he would not adventure himself into the theatre' (*Acts*, xix, 31).

To risk oneself, i.e. to venture: this sense, which arose in C. 14, was common in C. 15–17, rare in C. 18, archaic in C. 19, and obsolete in C. 20.

From Old Fr. *aventurer*, itself from the noun *aventure* (our *adventure*), which represents L. (*res*) *adventura*, (a thing), 'about to happen' (to a person), from *advenire*, 'to happen'. Cf. 'Thinking it unwise to adventure themselves abroad' (Potter, 1697: O.E.D.).

adversary. 1, adj., 'adverse, opposing', hence 'inimical, hostile', as in 'armed against all adversary powers' (heading to 2 *Corinthians*, x).

2, n. 'Opponent (in a lawsuit)', as in 'Agree with thine adversary quickly, whiles thou art in the way with him; lest at any time the adversary deliver thee to the judge, and the judge deliver thee to the officer, and thou be cast into prison' (*Matthew*, v, 25; cf. *Luke*, xii, 58, and xviii, 3).

The adj., deriving from the n., was current in late C. 14–18; in C. 19–20, extant only in law (*adversary suit*, a law-case in which an opposing party appears).

The n. comes from the L. adj., *adversarius*, 'opposed, opponent', itself from *adversus*, 'against'. *The Adversary* is the foe of mankind, i.e. the Devil; as in 1 *Peter*, v, 8, 'Be sober, be vigilant; because your adversary the devil, as a roaring lion, walketh about, seeking whom he may devour': Gr. Test., ὁ ἀντίδικος ὑμῶν διάβολος, ὡς λέων ὠρυόμενος, περιπατεῖ ξητῶν τινὰ καταπιεῖν: Vulgate, 'adversarius vester diabolus tanquam leo rugiens circuit, quaerens quam devoret'.

affect; affectioned; affections. 'They zealously affect you, but not well; yea, they would exclude you, that ye might affect them' (*Galatians*, iv, 17); 'Be kindly affectioned one to another with brotherly love . . .' (*Romans*, xii, 10); 'And they that are Christ's have crucified the flesh with the affections and lusts' (*Galatians*, v, 24)—cf. *Romans*, i, 26 ('vile affections'). *Affect* here='show a liking for' (mid C. 16–early 19): via Fr., from L. *affectare*, 'to aim at'; *affectioned*='disposed', esp. 'well

3

disposed' (ca. 1530–1700); from *affection*+*ed*; prob. on Fr. *affectionné*; *affections* here='passions'; via Fr. from L. *affectio*, 'disposition, inclination'.

after. According to. See quotation at **certify,** and cf. the first quotation at **mortify.**

This sense, which corresponds to Fr. *d'après* (lit., 'from after'), is archaic.

agree to. 'Thou art a Galilæan, and thy speech agreeth thereto' (*Mark* xiv, 70); 'To him they agreed' (*Acts*, v, 40); 'To this agree the words of the prophets, as it is written' (*ibid.*, xv, 15).

To agree with a person, as in the second quotation; with what has been written, as in the third; and with a fact, as in the first.

Agree to (or *unto*) belongs to C. 16–18, and its sense, defined more precisely, is 'to be consistent with, to correspond with', as in the first and third quotations; or, as in the second, 'to accede to the opinion of (a person)', which merges with the sense of *agree with*, 'to concur with (a person)'.

Via Old Fr. *agréer*, and ultimately from L. *gratus*, 'agreeable' (O.E.D.); the construction *agree to* is in imitation of the Fr. *agréer à*.

alien. '(Who) turned to flight'—i.e., put to flight—'the armies of the aliens' (*Hebrews*, xi, 34): i.e., of the foreigners.— 'At that time ye were without Christ, being aliens from the commonwealth of Israel' (*Ephesians*, ii, 12): i.e., 'persons excluded from (the citizenship and privileges of a nation)', as the O.E.D. makes clear: a theological and religious-history sense.

Alien, n., is the adj. used absolutely or substantivized. Via Old Fr. *al*(*l*)*ien* from L. *alienus*, 'belonging to another person' (cf. Shakespeare's 'Every alien pen hath got my use', Sonnet 78), hence 'belonging to another place' (O.E.D.).

allow. 'Truly ye bear witness that ye allow the deeds of your fathers: for they indeed killed them, and ye build their sepulchres' (*Luke*, xi, 48).

4

I.e., that ye sanction, approve, the deeds of your fathers. This *allow* comes, via Fr., from L. *allaudare*, 'to praise'; and the two nuances—'approve', 'sanction'—were current in C. 14–18, this sense being contemporary with the very closely allied one, 'to praise, to commend'. (The other *allow*—'to grant or bestow; to give credit for'—comes, via the same Old Fr. *alouer*, from L. *allocare*, 'to allocate' (O.E.D.).

alms; almsdeed. 'Who seeing Peter and John about to go into the temple asked an alms' (*Acts*, iii, 3); 'Now there was at Joppa a certain disciple named Tabitha, which by interpretation is called Dorcas: this woman was full of good works and almsdeeds which she did' (*ibid.*, ix, 36).

An *alms* (for properly and originally the word is a singular) is a charitable donation, a gift of charity, as here. In *Acts*, x, 4, 'Thy prayers and thine alms are come up for a memorial before God', *alms* is a plural, with sense 'things given in charity' (Gr. ἐλεημοσύναι). *Alms* comes via Germanic from a Low Latin perversion of L. *elemosina*, which = Gr. ἐλεημοσύνη, 'compassionateness'.

An *almsdeed* (better *alms-deed*) is a deed of charity to the poor, esp. if for a religious motive; the word is archaic.

amazed; amazement. 'And he taketh with them Peter and James and John, and began to be sore amazed, and to be very heavy' (sorrowful), *Mark*, xiv, 33; 'Even as Sara obeyed Abraham, calling him lord; whose daughters ye are, as long as ye do well, and are not afraid with any amazement' (1 *Peter*, iii, 6).

I.e., bewildered; bewilderment, confusion: common in late C. 16–mid 18. 'To *amaze*' is from *maze*, 'a state of bewilderment'; the *a* is almost certainly an intensive. *Amazement* derives from that verb.

The C. 20 ascending scale is: *surprise—astonishment—amazement—astoundment* (rare) or *astoundedness* (uncommon); *surprised—astonished—amazed—astounded*. Note that *wonder* (*wonderment*), which connotes thought, reflection, stands apart.

ambassage. 'Or else, while the other is yet a great way off, he sendeth an ambassage, and desireth conditions of peace' (*Luke*, xiv, 32). An embassy: from L. *ambo*, 'both'.

amethyst. See the quotation at **chrysolite.**

In C. 13–16, *ametist(e)*, *amatist*, *amatyst(e)*, on the analogy of its immediate origin, the Old Fr. *ametiste* (or *amatiste*). In the late C. 16, the English word 'began to be refashioned after the Latin' *amethystus*, which is a transliteration of the Gr. adj. ἀμέθυστος, 'not drunken', from the privative ἀ and μεθύσκειν, 'to intoxicate': 'from a notion that it was a preventive of intoxication' (O.E.D.), or from the fact that 'the best specimens are the colour of unmixed wine' (Souter).

anon. 'But he that received the seed into stony places, the same is he that heareth the word, and anon with joy receiveth it' (*Matthew*, xiii, 20); cf. *Mark*, i, 20.

At once; instantly; immediately; straightway, forthwith. From O.E. *on ane*, 'in one', i.e. in one mind, mood, act, movement, moment: cf. the C. 20 slang, *to guess a thing in one*, i.e. in one guess, hence immediately. Arising ca. 1000, it has in this—the correct—sense, been archaic since C. 17. Its modern sense (now affected and cheaply elegant) is 'soon; in a little while' (O.E.D.).

Apostles, the. *The Acts of the Apostles:* the records or transactions of the doings of the Apostles. (This sense of *acts* is a translation of the L. *acta*.)

The Gr. Test. title is: *ΠΡΑΞΕΙΣ ΤΩΝ ΑΠΟΣΤΟΛΩΝ:* The Deeds of the Apostles. Verdunoy, by the way, remarks that 'Le titre "Actes d'apôtres", beaucoup mieux garanti que "Actes des apôtres", est plus adéquat au contenu du livre; ce n'est pas, en effet, l'histoire de *tous* les apôtres que l'auteur raconte, mais seulement quelques faits saillants dans le ministère de Pierre et de Paul.'

Apostle:—'And he gave some, apostles; and some, prophets; and some, evangelists; and some, pastors and teachers' (*Ephesians*, iv, 11): Gr. Test., καὶ αὐτὸς ἔδωκε τοὺς μὲν ἀποστόλους, τοὺς δὲ προφητάς, τοὺς δὲ εὐαγγελιστάς, τοὺς δὲ ποιμένας καὶ διδασκάλους : Vulgate, 'Et ipse dedit quosdam quidem apostolos, quosdam autem prophetas, alios vero evangelistas, alios autem pastores, et doctores.'

Apostle comes from Old Fr. *apostle* (C. 12), whereas O.E. *apostol* came direct from L. *apostolus*. The L. word merely transliterates Gr. ἀπόστολος, which, lit. 'a messenger', became in the N.T. 'a delegate': 'one commissioned by another to represent him in some way, especially a man sent out by Jesus Christ Himself to preach the Gospel, *an apostle*' (Souter); ἀπόστολος derives from ἀποστέλλειν , 'to send away' (hence, in N.T., 'to commission'). The Apostles are 'the twelve witnesses whom Jesus Christ sent forth to preach his Gospel to the world; also the subsequently-commissioned Barnabas (*Acts*, xiii, 2; xiv, 14), and Paul, the "Apostle of the Gentiles" ' (O.E.D.).

approve. 1. To prove or demonstrate, as in 'Ye men of Israel, hear these words; Jesus of Nazareth, a man approved of God among you by miracles and wonders and signs, which God did by him, as ye yourselves also know' (*Acts*, ii, 22), and 'But in all things approving ourselves as the ministers of God, in much patience, in afflictions, in necessities, in distresses' (2 *Corinthians*, vi, 4).

2. To try or test; to put to the proof, to put to the test of experience, as in 'That ye may approve things that are excellent; that ye may be sincere and without offence till the day of Christ' (*Philippians*, i, 10) and 'And knowest his will, and approvest the things that are more excellent, being instructed out of the law' (*Romans*, ii, 18).

With sense 1, cf. Shakespeare's 'In religion, | What damned error, but some sober brow | Will bless it and approve it with a text?' (*The Merchant of Venice*, III, ii, 79), where the precise nuance is 'to confirm, to corroborate'. And with sense 2, cf. Shakespeare's 'Nay, task me to my word; approve me, lord' (1 *Henry IV*, IV, i, 9: Wright).

Both senses come from Old Fr. *aprover* (= Modern Fr. *approuver*, for sense 1; = *éprouver*, for sense 2), from L.

approbare (*ad* + *probare*, from *probus*, 'good'), 'to assent to as good', *probare* being 'to try, hence to ascertain, the goodness of' (O.E.D.).

apt. 'A bishop then must be blameless, the husband of one wife, vigilant, sober, of good behaviour, given to hospitality, apt to teach' (1 *Timothy*, iii, 2; cf. 2 *Timothy*, ii, 24).

In the Gr. Test., 'apt to teach' is represented by the one word διδακτικός, 'able to teach'; the Vulgate has *doctor*, which Verdunoy renders as 'capable d'enseigner'. In the phrase *apt to teach*, there is not only an explicit ability but also an implicit preparedness and willingness; there is a merging of 'fitness' and 'inclination'.

are not. 'Rachel weeping for her children . . . because they are not' (*Matthew*, ii, 18), i.e. are not alive; cf. 'Enoch walked with God: and he was not, for God took him' (*Genesis*, v, 24), Shakespeare's 'For those that were, it is not square [i.e., equitable] to take | On those that are, revenges' (*Timon of Athens*, v, iv, 36), and Byron's 'Tyrants and sycophants have been and are'.

This nuance, 'to exist in life, i.e. to be alive, to live', constitutes the human aspect of the generic sense, 'to have a place in the objective universe, to be within the realm of fact', as in Bacon's 'Men create oppositions, which are not' (i.e., they imagine them), Dryden's 'Troy is no more, and Ilium was a town', and Carlyle's 'So much that was not is beginning to be' (in reference to the French Revolution).

Wright; the O.E.D.

as = 'as if' in *Acts*, x, 11; *Revelation*, v, 6, and xiii, 3. Wright compares Shakespeare's 'Men, wives and children stare, cry out and run | As it were doomsday' (*Julius Cæsar*, III, i, 98) and 'And my fell of hair | Would at a dismal treatise rouse and stir | As life were in it' (*Macbeth*, v, v, 13).

as it were, in *Revelation*, viii, 10 ('The second angel . . . as it were a great mountain . . . was cast into the sea'), = *as if he were*, i.e. *like* (preposition): an archaic formula.

asp. 'Their throat is an open sepulchre; with their tongues they have used deceit; the poison of asps is under their lips' (*Romans*, iii, 13).

The asp is a small serpent, venomous and hooded; and it belongs to Egypt (and Libya), and is also known as the *Naja Haje*; its bite kills within a few minutes (cf. Ruskin's 'There is more poison in an ill-kept drain . . . than in the deadliest asp of Nile').

In C. 14–15, the English form of the word was the Latin one: *aspis* (a transliteration of Gr. ἀσπίς); Tyndale, 1526, has 'the poyson of Aspes'; only in the early C. 17, however, did *asp* become a genuinely English word. Shakespeare, for instance, in 1606 uses *aspick* (Fr. *aspic*); Florio, 1611, defines Italian *aspide* as 'an aspike or aspe'; Tennyson, in 1830, has 'Shewing the aspic's bite' (O.E.D.).

assay. 'By faith they passed through the Red Sea as by dry land: which the Egyptians assaying to do were drowned' (*Hebrews*, xi, 29).—Cf. *Acts*, ix, 26 and xvi, 7.

To make an attempt; to venture; set oneself to. These intransitive nuances, which arose in C. 14, are all obsolete. The modern form is *essay* (now rather literary).

From Old Fr. *as(s)aier*, or *as(s)ayer*, ultimately from L. *exagium*, 'a weighing', which is 'used in Romanic in wider sense of "examination, trial, testing" ' (O.E.D.).

assure. 'And hereby we know that we are of the truth, and shall assure our hearts before him' (*1st Epistle of John*, iii, 19).

Wright explains *assure*, in this passage, as 'to convince, to persuade', but the sense appears rather to be, 'to give confidence or courage to'—a sense current ca. 1370–1630, and then archaic.

Via Old Fr. from late L. *adsecurare* (on Classical L. *securus*, 'safe').

at one; atonement. 'And the next day he shewed himself unto them as they strove, and would have set them at one again, saying, Sirs, ye are brethren; why do ye wrong one to another?' (*Acts*, vii, 26).—'We also joy in God through our

9

Lord Jesus Christ, by whom we have now received the atonement' (*Romans*, v, 11): Gr. Test., δι' οὗ νῦν τὴν καταλλαγὴν
ἐλάβομεν: Vulgate, 'per quem nunc reconciliationem
accepimus'.

To set at one is 'to reconcile'; *to be at one* is 'to be reconciled,
to be agreed, to be united'; *atonement* = 'at-one-ment',
ment being a common suffix expressive of action, means or
instrument of action, or result of action: as in *abridgement,
aliment, fragment*. The noun *onement*, 'physical union; hence,
reconciliation', preceded *atonement*; 'He should . . . reconcile
himself and make an onement with God' affords an interesting
sidelight. The verb *atone* being later than the noun, *atonement*
is either *at-onement* or *atone-ment*; 'to be *at one*' was often
written '. . . *atone*'. In course of time, the pronunciation
changed from 'at-one-ment' to 'a-tone-ment'. Originally,
atonement signified both 'the condition of being *at one* with
others', i.e. 'in concord or harmony with them', and 'the
action of setting persons *at one*', i.e. of reconciling them. Here
arose the senses 'expiation' ('The best atonement he can make
. . . is to warn others', Addison) and 'propitiation of God by
expiation of sin' (see *Leviticus*, i, 4). None of the various
theological senses 'reconciliation, propitiation, expiation', as
applied to the redemptive work of Christ, occurs in any
version whatsoever of the N.T., the O.E.D. tells us; in the
passage cited at the head of this entry, *atonement* = 'reconciliation or restoration of friendly relations between God and
sinners', a sense rarely used after ca. 1660.

attendance. 'Till I come, give attendance to reading, to
exhortation, to doctrine' (1 *Timothy*, iv, 13).

Attention: a sense current ca. 1370–1800; rare after
ca. 1620. Via Old Fr. *attendance*, from L. *attendere* (*tendere*,
'to stretch'): the psychological origin—the semantics—being,
'the stretching of one's mind' in the effort of concentration.

Cf. 'Men generally think that . . . attendance unto the
word, is for old age', Thomas Taylor, *A Commentarie upon the
Epistle of St Paul to Titus*, 1612, in reference to *Titus*, ii, 6
(O.E.D.).

avenge of is archaic for *avenge (up)on* in 'Avenge me of mine adversary' (*Luke*, xviii, 3).

avouch. 'Christ avoucheth his authority by a question of John's baptism' (*Luke*, xx, heading); cf. the heading to *Acts*, iv, '. . . Peter boldly avouching the lame man to be healed by the name of Jesus.'

Stronger than 'acknowledge', stronger even than 'avow', *avouch* in these two passages='to declare, to affirm'.

From Old Fr. *avochier*, itself from Late L. *advocare*, 'to call to or upon' (especially 'to call in as a defender—or as a patron'). It is thus a doublet of *avow*.

await, n. 'But their laying await was known of Saul. And they watched the gates day and night to kill him' (*Acts*, ix,24).

To *lay await* is the C. 16-mid 17 form—cf. the C. 14 *lie in await*—of the phrase now represented by *lie in wait*, 'to be in ambush'. By itself *await* is 'a lying in wait or waylaying with hostile intent; ambush, ambuscade; a snare, plot' (O.E.D.): obsolete by the end of the 17th Century.

Tyndale, 1526, 'Their awayte was knowen of Saul';

R.V., 'Their plot . . .'

The word comes direct from Old Norman Fr. *await* or *aweit*, which corresponds to proper Old Fr. *aguait*, itself from the v. *aguaitier*, a Frenchifying of Old High Ger. *wahten* (Modern Ger. *wachten*): for the change from Old Fr. *gu* to English *w*, cf. **ward,** n.

B

babbler; babbling. 'Then certain philosophers of the Epicureans, and of the Stoicks, encountered him. And some said, what will this babbler say? other some,'—i.e., some others, certain others—'He seemeth to be a setter forth of strange gods: because he preached unto them Jesus, and the resurrection' (*Acts*, xvii, 18); 'O Timothy, keep that which is committed to thy trust, avoiding profane and vain babblings, and oppositions of science falsely so called' (1 *Timothy*, vi, 20).

A prater, a foolish or idle talker; idle talk (idle talking), foolish chatter. Both words derive directly from 'to *babble*', an echoic verb: cf. Low Ger. *babbelen* and the Fr. *babiller*: apparently it occurs in English as early as anywhere else (O.E.D.).

Babylon. *Revelation*, xvii, heading, 'A woman arrayed in purple and scarlet, with a golden cup in her hand, sitteth upon the beast, which [the woman, not the beast] is great Babylon, the mother of all abominations'; verse 5, 'And upon her forehead was a name written, MYSTERY, BABYLON THE GREAT, THE MOTHER OF HARLOTS AND ABOMINATIONS OF THE EARTH'.

This, the mystical Babylon of the Apocalypse, is based on the magnificent Babylon of history—the capital of the Chaldee Empire. In theological polemics, Babylon is the papal power (or its seat, Rome): to Protestants. To Roman Catholics, it is an historical city. *The Modern Babylon* is London.

The Heb. *Babel* becomes the Gr. Βαβυλών, transliterated into L. as *Babylon*. The Heb. form probably represents the Assyrian *bab-ilu*, 'gate of God', or *bab-ili*, 'gate of the gods': cf. *Bab el Mandeb*, Arabic for 'The Gate of Tears'. See esp. Sir James Frazer, *Folklore in the Old Testament*, 1918.

backside. 'And I saw in the right hand of him that sat on the throne a book written within and on the backside, sealed with seven seals' (*Revelation*, v, 1): i.e., on the back. As the back part, the rear, e.g. of a house, *backside* is now a provincialism.

Lit., the 'side' at the back; the part at the back.

band. A body of soldiers, as in 'There was a certain man in Cæsarea called Cornelius, a centurion of the band called the Italian band' (*Acts*, x, 1).

Via French, it is of Germanic origin; ultimately of the same origin as **bands** (q.v.): a *band* (or *bond*) 'binds'; a *band* (of men) is a 'binding' of men 'bound' together in interest. This *band* does not appear in English until late C. 15.

band, v. To combine, as in 'And when it was day, certain of
the Jews banded together, and bound themselves under a
curse,'—merely an oath, not a malediction—'saying that they
would neither eat nor drink till they had killed Paul' (*Acts*,
xxiii, 12): Vulgate, 'Collegerunt se quidam ex Judæis'.

Either from Fr. *bander* or direct from **band,** n., this verb is
generally, as here, intransitive.

bands. 'On the morrow, because he [a Roman captain]
would have known'—i.e., wished to know—'the certainty
wherefore he [Paul] was accused of the Jews, he loosed him
from his bands, and commanded the chief priests and all their
council to appear, and brought Paul down, and set him before
them' (*Acts*, xxii, 30); also in *Luke*, viii, 29; *Acts*, xvi, 26; and
Colossians, ii, 19.

I.e., material chains—bonds. After C. 17, the word was
archaic.

'*Band* and *bond* were at first merely phonetic variants'
(O.E.D.).

From Old Norse, the word is connected with 'to *bind*'.

baptist, as in *John the Baptist*.

John the Baptizer—the forerunner of Jesus Christ—was so
called because of his institution of baptism as a religious rite
of purification and preparation: 'Sein Johan . . . was Godes
baptiste' (St John, as baptizer, was God's deputy), *Ancrene
Riwle*, a religious work of the early 13th Century.

The sect of *Baptists* were in C. 17–18 called *Ana*baptists by
their opponents, for they insist on a re-baptism.

Baptist comes, via Old Fr., from L. *baptista*, itself from
Gr. βαπτιστής the agential n. of βαπτίξειν 'to baptize':
'βαπτίξω, lit. *I dip, submerge*, but specifically of ceremonial
dipping (whether immersion or affusion [a pouring-on]), *I
baptize*' (Souter).

On *baptism* see Cruden; Hastings and Sir James Frazer are
admirable on the practice.

barbarian; barbarous people. 'Therefore if I know not
the meaning of the voice, I shall be unto him that speaketh a

barbarian, and he that speaketh shall be a barbarian unto me'
(1 *Corinthians*, xiv, 11); 'And the barbarous people shewed
us no little kindness: for they kindled a fire, and received us
every one, because of the present rain, and because of the
cold' (*Acts*, xxviii, 2).

A foreigner; foreigners. In neither passage is there any
connotation of barbarism in its modern sense of 'uncivilized
ignorance and rudeness'. In mid C. 16–17, the predominant
senses of *barbarian* and *barbarous* were 'a foreigner, one whose
language and customs differ from the speakers' and 'speaking
a foreign language' (O.E.D.). The Gr. Test. has βάρβαρος
and οἵ τε βάρβαροι; the Vulgate, *barbarus* and *barbari* ('les
indigènes parlant punique, et non grec ou latin', Verdunoy).
In the N.T., in short, the sense of *barbarian* is 'one who speaks
neither Greek nor Latin'; of *barbarous*, merely 'foreign'.
Etymologically, the Gr. βάρβαρος (*barbaros*) has reference to
ba-ba as a reduplication characteristic of stammering; cf. L.
balbus, 'stammering' (O.E.D.). Barbarians stammered when
they spoke Greek.

base. 'And base things of the world, and things which are
despised, hath God chosen, yea, and things which are not, to
bring to nought things that are' (1 *Corinthians*, i, 28); 'Now I
Paul myself beseech you by the meekness and gentleness of
Christ, who in presence am base among you, but being absent
am bold toward you' (2 *Corinthians*, x, 1); 'But the Jews,
which believed not, moved with envy, took unto them
certain lewd fellows of the baser sort, and gathered a company, and set all the city upon an uproar, and assaulted the
house of Jason, and sought to bring them out to the people'
(*Acts*, xvii, 5).

From the Fr. *bas* (late L. *bassus*, short or low), *base*
means 'of humble birth', but not necessarily—nor even by
implication—worthless—much less, wicked.

be, 'to be alive; to exist'. See **are not.**

bear record. See **record.**

beast. A viper, as in 'And he shook off the beast into the fire, and felt no harm' (*Acts*, xxviii, 5).—A living creature, especially one in the likeness of an animal, as in *Revelation*, iv, 6–7, 'And before the throne there was a sea of glass like unto crystal: and in the midst of the throne, and round about the throne, were four beasts full of eyes before and behind. And the first beast was like a lion, and the second beast like a calf, and the third beast had a face as a man, and the fourth beast was like a flying eagle.'

From Old Fr. *beste*, which = L. *bestia*.

'Used to translate Gr. ξῶον or L. *animal*, esp. in versions of the Bible' (O.E.D.).

beast, number of the. See **number of the beast.**

because. In order that.

'And the multitude rebuked them, because they should hold their peace: but they cried the more, saying, Have mercy on us, O Lord, thou son of David' (*Matthew*, xx, 31).

This sense of *because* has been obsolete since the 17th Century in S.E.; it is, however, extant in dialect.

behalf, on this. On this account, on account of this.

'Yet if any man suffer as a Christian, let him not be ashamed; but let him glorify God on this behalf' (1 *Peter*, iv, 16).

Cf. Shakespeare's 'And in that behalf . . . we single you | As our best-moving fair solicitor' (*Love's Labour's Lost*, II, i, 27).

For the modern distinction between *in behalf of* and *on behalf of*, see my book on English usage and abusage.

beryl. See the quotation at **chrysolite.**

A pale-green, transparent precious stone. 'When of pale bluish green it is called an *aquamarine*; its yellow or yellowish varieties are the chrysoberyl, and, perhaps, the chrysoprase and chrysolite of the ancients. (The name is used in early literature without scientific precision . . .)', O.E.D.

Via Fr. from L. *beryllus* from Gr. βήρυλλος (probably of foreign origin: cf. Arabic and Persian *ballur*, crystal).—As a baptismal name, *Beryl* hardly antedates the C. 19.

bestow. 1. To *stow* away, put in a place (esp. a place of safety); hence, to dispose of. 'And he spake a parable unto them, saying, The ground of a certain rich man brought forth plentifully: And he thought within himself, saying, What shall I do, because I have no room where to bestow my fruits? And he said, This will I do: I will pull down my barns and build greater; and there will I bestow all my fruits and my goods' (*Luke*, xii, 16–18). Here, *fruits* = 'vegetable products in general, that are fit to be used as food by men and animals' (O.E.D.).

2. To lay out (goods or money), to expend (them or it); i.e., to *place* (goods or money) as investment. 'And though I bestow all my goods to feed the poor, and though I give my body to be burned, and have not charity, it profiteth nothing' (1 *Corinthians*, xiii, 3).

The second sense follows from the first. The M.E. verb *stow*, 'to place', derives from the O.E. noun, *stow*, 'a place' (cf. *Stow on the Wold*).

Bethlehem. 'Now when Jesus was born in Bethlehem of Judæa ...' (*Matthew*, ii, 1); 'Hath not the scripture said; That Christ cometh of the seed of David, and out of the town of Bethlehem, where David was?' (*John*, vii, 42).

Beth is a common first element in Jewish place-names (there must be at least fifteen in *The Bible* alone); it means 'house' (? also 'a group of houses'), as in *Bethel* ('the house of God'), *Bethlehem* ('the house of bread—or of war'), *Bethsaida* ('the house of fruits—or hunters').

bewray. 'And after a while came unto him they that stood by, and said to Peter, Surely thou also art one of them; for thy speech bewrayeth thee' (*Matthew*, xxvi, 73).

Here, *bewray* = to reveal or expose the true character of; cf. 'A man's speech and gesture will bewray his thoughts', Archbishop Edwin Sandys, a sermon preached in 1585; 'Here comes the queen, whose looks bewray her anger', where *bewray* = 'reveal' or 'indicate'.

'Probably more or less of a conscious archaism since the

17th Century; the ordinary modern equivalent is *expose'*
(O.E.D.).

M.E. *bewreien*: intensive *be* + O.E. *wreian*, 'to accuse or
unfavourably expose': of common Germanic stock.

bibber. See the quotation at **wine** and cf. *Luke*, vii, 34, 'The
Son of man is come eating and drinking; and ye say, Behold
a gluttonous man, and a winebibber, a friend of publicans
and sinners!'

A *bibber* is a tippler, one who drinks too frequently. From
the now archaic *bib*, 'to drink'; esp., 'to drink frequently',
itself probably from L. *bibere*, 'to drink'.

blase or **blaze,** the former being the earlier. To divulge,
make known. 'But he went out, and began to publish it
much,'—i.e., make it very public—'and to blaze abroad the
matter, insomuch'—to such an extent—'that Jesus could no
more openly enter into the city . . .' (*Mark*, i, 45).

From the sense, 'to proclaim (as with a trumpet)', itself
from the sense, 'to blow (e.g., with a musical instrument)':
cf. the O.E. *blæst*, a blast or blowing (O.E.D.).

bondmaid. A female slave, as in *Galatians*, iv, 22, 'For it is
written, that Abraham had two sons, the one by a bondmaid,
the other by a freewoman'.

In *Genesis*, xxi, 10, the word is *bondwoman*; cf. *bondman,
bondservant, bondslave*, all of which mean 'a slave', and *bond-
service* (1 *Kings*, ix, 21), 'enforced service', i.e. slavery.

Here, *bond* = *band*, 'a shackle, fetter, manacle'. In this
sense, both *band* and *bond* are archaic.

bottomless pit, the, which occurs seven times in *Revelation*
(e.g. ix, 1 and 2), is a rendering of the Gr. τὸ φρέαρ τοῦ
ἀβύσσου, lit. 'the well of the abyss (or, unfathomable depth)',
which in the Vulgate becomes *puteum abyssi*. Concerning
ἄβυσσος, Souter glosses thus, 'an especially Jewish conception,
the home of the dead and of evil spirits'.

bowels. 'For God is my record [= witness], how greatly I
long after you all in the bowels of Jesus Christ' (*Philippians*,

i, 8); 'If there be therefore any consolation in Christ, if any comfort of love, if any fellowship of the Spirit, if any bowels and mercies, Fulfil ye my joy, that ye be likeminded, having the same love, being of one accord, of one mind' (*ibid.*, ii, 1–2).

'The bowels were supposed by the old anatomists to be the seat of the emotions'—or rather, of the tender, the sympathetic emotions. 'The usage was transferred to our language from the translations of the Bible', as in 'There is no lady of more softer bowels' (Shakespeare, *Troilus and Cressida*, II, ii, 11) and 'Thou thing of no bowels, thou!' (*ibid.*, II, i, 54): Wright. This is an archaism—or, at best, a literarism.

From Old Fr. *boel* (or *bouel* or *buel*), itself from Late L. *botellus*, 'a sausage' (in Low L., 'a small intestine': O.E.D.).

brass. 'Provide neither gold, nor silver, nor brass in your purses' (*Matthew*, x, 9).

Collective for 'copper or bronze coins': C. 16–18. Tyndale uses it in 1526 in his rendering of this passage. As 'cash', *brass* is a slang (when not a dialectal) term that arose ca. 1590.

'O.E. *bræs*, of unknown origin' (O.E.D.).

broided. Braided.

(Of women) 'with broided hair' (1 *Timothy*, ii, 9).

Broid, 'to plait, interweave', belongs to mid C. 14–mid 17; it is a variant of *braid*, which, radically (in the common Germanic stock), signifies 'to pull quickly hither and thither' (O.E.D.).

buffet, v. 'And lest I should be exalted above measure through the abundance of the revelations, there was given to me a thorn in the flesh, the messenger of Satan to buffet me, lest I should be exalted above measure' (2 *Corinthians*, xii, 7).

I.e., to strike me. *Buffet* is used esp. of striking with the hand. i.e., to cuff or thump. Perhaps from the synonymous Fr. *buffeter*; ultimately, it is an echo word.

Gr. Test., ἐδόθη μοι σκόλοψ τῇ σαρκί, ἄγγελος Σατᾶν ἵνα με κολαφίξῃ, ἵνα μὴ ὑπεραίρωμαι : ⸀κολαφίξω, *I strike with*

18

the fist; hence, *I maltreat violently*' (Souter).—Vulgate, 'qui me colaphizet' ('qui me souffletât', Verdunoy, who glosses it as 'frapper à corps de poings').—Cf. the virulent Bentley's 'They must be bang'd and buffeted into reason' (1692).

builded (*Luke*, xvii, 28; *Ephesians*, ii, 22; *Hebrews*, iii, 3 and 4) is archaic for *built*, the preterite and past participle of *build*. Not much used after C. 17. In 'He (or they) builded better than he (or they) knew' it is a literarism—almost a literary cliché.

burn, v.i. See at **contain** (para. 3).

by. 1. In reference to; esp., in adverse reference to, i.e., against.

'For I know nothing by myself; yet am I not hereby justified: but he that judgeth me is the Lord' (1 *Corinthians*, iv, 4); i.e., 'am not conscious of guilt in the things laid [or charged] against me, yet am I not justified by that consciousness of rectitude, &c.' (Wright).

A fairly frequent M.E. use of *by*.

2. During.

'O ye house of Israel, have ye offered to me slain beasts and sacrifices, by the space of forty years in the wilderness?' (*Acts*, vii, 42; cf. *ibid.*, xiii, 21—xix, 10—xx, 31; *Revelation* xiv, 20).

Cf. Langland (*Piers Plowman*, B text, vi, 103), 'I wil worschip ther-with treuthe bi my lyve' (during my life, all my life).

This too is a fairly common M.E. usage.

C

Calvary. 'And when they were come to the place, which is called Calvary, there they crucified him, and the malefactors, one on the right hand, and the other on the left' (*Luke*, xxiii, 33): Gr. Test., Καὶ ὅτε ἦλθον ἐπὶ τὸν τόπον τὸν καλούμενον Κρανίον, lit., 'the place called [the] Skull',—not, as at *Matthew*, xxvii, 33, Κρανίον, 'of a Skull' (see *Golgotha*) : Vulgate,

'Et postquam venerunt in locum qui vocatur Calvariæ, ibi crucifixerent eum' (Verdunoy, 'Lorsqu'ils furent arrivés au lieu appelé Crâne [as in the Greek], ils l'y crucifièrent').

Calvary is 'the place of a skull': 'skull' in Latin being *calvaria*, 'used to translate Aramaic *gogultho* or *gogoltha* "the skull"' (Heb. *gulgoleth* skull, poll), in Gr. transliteration γολγοθά [Golgotha], the name of the mount of the Crucifixion, near Jerusalem' (O.E.D.): cf. L. *calvus*, 'bald' (and *calvities*, 'baldness'), a skull being bald.

Hence, *calvary*, a life-size representation of the Crucifixion, in the open air and generally on raised ground; a chapel of devotion; and a series of representations, in cathedral or chapel, of the Passion: these are Roman Catholic senses.

candlestick. 'Neither do men light a candle, and put it under a bushel, but on a candlestick; and it giveth light unto all that are in the house' (*Matthew*, v, 15).

'Like "inkhorn", "milestone", and other words, "*candlestick*" is used in a sense somewhat different from that which it originally bore, when it is the rendering of the Greek λυχνία or lampstand. The usage is as old as the time of Wiclif, and the Anglo-Saxon version has "Candel-stæf", to represent the same word, or rather the "candelabrum" of the Vulgate. In Cotgrave's *French Dictionary*, we find,

Lampier . . . A *candlesticke*, or branch, for a Lampe.' (Wright.)

canker; cankered. 'But shun profane and vain babblings: for they will increase unto more ungodliness. And their word will eat as doth a canker' (2 *Timothy*, ii, 16–17).

The old spelling of *cancer*, a malignant tumour or growth. 'It eats away or corrodes the part in which it is situated.' From L. *cancer*, 'a crab; the tumour so called': cf. Gr. καρκίνος (or καρκίνωμα): 'the tumour, according to Galen, was so called from the swollen veins surrounding the part affected bearing a resemblance to a crab's limbs' (O.E.D.).

Cankered:—'Your gold and silver is cankered; and the rust of them shall be a witness against you, and shall eat your flesh as it were fire. Ye have heaped treasure together for the last days' (*James*, v, 3).

From the sense 'cancerated, ulcerated', comes that of 'corroded or rusted'.

carefulness. 'But I would have you without carefulness. He that is unmarried careth for the things that belong to the Lord, how he may please the Lord' (1 *Corinthians*, vii, 32); 'For behold this selfsame thing, that ye sorrowed after a godly sort, what carefulness it wrought in you, yea, what clearing of yourselves, yea, what indignation, yea, what fear . . .' (2 *Corinthians*, vii, 11).

Care; anxiety. Lit., a being-full-of-care. This sense has been archaic since ca. 1870.

It is a very English word from the common Germanic stock, and it is 'in no way related to L. *cura*' (O.E.D.).

Cf. *careful* in *Luke*, x, 41, and *Philippians*, iv, 6.

carriage. 'And after those days we took up our carriages' and went up to Jerusalem' (*Acts*, xxi, 15).

Not vehicles, but such baggage or luggage as one carries with one on a journey: the Gr. Test. having μετὰ δὲ τὰς ἡμέρας ταύτας ἐπισκευάσμενοι (having equipped horses) ἀνεβαίνομεν εἰς Ἱερουσαλήμ; the Vulgate, simply '. . . præparati . . .' (Verdunoy 'nous fîmes nos préparatifs').

This is a late C. 14-mid 17 use of the word; a sense coming immediately from the mid C. 14–early 17 sense, 'a burden, a load'. The word *carriage* derives from Old Norman Fr. *cariage*: Late L. *carricare*, 'to load', from *carrus*, a waggon.

cast. 1, n. A throw, as in 'And he was withdrawn from them about a stone's cast, and kneeled down, and prayed' (*Luke*, xxii, 41).

2, v. To consider; to plan or devise; to contrive. 'Consider' or 'think over' is the sense in 'And when she saw him, she was troubled at his saying, and cast in her mind what manner of salutation this should be' (*Luke*, i, 29).

The n. comes direct from the v. *cast*, 'to throw' (from Old Norse).—*Cast*, 'to consider, to ponder', is a C. 14–17 usage: cf. *cast about* (*in one's mind*), dating from late C. 16.

castaway. 'But I keep under my body, and bring it into subjection: lest that by any means, when I have preached to others, I myself should be a castaway' (1 *Corinthians*, ix, 27).

(In opposition to the cynical *laisser faire* of 'Do as I say, not as I do'.) This sense, not an 'outcast' (as Wright explains it) but 'a reprobate', is much earlier than the nautical one ('a shipwrecked person').

catholic. 'He warneth them not to believe all teachers, who boast of the Spirit, but to try'—i.e., test—'them by the rules of the catholick faith: and by many reasons exhorteth to brotherly love' (1 *John*, iv, heading).

Here, *catholic* is 'in its original and literal sense of "universal", which is the sense in which the word is always used in the Prayer Book' (Wright): 'Catholike being a greeke word signifieth nothing in English but universall or common', T. Wilson, *Logike*, 1551, as in 'Science is truly catholic, and is bounded only by the universe', *The Times Weekly Edition*, Sept. 11, 1885 (cited by the O.E.D.).

The Catholic Epistles are the epistles of James, Peter, Jude: for they are addressed neither to a particular church nor to a particular person: they are general.

In the British Empire, *Catholic* has, in C. 19–20, been very common for *Roman Catholic*. English writers and historians should speak of the Roman Catholic Church (*Ecclesia apostolica catholica Romana*). In mid C. 16–17, the *Catholic Church* or the *Church Catholic* predominantly denoted *the Church universal*, i.e. the entire corpus of Christians.—See Hastings: Leclercq: and Lightfoot's *Ignatius*.

The word *catholic* comes, via Old Fr., either from Late L. *catholicus* or direct from its Gr. original καθολικός, which was formed from καθ' ὅλου (later, καθόλου), 'on the whole, in general'; hence, 'generally, universally'.

certain, n. See at **vex.**

certainty. 'And some cried one thing, some another, among the multitude: and when he could not know the certainty for the tumult, he commanded him to be carried into the castle' (*Acts*, xxi, 34); 'On the morrow, because he would have known'—i.e., he wished to know or learn—'the certainty wherefore he was accused of the Jews, he loosed him from his bands . . .' (*ibid.*, xxii, 30).

In verse 34, 'the truth of the case'; in 30, 'the actual circumstances': the Gr. Test., in both of these passages, has τὸ ἀσφαλές, 'that which is reliable': the Vulgate, 'certum cognoscere' and 'qua ex causa accusaretur'. This sense has been archaic since C. 17.

From Anglo-Fr.; ultimately from L. *certus*, 'settled, sure'.

certify. 'But I certify you, brethren, that the gospel which was preached of me is not after man' (*Galatians*, i, 11).

Make (a person) certain or sure that . . . ; to assure him that . . . : a usage deriving from *certify* (a person) *of*, to make him sure of (something): cf. Shakespeare's 'I go to certify her Talbot's here' (1 *Henry VI*) and 'Besides, Antonio certified the Duke | They were not with Bassanio in his ship' (*The Merchant of Venice*): archaic after C. 18.

chalcedony. See the quotation at **chrysolite.**

In *Revelation*, xxi, 19, the Vulgate has *chalcedonius*, which transliterates the Gr. Test. χαλκηδών, for which Souter prudently essays nothing more precise than '*a chalcedony*, a small stone of various colours'. The O.E.D. :—'A precious (or semi-precious) stone . . . : a cryptocrystalline sub-species of quartz (a true quartz, with some disseminated opal-quartz), having the lustre nearly of wax, and being either transparent or translucent.'

chambering. 'Let us walk honestly, as in the day; not in rioting and drunkenness, not in chambering and wantonness, not in strife and envying' (*Romans*, xiii, 13). The Gr. text has: ὡς ἐν ἡμέρᾳ εὐσχημόνως περιπατήσωμεν, μὴ κώμοις καὶ μέθαις, μὴ κοίταις καὶ ἀσελγείαις, μὴ ἔριδι καὶ ξήλῳ. Here, κοῖται (plural) = repeated immoral sexual-intercourse (κοίτη being a bed), and ἀσελγείαι = wantonness, lewdness (Souter).

For *chambering*, Wyclif has *couches* in one edition, *beds* in another. A gloss of 1613 reads, '*Chambering*, lightness, and wanton behaviour in private places': with which cf. Latimer's two comments:—'St Paul useth this word "*chambering*"; for when folks will be wanton, they get themselves in corners'; 'By this word "*chambering*" understand the circumstances of whoredom and lechery and filthy living'. From *chamber*, 'a private room, esp. a bed-room'.

chance, v. 'And that which thou sowest, thou sowest not that body that shall be, but bare grain, it may chance of wheat, or of some other grain' (1 *Corinthians*, xv, 37).

It may chance = it may happen (to be) = perchance = perhaps: an archaism. Cf. Shakespeare's 'It may chance cost some of us our lives' (2 *Henry IV*, II, i, 12), which in modern English would be 'It may (perhaps) cost . . .'

The v. *chance* derives directly from the n., which comes, via Old Fr. *cheance*, from Late L. *cadentia*, 'a falling' (Classical L. *cadere*, 'to fall'): cf. the archaic *it befalls*, *it befell* (it happened) (O.E.D.).

charge (charges). 'We have four men which have a vow on them; take them, and purify thyself with them, and be at charges with them, that they may shave their heads' (*Acts*, xxi, 23–24): be at the expense of their head-shaving. 'Who goeth a warfare any time at his own charges?' (1 *Corinthians*, ix, 7), at his own expense.

Charges = expenses. From *charge*, 'a pecuniary burden', a sense deriving from *charge*, 'a material burden'. Via Fr., from Late L. *carrica*, itself from *carricare*, 'to load'.

charge, give in. 'And these things give in charge, that they may be blameless' (1 *Timothy*, v, 7), i.e. charge yourselves with these things, assume the burden of, i.e. pay heed to, these things as your duties.

chargeable. 'For ye remember, brethren, our labour and travail: for labouring night and day, because we would not be chargeable unto any of you, we preached unto you the gospel of God' (1 *Thessalonians*, ii, 9).

Burdensome; cf. the etymology of **charge.**

Obsolete since ca. 1810, this sense arose in the latter half of C. 15. Its nuance 'expensive' occurs in 'Oxford is a chargeable place, sir, there is no living there without it [money]', Richard Estcourt, *The Fair Example*, 1706 (cited by O.E.D.).

charged, in 1 *Timothy*, v, 16 ('Let not the church be charged: that it may relieve them that are widows indeed'), = 'put to the expense and burden' (of maintaining widows that may not be truly widowed): a sense current in C. 14–mid 17.

Cf. **charge,** q.v.

charger. 'And his head was brought in a charger, and given to the damsel: and she brought it to her mother' (*Matthew*, xiv, 11); 'And she came in straightway with haste to the king, and asked, saying, I will that thou give me by and by in a charger the head of John the Baptist' (*Mark*, vi, 25).

A platter—a flat dish (or a large plate) for carrying a large joint of meat.

From *charge*, 'to load'.

charity. 'Though I speak with the tongues of men and of angels, and have not charity, I am become as sounding brass, or a tinkling cymbal' (1 *Corinthians*, xiii, 1): Gr. Test. ἀγάπη (see below): Vulgate, *caritas.*

'The Christian love of our fellow-men; Christian benignity of disposition expressing itself in Christ-like conduct: one of the "three Christian graces", fully described by St. Paul, 1 Cor. xiii; in devotional writings, now usually *Christian charity*; 'in the Revised Version, the word has disappeared, and *love* has been substituted'.

Bacon, in *Certain Considerations touching the Church of England:*—'I did ever allow the discretion and tenderness of the Rhemish translation . . . , that finding in the original the word ἀγάπη and never ἤρος, do ever translate *Charitie*, and never *Love*, because of the indifferency [lack of difference] and æquivocation [equivalence, synonymousness] of the word with impure love' (Wright). Of ἀγάπη, Souter remarks that it is the Biblical synonym of ἀγάπησις (from ἀγαπάω, I love with reverent affection (as Christ is loved by mankind) or with tender and kindly consideration (as Christ loves us)—not sexually); it was not used in this higher sense before ca. 100 B.C.

In *Jude*, 12 ('your feasts of charity'), the plural ἀγάπαι is used concretely of 'the *love-feasts* of the Christians, evening meals . . . either accompanied or followed by the Eucharist . . . sacred, and intended to be expressive of the union of Christians in their Head' (Souter).

Via Fr. from L. *caritas*, lit. 'high price, dearness', fig. 'fondness, affection'.

cheer, be of good. 'And, behold, they brought to him a man sick of the palsy, lying on a bed: and Jesus seeing their faith said unto the sick of the palsy; Son, be of good cheer; thy sins be forgiven thee' (*Matthew*, ix, 2); cf. xiv, 27.

Lit., 'be of good face', i.e., 'to exhibit in the countenance the signs of gratification and joy' (Wright); hence, 'be cheerful'. The phrase is a rendering of Fr. *faire bonne chère*: Latimer, in a sermon (ca. 1550), exhorted his congregation thus, 'While we live here, let us make bone chear'; later, *faire bonne chère* = to eat heartily.

Cheer, 'face', belongs to C. 13– early 18, being archaic thereafter; and its comes, via Old Fr., from Later L. *cara*, 'face; countenance' (O.E.D.).

cherub, cherubim, cherubims. See at **seraph.**

children of God. See second paragraph of next entry.

children of light and **children of this world.** 'And the lord commended the unjust steward, because he had done wisely: for the children of this world are in their generation wiser than the children of light' (*Luke*, xvi, 8); 'While ye have light, believe in the light, that ye may be the children of light'

(*John*, xii, 36); 'Ye were sometimes'—i.e., formerly—'darkness, but now are ye light in the Lord: walk as children of light' (*Ephesians*, v, 8); 'Ye are all the children of light, and the children of the day: we are not of the night, nor of darkness' (1 *Thessalonians*, v, 5).

Children of light is not necessarily synonymous with *children of God*, which = believers, so called because adopted by God (as, e.g., in *Luke*, xx, 36—*Romans*, viii, 16 and 21—*Galatians*, iii, 26, 'Ye are all the children of God by faith in Jesus Christ'); it is opposed to *children of darkness*, the latter a phrase that does not actually occur in the N.T., although it is implied in the third and fourth of the quotations cited above and also in *Ephesians*, v, 11, and esp. 2 *Corinthians*, vi, 14, 'Be ye not unequally yoked together with unbelievers: for what fellowship hath righteousness with unrighteousness? and what communion hath light with darkness?'

Children of light and *children of this world* are but two of a large group of such phrases as *children of darkness—disobedience—sin; children of truth—wisdom; children of the East; children of the time—the age—the century*: all on the analogy of a Hebraism retained in Scriptural translations (O.E.D.). The relevant Gr. passage is οἱ υἱοὶ τοῦ αἰῶνος τουτοῦ φρονιμώτεροι ὑπὲρ τοὺς υἱοὺς τοῦ φωτὸς, 'the sons of this age, more prudent (or sensible) than the sons of the light': οἱ υἱοὶ τοῦ φωτός recurs in *John*, xii, 36, and 1 *Thessalonians*, v, 5; in *Ephesians*, v, 8, it is varied as τέκνα φωτός. (In the second and third of the four illustrative passages—the *John* and *Ephesians* passages—light, 'as universal beneficence', has come 'to be associated . . . with God and the Messiah' (Souter).

Both τέκνον, 'a child', and υἱός, 'a son', are used Hebraistically, with the genitive, 'of those who show qualities like that expressed by the genitive' or of those persons 'who so perfectly exemplify these qualities, etc., that they can be spoken of as having a family likeness to them' (Souter), as in τέκνα (or υἱοὶ) τοῦ φωτός—τῆς σοφίας, 'those who show wisdom, are exemplars thereof'—τῆς ἀπειθείας, 'rebels *par excellence*', for the quality may be an evil quality.

Christ. See **Jesus Christ.**

chrysolite; chrysoprasus. 'And the foundations of the
wall of the city were garnished with all manner of precious
stones. The first foundation was jasper; the second, sapphire;
the third, a chalcedony; the fourth, an emerald; the fifth,
sardonyx; the sixth, sardius; the seventh, chrysolyte; the eighth,
beryl; the ninth, a topaz; the tenth, a chrysoprasus; the
eleventh, a jacinth; the twelfth, an amethyst' (*Revelation*,
xxi, 19–20).

Gr. χρυσόλιθος lit. 'gold stone' (Vulgate *chrysolithus*): 'The
golden colour in the topaz, gave it the name chrysolith',
Holland's *Pliny*. *Chrysolite* is 'a name formerly given to several
different gems of a green colour, such as zircon, tourmaline,
topaz, and apatite. Since about 1790 restricted to the precious
olivine . . . [of] pale yellowish-green' (O.E.D.).

Gr. χρυσόπρασος (from χρυσός, 'gold',+ πράσον, 'a leek'),
is, lit., 'golden-green'. *Chrysoprasus* is the L.—the Vulgate L.
—form of the word, preferred by the A.V. here to the more
English *chrysoprase*, which, however, occurs in the glosses of
Ezekiel, xxvii, 16, and xxviii, 13.

In *The Bible*, the *chrysoprase* is probably a variety of the
beryl. It was one of those precious stones which, in the Middle
Ages, were supposed to have the power of shining in the dark.
(In modern mineralogy, *chrysoprase* is the name given to 'an
apple-green variety of chalcedony', O.E.D.).

church. Used of a heathen temple in *Acts*, xix, 37, thus:—
'For ye have brought hither these men, which are neither
robbers of churches, nor yet blasphemers of your goddess',
Diana of the Ephesians: cf. 'Janus church' (Janus's church) in
Fairfax's *Tasso*, and 'the church of Castor and Pollux' in
Holland's *Pliny* (both adduced by Wright). The sense is that
of No. 6 in Cruden's discrimination of the senses in which
church is used:—

   1. A religious assembly selected from the world in accord-
      ance with Christ's word: as in 1 *Corinthians*, i, 2, and
      Revelation, ii, 7.

2. All the elect of God, no matter what their nationality, as in *Colossians*, i, 18.

3. The faithful of some one family, together with such friends as worship with them, as in *Romans*, xvi 5; *Colossians*, iv, 15; *Philemon*, 2.

4. The faithful within one province: 2 *Thessalonians*, i, 1.

5. The governors or official representatives of a church: *Matthew*, xviii, 17.

6. A multitude of people assembled together, whether Christian or pagan.

7. The Jews, whose congregation formerly constituted the church, and were the chosen people, of God: *Acts*, vii, 38.

From M.E. *chirche*, O.E. *circe*; the latter corresponding to Old Saxon and West Germanic *kirika*; the ultimate origin being 'the Greek word κυριακόν, properly adj. "of the Lord . . ." (from κύριος, lord), which occurs, from the 3rd Century at least, used substantively (sc. δῶμα . . .) = "house of the Lord", as a name of the Christian house of worship' (O.E.D.).

close, adj. 'And when the voice was past, Jesus was found alone. And they kept it close, and told no man in those days any of those things which they had seen' (*Luke*, ix, 36).

Kept it close = 'kept it a secret; concealed the fact': Gr. Test. ἐσίγησαν (fell silent): Vulgate, 'tacuerunt' (held their tongues). In Udall's *Erasmus*, 1548, we find: 'Keep close (quoth they) the things that ye have seen', of which the semantic origin appears in 'I pray you keep this letter close to your self', 1468, one of the Paston letters, cited by the O.E.D.

Close comes from Fr. *clos*, itself from L. *clausus*, 'closed, shut' (*cludere*, 'to shut or close').

clothed upon. 'For in this we groan, earnestly desiring to be clothed upon with our house which is from heaven . . . For we that are in this tabernacle do groan, being burdened: not for that we would be unclothed, but clothed upon, that mortality might be swallowed up of life' (2 *Corinthians* v, 2, 4).

Clothed upon = 'having a garment on, over other clothing.

This rendering of the Gr. ἐπενδύσασθαι is retained from Tyndale's translation of verse 4. Wiclif has "clothed above" ' (Wright).

coast. 'And, behold, the whole city came out to meet Jesus: and when they saw him, they besought him that he would depart out of their coasts' (*Matthew*, viii, 34).

Here, *coasts* = borders. *Coast* is 'the border, bound, or limit, of a country; territory on or near a boundary or frontier, borderland' (O.E.D.); to the ordinary reader, it is misleading. 'Among these misleading archaisms the word *coast* for "border" or "region" is perhaps the most frequent. It would be unreasonable to expect the English reader to understand that when S. Paul "passes through the *upper coasts*" (τὰ ἀνωτερικὰ μέρη) on his way to Ephesus (*Acts*, xix, 1) he does in fact traverse the high land which lies in the *interior* of Asia Minor. Again in the Gospels, when he hears of our Lord visiting "the *coasts* of Tyre and Sidon" (*Matthew*, xv, 21; *Mark*, vii, 31), he naturally thinks of the sea-board, whereas the word in one passage stands for μέρη "parts", and in the other for ὅρια "borders", and the circumstances suggest rather the eastern than the western frontier of the region. And perhaps also his notions of the geography of Palestine may be utterly confused by reading that Capernaum is situated "upon the sea-coast" (*Matthew*, iv, 3)', Joseph Lightfoot, *On a fresh Revision of the New Testament* (quoted by Wright).

Colosse and **Colossians.** THE EPISTLE OF PAUL THE APOSTLE TO THE COLOSSIANS, i, 2, 'To the saints and faithful brethren in Christ which are at Colosse: Grace be unto you', where *saints* = 'the godly' (saints *in posse* though not *in esse*, or, at a higher level, saints *de facto* but not *de jure—ecclesiastico*).

Most of the Colossians (among them Epaphras) were Gentiles. Of Colossæ, a town in the Roman province *Asia*, Verdunoy speaks thus:—'Colosses était située en Phrygie, dans la fertile vallée du Lycos, affluent du Méandre, à 16 kilomètres de Laodicée et de Hiérapolis, sur la grande voie commerciale

et stratégique qui allait de la mer à l'Euphrate.—L'église de
Colosses avait eu pour fondateur Epaphras, peut-être converti
par saint Paul.'

colour. 'And as the shipmen were about to flee out of the
ship, when they had let down the boat into the sea, under
colour as though they would have cast anchors out of the foreship . . .' (*Acts*, xxvii, 30): under the pretext of casting. . . .

Colour = pretext or excuse; L. *color* also has this sense, as in
*Res illo colore defenditur apud judicem, ut videatur ille non sanæ
mentis fuisse*, 'The lawsuit is defended on that ground (or pretext or excuse), in order that the plaintiff may seem to have
been not in his right mind'. *Under colour of*, 'under pretext or
pretence of', dates from the 14th Century.

come. 'Unto which promise our twelve tribes, instantly
serving God day by day, hope to come' (*Acts*, xxvi, 7).

To attain: a dignified sense that has been obsolete, or, at
best, archaic, since C. 18.

comfort; comforter; comfortless. In *The Bible*, *comfort*
generally means 'to strengthen', literally or figuratively; 'to
refresh' is in a few contexts a better rendering. Thus *comforter*
= 'one who strengthens or invigorates; a consoler', as in 'And
I will pray the Father, and he shall give you another Comforter, that he may abide with you for ever' (*John*, xiv, 16); in
a later verse (26), we receive enlightenment, thus, 'But the
Comforter, which is the Holy Ghost', the Gr. text being ὁ δὲ
παράκλητος, τὸ Πνεῦμα τὸ ῞Αγιον, where ὁ παράκλητος is,
like L. *advocatus*, an intercessor; a helper; a consoler ('corresponding to the name Menahem [2 *Kings*, xv, 14, 16, 20] given
to the Messiah', Souter). In the same chapter (verse 18), we
have 'I will not leave you comfortless: I will come to you',
where *comfortless* = without assistance, without consolation,
without spiritual refreshment and help. In *Psalms*, liv, 4,
comfortable signifies 'consoling; invigorating'.

Through Old Fr. from L. *confortare*, 'to strengthen': *con*, an
intensive prefix + *fortis*, 'strong' + *are*, verbal ending.

commend; commendation. 'And when they had ordained them elders in every church, and had prayed with fasting, they commended them to the Lord, on whom they believed' (*Acts*, xiv, 23); 'Do we begin again to commend ourselves? or need we, as some others, epistles of commendation to you, or letters of commendation from you?' (2 *Corinthians*, iii, 1).

Commend to = 'to commit to the charge of' (L. *commendare*), with the connotation 'with a recommendation': cf. Shakespeare's 'Are journeying to salute the emperor | And to commend their service to his will' (*Two Gentlemen of Verona*, I, iii, 42).

Commendation = 'recommendation', the modern word for this Biblical one. 'Epistles of *commendation* [as above], and in early Canons, were letters commendatory, by which the bearers, when leaving their own congregations, were recommended to distant churches, as guarantees of character' (Wright).

commune, v.; communicate, communication. 'And they were filled with madness; and communed one with another what they might do to Jesus' (*Luke*, vi, 11), where *commune* = to consult or, perhaps, merely to converse. *Communicate* is sometimes transitive, 'to impart' (to others), in 'And I went up by revelation, and communicated unto them that gospel which I preach among the Gentiles . . .' (*Galatians*, ii, 2); sometimes intransitive, 'to share or participate', as in 'Notwithstanding ye have well done, that ye did communicate with my affliction' (*Philippians*, iv, 14), where *communicate with* = share in. 'Let no corrupt communication proceed out of your mouth, but that which is good to the use of edifying, that it may minister grace unto the hearers' (*Ephesians*, iv, 29); 'And he said unto them, What manner of communications are these that ye have one to another, as ye walk, and are sad?' (*Luke*, xxiv, 17); 'Evil communications corrupt good manners' (1 *Corinthians*, xv, 33), the R.V. having 'evil company' and the American Revisers preferring 'evil companionships'; but in any case *communication* in these three quotations = talk, conversation. The Vulgate has *colloquia*; the Gr. Test., ὁμιλίαι (φθείρουσιν ἤθη χρήσθ' ὁμιλίαι κακαί), which, in the singular, Souter translates as 'intercourse, companionship, conversation': a sense that, in English, was archaic after the 17th Century.

The three words—*commune, communicate, communication*—come, via Fr., from L. *communis*, 'common', '(held) in common': cf. *make common cause with*.

companion, n., and **company,** v. 'Epaphroditus, my brother and companion in labour, and fellowsoldier' (*Philippians*, ii, 25; cf. *Revelation*, i, 9); 'I wrote to you in an epistle, not to company with fornicators' (1 *Corinthians*, v, 9; cf. *Acts*, i, 21).

Companion comes, via Old Fr. *compa(i)gnon*, from the (accusative of the) Late L. *companio*: *com = cum*, together; *panis*, bread: lit., one who shares bread with another.

With *company*, v., as used above, cf. Trevisa's 'Bicause they companye with englisshmen' (1387), Latimer's 'How many such prelates, how many such bishops, Lord, . . . are there now in England? And . . . shall we company with them?' (ca. 1555), and H. E. Manning's 'Those with whom we have here companied through the long years of our earthly sojourn' (1842): to associate with.

Either direct from the n. or from Old Fr. *compaignier* (O.E.D.; Wright).

compass. 'Woe unto you, Scribes and Pharisees, hypocrites! for ye compass sea and land to make one proselyte' (*Matthew*, xxiii, 15); 'For the days shall come upon thee, that thine enemies shall cast a trench about thee, and compass thee round, and keep thee in on every side' (*Luke*, xix, 43).

'To encompass', as we say to-day: in the quotation from *Matthew*, it = 'to go round'; in that from *Luke*, it = 'to surround'.

From Fr. *compasser*, 'to measure'; cf.:—

compass, fetch a. 'And from thence we fetched a compass, and came to Rhegium' (*Acts*, xxviii, 13): made a circuit, went round.

Compass, 'a circle or a circumference', dates from the 14th Century and comes from Old Fr. *compas*, 'measure, pair of compasses, circle', probably from Medieval L. *compassus* (*passus*, 'a pace').

concision. 'Beware of dogs, beware of evil workers, beware of the concision' (*Philippians*, iii, 2).

The chapter heading explains 'concision' (an obsolete variant of *circumcision*) thus:—'He [Paul] warneth them to beware of the false teachers of the circumcision', and in a marginal note the Geneva Translators remark that 'the false apostles gloried in their Circumcision, wher unto S. Paul here alludeth, calling them *concision* [Vulgate: *concisionem*], which is cutting of & tearing a sunder of the Church'. (Wright.)

conclude. To resolve; to decide.

'As touching the Gentiles which believe, we have written and concluded that they observe no such thing . . .' (*Acts*, xxi, 25).

L. *concludere*, 'to shut up closely, to close, to end'.

concupiscence. 'But sin, taking occasion by the commandment, wrought in me all manner of concupiscence. For without the law sin was dead' (*Romans*, vii, 8); 'Mortify therefore your members which are upon the earth; fornication, uncleanness, inordinate affection, evil concupiscence, and covetousness, which is idolatry' (*Colossians*, iii, 5); 'That every one of you should know how to possess his vessel in sanctification and honour; Not in the lust of concupiscence, even as the Gentiles which know not God' (1 *Thessalonians*, iv, 4–5).

From L. *concupiscentia*, 'evil desire, lust'. In the *Romans* passage, the Gr. word is ἐπιθυμία, as it is also in *Colossians* and *Thessalonians*; Souter renders it as 'eager (passionate) desire, passion'; and the O.E.D. makes it clear that in the N.T., *concupiscence* = 'the coveting of "carnal things", desire for the "things of the world"'.

conscience. 'Howbeit'—however or nevertheless—'there is not in every man that knowledge: for some with conscience of the idol unto this hour eat it as a thing offered unto an idol; and their conscience being weak is defiled' (1 *Corinthians*, viii, 7); 'For then would they not have ceased to be offered? because that the worshippers once purged should have had no more conscience of sins' (*Hebrews*, x, 2).

Gr. Test. τῇ συνηθείᾳ . . . τοῦ εἰδώλου, 'by familiarity with the idol', and ἡ συνείδησις αὐτῶν ἀσθενὴς οὖσα, their innate power-to-discern-what-is-good being weak'; συνείδησις recurs in the *Hebrews* passage.

The Vulgate has *conscientia* in all three places.

'Consciousness' fits the third and second, 'knowledge' or 'internal conviction' the first of these three instances of *conscience*: three nuances of the one sense, which was current in C. 14–mid 18. Via Fr., from L. *conscientia*—*conscire*, lit. 'to share knowledge, to know along with'.

consent unto. 'And Saul was consenting unto his [Stephen's] death' (*Acts*, viii, 1), the Gr. Test. having Σαῦλος δὲ ἦν συνευδοκῶν [entirely approving of] τῇ ἀναιρέσει αὐτοῦ; 'If then I do that which I would not, I consent unto the law that it is good' (*Romans*, vii, 16), the Gr. being . . . σύμφημι [I express agreement with] τῷ νόμῳ ὅτι καλός.

'Voluntarily to accede to or acquiesce in what another proposes or desires; to agree, comply, yield' (O.E.D.); almost 'to take pleasure in', the Gr. word in *Acts*, viii, 1 recurs in *Romans*, i, 32, where it (συνευδοκοῦσι) is translated 'they have pleasure in'—thus, 'Who knowing the judgment of God, that they which commit such things are worthy of death, not only do the same, but have pleasure in them that do them'. From L. *consentire*, 'to feel together; to agree'.

consist. 'And he [God] is before all things, and by him all things consist' (*Colossians*, i, 17).

The modern equivalent is 'to subsist', and in this sense *consist* has been archaic since early C. 18 and is now only historic (in reference to the above passage): cf. 'Of those things which

consist by nature, nothing can be changed by custom'
(Bacon); R.V., 1881, 'In him all things consist', marginal
gloss, 'That is, hold together'.

Perhaps via Fr., and certainly from L. *consistere*, 'to remain
firm, to exist'.

consort. 'And some of them believed, and consorted with
Paul and Silas; and of the devout Greeks a great multitude,
and of the chief women not a few' (*Acts*, xvii, 4).

To associate, as in 'They wilfully themselves exile from
light, | And must for aye consort with black-brow'd night'
(Shakespeare, *Midsummer Night's Dream*, III, ii, 387) and 'If
Death | Consort with thee, Death is to me as Life' (Milton)
and 'They consorted with Lutherans' (Macaulay).

Perhaps from the obsolete Italian *consortare*, 'to consort
together'; cf. Medieval L. *consortari*, 'to have common
boundaries' (O.E.D.). Ultimately there must be a connexion
with L. *sors*, 'lot' or 'fate': cf. L. *consors*, 'one who casts in his
lot with others, and shares in common with them' (Wright).

constantly. 'This is a faithful saying, and these things I will
that thou affirm constantly, that they which have believed
in God might be careful to maintain good works' (*Titus*, iii,
8); cf. *Acts*, xii, 15, 'And they said unto her, Thou art mad.
But she constantly affirmed that it was even so.' The corresponding Gr. words are διαβεβαιοῦσθαι, 'to assert emphatically', and διϊσχυρίζετο, 'she asserted emphatically'.

Rather, therefore, 'emphatically' than 'consistently' (another obsolete sense of the adv.). From L. *constanter*, from
constare, a strengthened form of *stare*, 'to stand'.

consult. 'Or what king, going to make war against another
king, sitteth not down first, and consulteth whether he be able
with ten thousand men to meet him that cometh against him
with twenty thousand?' (*Luke*, xiv, 31).

Gr. Test. βουλεύσεται, 'will deliberate, or take counsel'.

In modern usage, one consults another about something,
or, absolutely, consults with another. With this Biblical use,

cf. Shakespeare's 'Every man . . . , not consulting, broke into a general prophecy' (*Henry VIII*, I, i, 91).

Via Fr. from L. *consultare*, 'to consult frequently'.

contain. 'I say therefore to the unmarried and widows, it is good for them if they abide even as I'—a celibate. 'But if they cannot contain, let them marry: for it is better to marry than to burn' (Paul to the Corinthians, I, vii, 8–9).

Contain (v.i. of C. 17–18, from v. reflexive of late C. 13–20, now archaic) is 'to refrain from yielding to passion, to be continent, preserve one's chastity': via Old Fr. from L. *continere*, 'to hold together'.

Burn = 'to be on fire with lust' (cf. *Romans*, i, 27), an intensification of *to be ardent* (L. *ardere*, to burn).

contrariwise. 'So that contrariwise, ye ought rather to forgive him, and comfort him, lest perhaps such a one should be swallowed up with overmuch sorrow' (2 *Corinthians*, ii, 7), where *swallowed up*, by the way, = 'absorbed, engrossed, excessively preoccupied'; cf. *Galatians*, ii, 7, and 1 *Peter*, iii, 9.

Grindal, in his *Injunctions to the Clergy*, 1571, writes, 'But contrariwise, at all times, when ye shall have leisure, ye shall hear or read some part of holy scripture, or some other good authors' (Wright). In both passages, *contrariwise* (contrary ways) = on the contrary. A hybrid of L. and English origin: *contra*, 'against'.

The Gr. Test. has τοὐναντίον 'syncopated from τὸ ἐναντίον, *the opposite*' (Souter).

controversy. 'And without controversy great is the mystery of godliness: God was manifest in the flesh, justified in the Spirit, seen of angels, preached unto the Gentiles, believed on in the world, received up into glory' (1 *Timothy*, iii, 16).

Without controversy (ca. 1540–1800), like *beyond controversy* (C. 19–20) and the rare *out of controversy* (Milton, 1644), means 'without or beyond dispute; without doubt, doubtless', and corresponds to the L. *sine controversia*.

Perhaps via Fr.; from L. *controversia*, from *controversus*, 'turned (*versus*) against (*contra*)', i.e. 'disputed'.

convenient. 'Wherefore, though I might be much bold in Christ to enjoin thee that which is convenient' (*Philemon*, 8); 'Neither filthiness, nor foolish talking, nor jesting, which are not convenient: but rather giving of thanks' (*Ephesians*, v, 4); 'And even as they did not like to retain God in their knowledge, God gave them over'—abandoned them—'to a reprobate mind, to do those things which are not convenient' (*Romans*, i, 28).

'Ethically suitable, morally becoming; proper' is the sense in these passages, as also in 'a convenient chastity' (1497) and 'She sang and danced more exquisitely than was convenient for an honest [i.e., respectable] woman' (1684); a sense current in C. 15–mid 18 (O.E.D.).

L. *conveniens* (accusative, *-entem*), from *convenire*, 'to come together', hence 'to suit'.

conversation; converse. In the N.T., *conversation* 'means general deportment or behaviour, especially as regards morals; and, in all but two passages, corresponds very exactly to the word in the original (ἀναστροφή ["*dealing with other men, going up and down* among men, *life, manner of life*", Souter]). In Heb. xiii. 5, however, the Greek word means "disposition"; and in Phil. iii. 20, "citizenship" ' (Wright).

From L. *conversatio*, 'intercourse', via Old Fr.

Converse. '. . . Who afterwards devoutly and charitably converse together' (*Acts*, ii, heading).

'To associate familiarly, to consort, keep company' (O.E.D.). Ultimately from L., but immediately from Old Fr. *converser*, 'to pass one's life'.

convince. 'Which of you convinceth me of sin? And if I say the truth, why do ye not believe me?' (*John*, viii, 46); 'The Jews' prerogative: which they have not lost: howbeit the law convinceth them also of sin' (*Romans*, iii, heading), where *howbeit* = although.

To *convince of* is now to *convict of*: to prove a person, or find him, guilty of (offence or error). The latest example quoted by the O.E.D. is 'Instead of clearing, this paper only serves to convince her' (playwright Foote, 1776); the sense arose ca. 1530.

From L. *convincere*, 'to conquer; to convict': *con*, 'wholly', + *vincere*, 'to conquer'.

Corinthians. In L., *Corinthii* (from Gr. Κορίνθιοι).

Κόρινθος, Corinth (via Fr. *Corinthe*) was, in ancient Greece, a city 'celebrated for its artistic adornment, and for its luxury and licentiousness' (O.E.D.),—whence the slang *Corinth*, 'a brothel', and *Corinthian*, 'a fashionable rake'. Tyndale's rendering (1526) of 2 *Corinthians*, vi, 11, is 'O ye Corinthyans! oure mouth is open unto you'.

corrupt; corruptible and **uncorruptible.** '*Corrupt*, in its primitive use, means, to *destroy*, to *cause decay*, to *spoil*; and is employed in this signification more frequently than in its after application to *moral tainting*, the meaning to which the word is now restricted. *Matthew*, vi, 19: "Where moth and rust doth *corrupt*", ἀφανίξει. *James*, v, 2: "Your riches are *corrupt*[ed]", σέσηπε—an allusion to the [preceding]. 1 *Corinthians*, ix, 25: "Now they do it to obtain a corruptible crown, φθαρτόν; but we an uncorruptible", ἄφθαρτον; alluding to the garland of leaves with which the victors in the Grecian Games were crowned, and which, after a time, faded. So, in *Romans*, i, 23, the *uncorruptible* God, ἀφθάρτου, is contrasted with *corruptible* man, φθαρτοῦ, meaning, it would seem, not the difference in respect of liability to *moral* depravation and exemption from it, but between the *perishable* nature of man, and the *imperishable* nature of God' (Bishop Hinds, glossary to *Scripture and the Authorized Version of Scripture*: quoted by Wright). The Gr. φθαρτός = 'perishable'. To *corrupt* is from L. *corrumpere* (passive participle, *corruptus*), from *rumpere*, 'to break'.

course, by. 'If any man speak in an unknown tongue, let it be by two, or at the most by three, and that by course; and let one interpret' (1 *Corinthians*, xiv, 27).

'By turns, in turn', or rather, 'in due order': cf. Bacon's

in course, which is synonymous, thus, 'History of nature is of
three sorts: of nature in course; of nature erring or varying;
and of nature altered or wrought' (quoted by Wright). Here
course = 'systematic or, at the least, appointed order':· a
C. 16–17 sense. *Course*, applied to time, action, events,
derives from the sense 'path, or direction, of running': L.
cursum, 'a running; race; course', from *currere*, to run.

cousin. 'And, behold, thy cousin Elisabeth, she hath also
conceived a son in her old age' (*Luke*, i, 36); 'And her neigh-
bours and her cousins heard how the Lord had shewed great
mercy upon her; and they rejoiced with her' (*ibid.*, i, 58).

The senses, here, are 'kinswoman' and 'kinsmen and kins-
women'. In C. 14–mid 18, *cousin* was very often applied to
'a collateral relative more distant than a brother or sister'
and it included nephews and nieces and first and second
cousins and other relatives. Via Fr. from L. *consobrinus*, 'a
cousin by the mother's side'; one of the Medieval L. forms
was *cosinus* (O.E.D.).

covenant, v. 'And [Judas Iscariot] said unto them, What
will ye give me, and I will deliver him unto you? And they
covenanted with him for thirty pieces of silver' (*Matthew*,
xxvi, 15); 'And he went his way, and communed with the
chief priests and captains, how he might betray him unto
them. And they were glad, and covenanted to give him
money' (*Luke*, xxii, 4–5).

'To enter into a covenant', i.e. into a formal agreement;
'to agree solemnly; to contract'. Spenser, in *The State of
Ireland*, 1596, has 'The reason why the landlord will no longer
covenant with him' (O.E.D.); the word is slightly archaic.

Direct from the noun, which is an adoption of Old Fr.
covenant, ultimately from L. *convenire*, 'to come together'
(lit.), hence 'to agree'.

covet. 'But covet earnestly the best gifts: and yet shew I unto
you a more excellent way' (1 *Corinthians*, xii, 31); 'Wherefore, brethren, covet to prophesy, and forbid not to speak with
tongues' (*ibid.*, xiv, 39).

To desire eagerly: cf. the C. 16–17 proverb, *all covet, all lose*. The use with the infinitive has been archaic since ca. 1870, and in C. 19–20 the predominant sense has been 'to desire culpably, enviously'.

Via Old Fr. *coveiter* (or *cuveitier*) from some(? Low) L. verb formed from Classical L. *cupere*, 'to desire', or from its derivative n., *cupiditas* (O.E.D.).

crave. 'Joseph of Arimathæa, an honourable counsellor' which also waited for the kingdom of God, came, and went in boldly unto Pilate, and craved the body of Jesus' (*Mark*, xv, 43).

To ask earnestly for, to beg for: dating from the late 13th Century, this sense is, in the present century, slightly archaic, for the dominant C. 20 sense is 'to long for, have a craving for'. Cf. these two quotations from Shakespeare: 'I, poor Margaret, . . . Am come to crave thy just and lawful aid' (3 *Henry VI*, III, iii, 32); 'Madam, your mother craves a word with you' (*Romeo and Juliet*, I, v, 113).

O.E. *crafian*, of Scandinavian origin: the Scandinavian radical *kraf* = 'to force, to exact' (O.E.D.).

creature. 'Who changed the truth of God into a lie, and worshipped and served the creature more than the Creator, who is blessed for ever' (*Romans*, i, 25); 'For the earnest expectation of the creature waiteth for the manifestation of the sons of God' (*ibid.*, viii, 19); 'For every creature of God is good, and nothing to be refused, if it be received with thanksgiving' (1 *Timothy*, iv, 4); 'Of his own will begat he us with the word of truth, that we should be a kind of firstfruits of his creatures' (*James*, i, 18).

Since C. 18 an archaism, *creature* in C. 14–17 very often signified a thing created, anything created, *any* product (animate or inanimate) of creative action, any creation: cf. Shakespeare's 'Fierce fire and iron . . . Creatures of note for mercy-lacking uses' (1595) and R. Brooke's 'Light was one of the first creatures' (1641).

Via Fr., from L. *creatura*, 'a thing created', formed from *creare*, 'to create', (O.E.D.).

Cretians (*Titus*, i, 12) is an occasional C. 16–17 variant of *Cretans*.

crucify. See the quotation at **Calvary** where the Gr. Test. has ἔϰει ἐσταύϱωσαν αὐτόν and the Vulgate, 'ibi crucifixerunt eum'. The Gr. v. σταυϱόω, 'I crucify', is formed from σταυϱός, 'a stake', hence the transverse beam of a cross (the top of the *T*), hence a cross, hence the crucifixion of Christ. The Vulgate v. is *crucifigere*, i.e. *cruci figere*, to fasten to the cross.

Crucify comes, via Fr. *crucifier*, from a presumed late Low L. *crucificare* (cf. Spanish *crucificar*): O.E.D.

To crucify a person was, by the Greeks and Romans, considered an extremely ignominious death; crucifixion seems to have been one of the Phœnicians' principal contributions to civilization.

In *Galatians*, vi, 14, *crucify* is used metaphorically.

cumber. 'But Martha was cumbered about much serving, and came to him, and said, Lord, dost thou not care that my sister hath left me to serve alone? bid her therefore that she help me' (*Luke*, x, 40).

(Concerning a barren fig-tree) 'Why cumbereth it the ground?' (*ibid.*, xiii, 7). Martha was distressed or troubled, with a connotation of incommodation or inconvenience; why does this fig-tree burden (or occupy obstructively or improfitably) the ground? In much the same sense as *encumber*, of which it may, despite the dates so far recorded, be an aphesis (a foreshortening); ultimately connected with L. *cumulus*, 'a heap'.

cunning, adj.; **cunningly.** In *The Bible*, these words mean 'skilful' or 'expert' (as in the American Revision) and 'skilfully', 'expertly'. The sole instance of the adv. occurs in 2 *Peter*, i, 16, thus, 'For we have not followed cunningly devised fables, when we made known unto you the power and coming of our Lord Jesus Christ, but were eyewitnesses of his majesty'. The adj. occurs nineteen times, of which only one occasion is afforded by the N.T.: 'Carried about with every wind of doctrine, by the sleight'—trickery or (in the modern sense) cunning—'of men, and cunning craftiness' or expert guile, 'whereby they lie in wait to deceive' (*Ephesians*, iv, 14).

Lit., the adj. = 'knowing'; cf. a *knowing blade*.

curse, n. See at **band, v.**

custom, as in the phrase *sitting at the receipt of custom*, occurs in *Matthew*, ix, 9; *Mark*, ii, 14; *Luke*, v, 27.

Read the entry at **receipt** before passing on to:—In *the receipt of custom*, *custom* is the generic ('taxes' or 'revenue') of the particular *custom*, 'any customary tax or tribute paid to a lord or ruler' (the O.E.D.), a sense current in C. 14–18; cf. Coverdale's rendering of *Ezra*, iv, 13, 'Then shall they not geve [i.e., give] tribute, toll, and yearly custome'.

Via Old Fr. *custume* (or *costume*), from a Romanic variation of Classical L. *consuetudo*, 'custom, habit, usage', with which cf. the legal (and Scottish) *consuetude*.

cymbal. See **tinkling cymbal.**

D

damnable; damnation; damned. 'False teachers . . . , who privily shall bring in damnable heresies' (2 *Peter*, ii, 1), i.e., heresies of perdition or destruction.

Damnation = 'judgement' or 'condemnation' in *Mark*, xii, 40; *Luke*, xx, 47; *Matthew*, xxiii, 33; *John*, v, 29; *Romans*, iii, 8, and xiii, 2; 1 *Corinthians*, xi, 29; 1 *Timothy*, v, 12. In *Matthew*, xxiii, 14; *Mark*, iii, 29; and 2 *Peter*, ii, 3: in these three passages, the sense of *damnation* is ' condemnation to eternal punishment in the world to come; the fact of being damned, or doomed to hell' (O.E.D.).

Damned:—'He that believeth and is baptized shall be saved; but he that believeth not shall be damned' (*Mark*, xvi, 16), i.e.,

judged; 'And he that doubteth is damned if he eat, because
he eateth not of faith; for whatsoever is not of faith is sin'
(*Romans*, xiv, 23), where *damned* = 'condemned'; 'That they
all might be damned who believed not the truth, but had
pleasure in unrighteousness' (2 *Thessalonians*, ii, 12), where the
same comment holds good.

In the Gr. Test., the word is ϰϱίνω, 'I judge', or a derivative,
esp. ϰϱίσις, '*judging, judgement*; generally *divine judgement*'
(Souter).

From Old Fr. *dam(p)ner*, itself from L. *dampnare* or *damnare*:
'taken early into Fr. in legal and theological use' (O.E.D.); the
earliest English sense being 'to pronounce adverse judgement
on'.

damsel. 'A certain damsel' (*Acts*, xvi, 16): see the quotation
at **soothsaying**. In C. 16–17, simply 'a young unmarried
woman', without any of that connotation of high rank which
resides in *damosel*.

Early M.E. *damaisele* or *dameisele*; adopted from Old Fr.,
where it arose on *dame*, with the sense 'a little, a young,
lady'; and so ultimately from L. *domina*, 'the mistress of the
house'. Since C. 17, *damsel* has been archaic; since ca. 1830,
literary too.

danger. 'But I say unto you, That whosoever is angry with
his brother without a cause shall be in danger of the judgement:
and whosoever shall say to his brother, Raca, shall be in
danger of the council: but whosoever shall say, Thou fool,
shall be in danger of hell fire' (*Matthew*, v, 22).

Gr. Test.: πᾶς ὁ ὀργιζόμενος τῷ ἀδελφῷ αὐτοῦ ἔνοχος
ἔσται τῇ ϰρίσει, '. . . shall be exposed to the (divine) judgement'; and ἔνοχος (liable) is used in the other two clauses.

With the Biblical phrase *in danger of*, cf. Tyndale's 'Even so
are our consciences bound and in danger to the law under old
Adam, as long as he liveth in us' and Latimer's 'Here we may
see how much we be bound and in danger unto God'
(Wright): the phrase belongs to C. 13–17. *Danger* comes, via
Old Fr. *dangier*, from some Late L. derivative of *dominium*,

'lordship, sovereignty' (*dominus*, 'master, lord'): originally, *danger* meant 'jurisdiction, dominion'; *in one's danger*, 'in his jurisdiction', hence 'under an obligation to' (O.E.D.).

day-spring or **dayspring**. 'Through the tender mercy of our God; whereby the dayspring from on high hath visited us, | To give light to them that sit in darkness and in the shadow of death . . .' (*Luke*, i, 78–9).

Gr. Test. ἀνατολὴ ἐξ ὕψους, 'the rising (of the sun) from heaven'. Cf. the next entry.

The spring of day ('As sudden | As flows congealed in the spring of day' (Shakespeare) is obviously the rising of the sun ('Soon as they forth were come to open sight | Of dayspring', Milton)—daybreak, dawn ('From dayspring to midnight, I sit not, nor rest not', Udall).

Mostly a C. 16–17 word.

day star or **daystar**. 'We have also a more sure word of prophecy; whereunto ye do well that ye take heed, as unto a light that shineth in a dark place, until the day dawn and the day star arise in your hearts' (2 *Peter*, i, 19).

The Morning Star—the planet Venus—is here figurative, as in Wesley's hymn, 'We lift our hearts to thee, O Day-Star from on High' and Philemon Holland's 'For all the while that she preventeth [or precedes; almost, announces] the morning, and riseth Oriental before, she taketh the name of Lucifer (or Day-Star) as a second sun hastening the day'. The L. name *Lucifer*, 'light-bearer', is a rendering of the Gr. name *Phosphor* (φωσφόρος ; sc. ἀστήρ, 'a star').

The Gr. Test. has ἕως οὗ ἡμέρα διαυγάσῃ, καὶ φωσφόρος ἀνατείλῃ ἐν ταῖς καρδίαις ὑμῶν: 'until the light pierce the shadows and the day-star shine'. The Vulgate: 'donec dies elucescat, et lucifer oriatur in cordibus vestris'.

dealing. 'Then saith the woman of Samaria unto him, How is it that thou, being a Jew, askest drink of me, which am a woman of Samaria? for the Jews have no dealings with the Samaritans' (*John*, iv, 9).

Dealings = 'intercourse; friendly or business communication' (O.E.D.), a sense arising not until ca. 1530. The v. *deal* originally meant 'to divide'; hence, 'to distribute'; it is of the common Germanic stock.

decease. To die, as in 'Now there were with us seven brethren: and the first, when he had married a wife, deceased, and, having no issue, left his wife unto his brother' (*Matthew*, xxii, 25). This v. has become obsolete, except in the participial adj., *deceased* (recently dead): commonest in C. 16–17. Stow, 'After infinite victories obtained, and an incomparable renown amongst all men for the same, he deceased at Florence' (*Annals*, 1592); Fuller, 'Queen Sibyl, who deceased of the plague' (*The Holy War*, 1639).

Immediately from the English n., which in M.E. was *deces*, from Fr. *décès*, from L. *decessus*, a euphemism ('departure') for *mors*, 'death' (Wright; O.E.D.).

deceivableness. 'And with all deceivableness of unrighteousness in them that perish; because they received not the love of the truth, that they might be saved' (2 *Thessalonians*, ii, 10).

Deceptiveness; the R.V. has 'deceit'; the Vulgate, 'in omni seductione iniquitatis'; Gr. Test., ἐν πάσῃ ἀπάτῃ [deception] ἀδικίας.

A C. 16–17 usage, retained thereafter as a reminiscent archaism: in C. 14–17, *deceivable* (as if 'able to deceive') very generally meant 'deceitful, deceptive'.

decently. 'Let all things be done decently and in order' (1 *Corinthians*, xiv, 40).

In a decent or becoming or fitting manner; with decency. From *decent*, 'becoming; appropriate': since ca. 1850, an archaism. Via Fr. from L. *decens* (*decere*, 'to be fitting').

declare. 'Then Jesus sent the multitude away, and went into the house: and his disciples came unto him, saying, Declare unto us the parable of the tares of the field' (*Matthew*, xiii, 36); cf. the quotation at **devotions.**

To make *clear*, to explain, elucidate, interpret: a C. 14–
early 18 sense; via Fr. from L. *declarare* (*de + clarus*, 'clear'),
'to make clear or evident'.

'. . . No need to declare it, the matter is plain enough',
Palsgrave, 1530; *Aggeus the Prophete, declared by a large Com-
mentarye*, Pilkington, 1560; 'To declare this a little, we must
assume that the surfaces of such bodies are exactly smooth',
Boyle, ca. 1691 (O.E.D.).

defer. 'And when Felix heard these things, having more perfect knowledge of that way, he deferred them, and said,
When Lysias the chief captain shall come down, I will know
the uttermost of your matter' (*Acts*, xxiv, 22).

Defer, 'to put off to a future occasion', is obsolete as applied
to a person-accusative: this use belongs to late C. 14–early
18 and occurs in Shakespeare's 2 *Henry VI* (at IV, vii, 142)
and *Richard III* (at III, vii, 107).

Via Fr., from L. *deferre*, 'to carry away'.

degree. 'For they that have used the office of a deacon well
purchase to themselves a good degree, and great boldness in
the faith which is in Christ Jesus' (1 *Timothy*, iii, 13). The
Gr. Test. has οἱ γὰρ καλῶς διακονήσαντες βαθμὸν ἑαυτοῖς
καλὸν περιποιοῦνται (those who have 'deaconed' well, gain
for themselves a fine promotion); the Vulgate, 'Qui enim
bene ministraverint gradum bonum sibi acquirent' ('s'acquièr-
ent un rang honorable', Verdunoy). This sense, dating from
C. 13 and exemplified in Shakespeare's 'Scorning the base
degrees | By which he did ascend' (*Julius Cæsar*, II, i, 25),
is simply a metaphor from the basic meaning 'a step; a rung
in a ladder'. Immediately from Old Fr. *degre(z)*, ultimately
L. *de* (down) + *gradus* (a step).

dehort. 'Christ instituteth his holy supper, covertly fore-
telleth of the traitor, dehorteth the rest of his apostles from
ambition' (*Luke*, xxii, heading); 'He dehorteth them from the
breach of charity' (1 *Peter*, ii, heading).

'To use exhortation to dissuade (a person) from a course or

purpose' (O.E.D.): a sense current ca. 1540–1710. In 1553, 'Rhetoric' Wilson could pointedly write, 'Whereby we doe perswade ... disswade ... exhorte, or dehorte ... any man'. From L. *dehortari*.

deliciously. (Concerning Babylon.) 'How much she hath glorified herself, and lived deliciously, so much torment and sorrow give her. . . . And the kings of the earth, who have committed fornication and lived deliciously with her, shall bewail her and lament for her, when they shall see the smoke of her burning' (*Revelation*, xviii, 7, 9).

Luxuriously, sumptuously; voluptuously: C. 14–early 19. 'The King . . . deliciously took his pleasure', Sir T. Herbert, 1634 (O.E.D.). From Anglo-Fr. (and Old Fr.) *delicious*, from Late L. *deliciosus*, formed on Classical L. *deliciæ*, 'pleasure; charm'.

deputy. '. . . A certain sorcerer, a false prophet, a Jew, whose name was Bar-jesus: | Which was with the deputy of the country, Sergius Paulus, a prudent man' (*Acts*, xiii, 7); 'And when Gallio was the deputy of Achaia . . .' (*ibid.*, xviii, 12); 'Wherefore if Demetrius, and the craftsmen which are with him, have a matter against any man, the law is open, and there are deputies: let them implead one another' (*ibid.*, xix, 38).

'Appropriately used by our Translators as the rendering of the Greek ἀνθύπατος, the *proconsul* or governor of a senatorial province. In the 16th century the Lord-Lieutenant of Ireland was called the Lord Deputy' (Wright): cf. Shakespeare, *Henry VIII*, III, ii, 260.

A substantivization of late M.E. *depute*, past participle = 'appointed'; this participle comes, via Old Fr., from L. *deputatus*, 'assigned' (*deputare*, i.e. *de* + *putare*, 'to hew').

determinate. 'Him, being delivered by the determinate counsel and foreknowledge of God, ye have taken, and by wicked hands have crucified and slain' (*Acts*, ii, 23).

Here, *determinate* = 'settled so as not to vary'; so late as 1855, critic Brimley spoke of Tennyson as one 'smitten with a determinate aversion to popularity' (O.E.D.); now an archaism. From L. *determinatus*, the passive participle of *determinare*, 'to bound, limit', hence 'to fix': *de* (intensive) + *terminare*, 'to set bounds to; to delimit'.

devotions. 'For as I passed by, and beheld your devotions, I found an altar with this inscription, TO THE UNKNOWN GOD. Whom therefore ye ignorantly worship, him declare I unto you' (*Acts*, xvii, 23).

The marginal gloss is 'Or, gods that you worship': the O.E.D. defines this *devotion* as 'an object of religious worship', i.e. *devotion* used objectively instead of, as usual, subjectively, but it adds, 'This sense is not very certain, the meaning of the quotations being in every sense [Sidney, *Arcadia*, 1580; the N.T. passage; dramatist Fletcher, ca. 1625] doubtful'. The Vulgate has 'videns simulacra vestra', rendered by Verdunoy as 'en considérant les objets du culte'; the Gr. Test. has σεβάσματα, 'objects of worship, things worshipped' (Souter).

Via Old Fr. from L. *devotio*, 'a devoting' (*devovere*, 'to devote').

Diana of the Ephesians. 'But when they knew that he was a Jew, all with one voice about the space of two hours cried out, Great is Diana of the Ephesians. And when the townclerk had appeased the people, he said, Ye men of Ephesus, what man is there that knoweth not how that the city of the Ephesians is a worshipper of the great goddess Diana, and of the image which fell down from Jupiter?' (*Acts*, xix, 34–5): νεωκόρον οὖσαν τῆς μεγάλης Ἀρτέμιδος.

The very name *Artemis* (or *Diana*) *of the Ephesians* indicates that the identification of the ancient Italian Diana, moongoddess, with the Greek Artemis had already taken place. 'At Rome Diana was the goddess of light, and her name contains the same root as . . . *dies* [day]', Blakeney.

Verse 24 of the same chapter of *Acts* gave rise to that odd C. 17 sense, 'source of gain': see the O.E.D.

diligence; diligently. 'Do thy diligence to come shortly unto me' (2 *Timothy*, iv, 9); 'Wherefore the rather, brethren, give diligence to make your calling and election sure: for if ye do these things, ye shall never fail' (2 *Peter*, i, 10); 'Bring Zenas the lawyer and Apollos on their journey diligently, that nothing be wanting unto them' (*Titus*, iii, 13).—'And he sent them to Bethlehem, and said, Go and search diligently for the young child' (*Matthew*, ii, 8); in the preceding verse, 'Then Herod, when he had privily called the wise men, enquired of them diligently what time the star appeared'.

Do diligence = do one's utmost; *give diligence* = take heed (or care); *diligently* = carefully, accurately. The first belongs to late C. 14–17 and occurs in Chaucer; the second, to C. 16–17; the third to late C. 14–early 18 (O.E.D.).

Diligence and *diligent* (whence the adverb): via Fr. from L. *diligentia* (on *diligens*, 'attentive, assiduous, careful').

disciple. The twelve Apostles are often called the Disciples; but, generally, *disciple* is, in the N.T., used in reference to believers in Christ (whether during his sojourn on earth or afterwards). In *Mark*, ii, 18, and *John*, iii, 25, the term is applied to the followers of John the Baptist; in *Mark*, ii, 18, it is also applied to the followers of Moses; so too in *John*, iii, 25.

The Gr. Test. has μαθητής (plural μαθηταί), whence μαθητεύω, 'I make—or make into—disciples' (*Matthew*, xiii, 52); from a v. meaning 'to learn'.

Lit., 'a pupil or learner', esp. 'one who believes in the doctrine of his teacher and follows him' (Irwin), *disciple* comes from L. *discipulus*, 'a pupil or learner' (*discere*, to learn); hence it also means a personal follower of *any* religious or philosophical teacher, master, authority.

dishonesty. 'But [we] have renounced the hidden things of dishonesty, not walking in craftiness, nor handling the word of God deceitfully' (2 *Corinthians*, iv, 2).

Disgrace, shame: ca. 1370–1630: 1386, Chaucer, 'Shame,

that eschueth alle deshonestee'; More, *Utopia,* 'It is a great reproche, and dishonesty for the husband to come home without his wife'; Shakespeare, *Twelfth Night,* III, iv, 421; *The Winter's Tale,* II, iii, 117; *The Merry Wives of Windsor,* IV, ii, 140.

Via Old Fr. *deshon(n)esté,* from Italian *disonesta,* from *dishonestus,* 'dishonourable; unrespectable, disreputable' (O.E.D.).

dispensation. 'For if I do this thing willingly, I have a reward: but if against my will, a dispensation of the gospel is committed unto me' (1 *Corinthians,* ix, 17); 'That in the dispensation of the fulness of times he might gather together in one all things in Christ . . .' (*Ephesians,* i, 10); 'Whereof [i.e., of the Church] I am made a minister, according to the dispensation of God which is given to me for you, to fulfil the word of God' (*Colossians,* i, 25).

Dispensation in the first two passages = 'the action of administering or managing'; in the third, it has the closely allied meaning, 'the system by which things are administered'; or more probably, according to the O.E.D., in the first and third it = 'office of an administrator', and, in the second, it = 'method or system of administration'. In the Vulgate, *dispensatio* renders the Gr. οἰκονομία, which Souter pertinently translates '*household management* [οἰκία, a house], *stewardship, the office of a steward*; hence met[aphorically, as here] of any position of trust or the duties of that position, *provision, arrangement, dispensation* (even God being sometimes regarded as steward)'.

The word *dispensation* = weighing out (and distributing); via Fr., it comes ultimately from L. *dispendere,* 'to dispend'.

disposition. 'Who have received the law by the disposition of angels, and have not kept it' (*Acts,* vii, 53): Gr. Test. εἰς διαταγὰς ἀγγέλων (according to the ordinances of angels); Vulgate, 'in dispositione angelorum' ('par l'intermédiaire d'anges', Verdunoy); R.V., 'as it was ordained by'—gloss, 'as the ordinance of'.

This sense, recorded first in Chaucer, has been archaic since C. 18. Via Fr. from a L. n. formed on *disponere*, 'to place here and there; to arrange'.

dispute. 'And he went into the synagogue, disputing and persuading the things concerning the kingdom of God' (*Acts*, xix, 8).

I.e., discussing or debating or arguing about the things concerning the kingdom of God (διαλεγόμενος καὶ πείθων τὰ περὶ τῆς βασιλείας τοῦ Θεοῦ: 'disputans et suadens de regno dei', brilliantly translated by Verdunoy as 'il discourait d'une manière persuasive sur les choses qui concernent le royaume de Dieu').—This usage was common in C. 16–17, but has been archaic since ca. 1830.

Ultimately ex *disputare*, which in Classical L. = 'to compute; investigate; treat of; discuss'.

divers, adj. 'Divers diseases and torments' (*Matthew*, iv, 24); 'There shall be famines, and pestilences, and earthquakes, in divers places'. There are, in the N.T., some eighteen instances of *divers* (see Cruden).

Several; various; sundry: in the first example, *divers* = 'several different'; in the second, 'various'. These nuances, which have been archaic since ca. 1850, derive immediately from the sense 'different, diverse' (C. 13–17), which represents Old Fr. *div(i)ers*, from L. *diversus*, lit. 'turned different ways', hence 'different' (O.E.D.).

doctor; doctrine. 'And it came to pass, that after three days they found him in the temple, sitting in the midst of the doctors, both hearing them, and asking them questions' (*Luke*, ii, 46); 'Pharisees and doctors of the law' (*ibid.*, v, 17); 'Gamaliel, a doctor of the law' (*Acts*, v, 34). '. . . When Jesus had ended these sayings, the people were astonished at his doctrine' (*Matthew*, vii, 28); 'And he taught them many things by parables, and said unto them in his doctrine' (*Mark*, iv, 2); *Acts*, v, 28 (see quotation at **Jerusalem**).

Here, *doctor* = 'a teacher': a C. 14–18 usage: via Fr., from

L. *doctor*, 'a teacher' (*docere*, to teach): in the late Middle Ages, Augustine, Gregory, Jerome and Ambrose were called 'the four doctors', as Langland also called Matthew, Mark, Luke, and John.

Doctrine, in the first passage, = 'manner of teaching'; in the second, 'act of teaching' (the R.V. has 'teaching'). Via Fr. from L. *doctrina*, 'teaching'.

done away. 'But when that which is perfect is come, then that which is in part shall be done away' (1 *Corinthians*, xiii, 10; cf. 2 *Corinthians*, iii, 11 and 14).

'Abolished' or 'done away *with*' (as we should now express it): cf. Shakespeare's 'So in thyself thyself art made away' (*Venus and Adonis*, 763). The Gr. Test. has, for the quoted passage, ὅταν δὲ ἔλθῃ τὸ τέλειον, τὸ ἐκ μέρους (the partial) καταργηθήσεται (will be abolished, annulled); the Vulgate, *evacuabitur* ('disparaîtra', Verdunoy).

dote. 'He is proud, knowing nothing, but doting about questions and strifes of words, whereof cometh envy, strife, railings, evil surmisings' (1 *Timothy*, vi, 4).

To be foolish or, more precisely, to talk foolishly: dating from C. 13, this sense has been little used since C. 17 and archaic since ca. 1830. From Middle Dutch *doten*, 'to be silly; to be crazy'. Tyndale vigorously renders νοσῶν (being diseased) as 'wasteth his brains'.

draught. 'Do not ye yet understand, that whatsoever entereth in at the mouth goeth into the belly, and is cast out into the draught?' (*Matthew*, xv, 17; cf. *Mark*, vii, 19). [In 2 *Kings*, x, 27: *draught-house.*]

A privy: a C. 16–17 sense of the word, found in More, Palsgrave, Shakespeare, 'Melancholy' Burton, and in W. Robertson's *Phraseologia Generalis*, 1681, 'A draught or Jakes, *latrina: secessus*', the latter being the word in the Vulgate.

Perhaps a shortening of *withdraught* in the same sense. From the Common Germanic *dragan*, 'to draw (or pull)'.

Wright; O.E.D.

dure. 'Yet hath he not root in himself, but dureth for a while' (*Matthew*, xiii, 21): 'Non habet autem in se radicem, sed est temporalis': οὐκ ἔχει δὲ ῥίζαν ἐν ἑαυτῷ ἀλλὰ πρόσκαιρός ἐστι (is transitory).

To endure, to last, continue to exist: from ca. 1270; but archaic since C. 17. Evelyn, *Sylva*, 1664, 'The wood being preserved dry, will dure a very long time'. Via Fr. *durer*, from L. *durare*, 'to hold out, to last' (*durus*, hard).

E

earnest. '(God) Who hath also sealed us, and given the earnest of the Spirit in our hearts' (2 *Corinthians*, i, 22), cf. *ibid.*, v, 5; 'Ye were sealed with that holy Spirit of promise, Which is the earnest of our inheritance until the redemption of the purchased possession, unto the praise of his glory' (*Ephesians*, i, 13–14).

'*Sealing* especially refers to the understanding; *earnest* to the affections. Though the *seal* assures us, yet it is not part of the inheritance; but the *earnest* so assures us, that it gives a part of the inheritance' (Cruden).

The Gr. Test. has δοὺς τὸν ἀρραβῶνα τοῦ Πνεύματος (having given the—as it were—earnest-money of the Holy Ghost) and ὅ ἐστιν ἀρραβὼν τῆς κληρονομίας ἡμῶν (which is the earnest-money—the prepaid deposit—of our inheritance); in 2 *Corinthians* i, 22, and v, 5, the Vulgate has the synonymous *pignus*. In M.E., it is *e(e)rnes*; the word is cognate with the synonymous *erles* (or *arles*) and *erres* (from Old Fr. *erres*); the latter reminds us that the Gr. ἀρραβών is of Semitic origin (*arra*).

edify. 'Then had the churches rest throughout all Judæa and Galilee and Samaria, and were edified' (*Acts*, ix, 31); 'Knowledge puffeth up, but charity edifieth' (1 *Corinthians*, viii, 1); 'He that speaketh in an unknown tongue edifieth himself; but he that prophesieth edifieth the church' (*ibid.*, xiv, 4).

In these passages, *edify* = to improve or benefit spiritually or intellectually (or both), to promote the spiritual and/or intellectual cause of: this religious metaphor, on the radical sense, 'to build (a house), to construct (a building)', arose, in C. 14, from the fact that the Christian Church was often called 'the house (or temple) of God'; or rather, the metaphor was already present in the Fr. *édifier*, which represents the L. *ædificare* (to make a dwelling).

effeminate. 'Know ye not that the unrighteous shall not inherit the kingdom of God? Be not deceived: neither fornicators, nor idolaters, nor adulterers, nor effeminate, nor abusers of themselves with mankind . . . shall inherit the kingdom of God' (1 *Corinthians*, vi, 9 (10)).

Effeminate renders μαλακοί, plural adj. used as n., 'effeminate persons', a euphemism here for *cinædi* or *pathici*; the Vulgate has *molles*, 'voluptuous persons' (another euphemism). 'Sodomites' is the word needed, not 'voluptuaries'.

elect. 'I charge thee before God, and the Lord Jesus Christ, and the elect angels, that thou observe these things' (1 *Timothy*, v, 21).

' "*Elect* angels" . . . seems to mean, "the angels, God's *chosen* ministers" ' (Wright). Cruden has this note:—'ELECT, or *Chosen*, is spoken, [1] of Christ . . . [2] of good angels, whom God chose from among the rest to eternal life and happiness. . . .' The Gr. Test. has ἐνώπιον . . . τῶν ἐκλεκτῶν ἀγγέλων, in the presence of the selected angels; Vulgate, 'Coram . . . electis angelis' ('devant les anges élus', Verdunoy).

From L. *electus*, passive participle of *eligere*, 'to pick out; to select'.

elements, the. See at **fervent** and at **rudiments.**

emerald. See the quotation at **chrysolite.**
'In early examples the word, like most other names of precious stones, is of vague meaning'; doubtfully to be identified with the Classical *smaragdus*; 'in the A.V. . . . *emerald* has been adopted as the rendering of Heb. *nóphek* ([Septuagint]

ἄνθραξ, Vulg[ate] *carbunculus*), a gem as to the nature of which there is no evidence' (O.E.D.).

Nevertheless, the actual word comes, via Old Fr. *esmeralde, esmeraude, emeraude*, from L. *smaragdus*, which transliterates Gr. σμάραγδος.

emulation. 'Now the works of the flesh are manifest, which are these; Adultery . . . Idolatry, witchcraft, hatred, variance, emulations, wrath, strife, seditions, heresies' (*Galatians*, v. 19–20).

Vulgate *æmulationes*, Gr. Test. ξῆλοι, Verdunoy 'la jalousie'. Jealousy; unpleasant and/or evil rivalry: a C. 16–17 usage. Cf. Shakespeare's 'I was advertised their great general slept, | Whilst emulation in the army crept' (*Troilus and Cressida*, II, ii, 212) and 'My heart laments that virtue cannot live | Out of the teeth of emulation' (*Julius Cæsar*, II, iii, 14).

The L. *æmulatio* was originally a n. of action formed from *æmulari*, 'to rival'.

enable. 'And I thank Jesus Christ our Lord, who hath enabled me, for that he counted me faithful, putting me into the ministry' (1 *Timothy*, i, 12).

I.e., hath made me able or capable or suitable to the purpose.

end.   'Ye have heard of the patience of Job, and have seen the end of the Lord; that the Lord is very pitiful [compassionate], and of tender mercy' (*James*, v, 11).

Here, *end* seems to mean 'aim or purpose'; cf. '(to serve) the ends of Justice' and the Gr. τέλος, 'end' (lit., and hence also fig.), as in that branch of philosophy which is called *Teleology*.

endeavour. 'Endeavouring to keep the unity of the Spirit' (*Ephesians*, iv, 3); 'I will endeavour that ye may be able after my decease to have these things always in remembrance' (2 *Peter*, i, 15).

Endeavour is more than merely 'to try': as F. D. Maurice said in his *Lincoln's Inn Sermons*, p. 156, the word implies 'the highest energy that could be directed to an object'; cf. Trench, *On the Authorized Version of the New Testament*, p. 44 (cited by Wright).

From Fr. *en devoir*; 'cf. the Fr. phrase *se mettre en devoir de faire quelquechose*, to make it one's duty to do something; hence, to set about, to endeavour' (O.E.D.).

ensample. 'Now all these things happened unto them for ensamples: and they are written for our admonition, upon whom the ends of the world are come' (1 *Corinthians*, x, 11); 'Brethren, be followers together of me, and mark them which walk so as ye have us for an ensample' (*Philippians*, iii, 17); 1 *Thessalonians*, i, 7.

An example; a precedent to be followed; a pattern of conduct. Latimer, in a sermon of ca. 1550, has, 'A bishop, not alonely giving good ensample, but teaching according to it, rebuking and punishing vice' (Wright); in 1847—by which date the term was already archaic—Emerson wrote, in his poem *To Rhea*, 'I make this maiden an ensample | To Nature' (O.E.D.).

Via Old Fr. *essample*, from L. *exemplum* (*eximere*, 'to take out').

ensue. See **eschew.**

entreat. 'For he shall be delivered unto the Gentiles, and shall be mocked, and spitefully entreated, and spitted on' (*Luke*, xviii, 32); 'And the next day we touched at Sidon. And Julius courteously entreated Paul, and gave him liberty to go unto his friends to refresh himself' (*Acts*, xxvii, 3); also *Matthew*, ii, 26.

To treat, to handle, to act towards: C. 15–18, then an archaism (also in form *intreat*). 'The pope ill entreated and imprisoned his messengers', Fuller, 1639.

From Old Fr. *entrait(i)er*, *en* + *traiter* (L. *tractare*): O.E.D.

envy. 'He knew that for envy they had delivered him' (*Matthew*, xxvii, 18), cf. *Mark*, xv, 10; 'And the patriarchs, moved with envy, sold Joseph into Egypt' (*Acts*, vii, 9); '. . . Full of envy, murder, debate, deceit, malignity' (*Romans*, i, 29).

Ill-will, spite, malice; malignant feeling; enmity: a sense current in C. 14–mid. 18. 'Envye proprely is malice, therfore it is proprely agayns the bounté of the Holy Gost', Chaucer, ca. 1386 (Wright); 'In Naseby-Fields both armies met, | Their envy, like their numbers, great', Edward Ward, 1707. Immediately from Fr. *envie*, which represents L. *invidia*, formed from *invidus*, 'envious' (*invidere*, 'to look maliciously upon', from *videre*, 'to see'): O.E.D.

Ephesians. *The Epistle of Paul the Apostle to the Ephesians:* 'Paul . . . to the saints which are at Ephesus': Παῦλος τοῖς ἁγίοις τοῖς οὖσιν ἐν Εφέσῳ: 'Paulus . . . omnibus sanctis qui sunt Ephesi.'

(For an admirable brief introduction to this Epistle, see Verdunoy.)

From L. *Ephesius* ('an Ephesian'), a transliteration of the Gr. Ἐφέσιος. '*Ephesus*, a coast city, capital of the Roman province Asia' (Souter).

In Shakespeare's time, *Ephesian* meant 'a boon companion' (2 *Henry IV*, II, ii, 164; *The Merry Wives of Windsor*, IV, v, 19): cf. *Corinthian*.

Epistle. *The Epistle of Paul the Apostle to the Romans*, and the various other Epistles of St. Paul; the word *epistle* occurs frequently in the Books of the N.T., and it is at least twice employed fig.: 'Ye are our epistle written in our hearts, known and read of all men' (2 *Corinthians*, iii, 2); and in the next verse, 'Forasmuch as ye are manifestly declared to be the epistle of Christ ministered by us, written not with ink, but with the Spirit of the living God; not in tables of stone, but in fleshly tables of the heart'.

Gr. ἐπιστολή (from ἐπιστέλλειν, 'to enjoin in writing', hence 'to write': lit., ἐπί, 'on the occasion of' + στέλλειν, 'to send') became L. *epistola*, which became Old Fr. *epist(o)le*: O.E.D.

The term *epistle*, as applied to an Apostle's letter that forms part of the canon of Scripture, arose ca. 1200; as applied to any letter, it had arisen at least three centuries earlier and has, since mid-Victorian days, been slightly archaic and, since ca. 1890, generally jocose or sarcastic.

err. 'Brethren, if any of you do err from the truth . . .'
(*James*, v, 19); 'For the love of money is the root of all evil:
which while some coveted after, they have erred from the
faith' (1 *Timothy*, vi, 10); 'Who concerning the truth have
erred, saying that the resurrection is past already' (2 *Timothy*,
ii, 18).

The Gr. Test. reads, respectively, Ἀδελφόι μου, ἐάν τις ἐν
ὑμῖν πλανηθῇ ἀπὸ τῆς ἀληθείας (wander from the truth);
ἀπεπλανήθησαν ἀπὸ τῆς πίστεως (have wandered away from
the faith); περὶ τὴν ἀλήθειαν ἠστόχησαν (have missed their
aim).

The L. *errare*, which, by the medium of Fr., is the origin
of 'to *err*', means 'to wander, to go astray' (cf. the cognate
German *irren*): and this is the sense here. A sense common
ca. 1370–1700, and obsolete since ca. 1750.

error in 1 *John*, iv, 6, 'Hereby know we the spirit of truth, and
the spirit of error', means 'false doctrine, which is not agreeable to the word of God'; in *Hebrews*, ix, 7, '. . . Blood, which
he offered for himself, and for the errors of the people', *errors*
= 'sins of all sorts'; and in *Romans*, i, 27, 'And likewise also the
men, leaving the natural use of the woman . . .', *their error*
means sodomy. (Cruden.)

L. *error*, 'a wandering, a straying from the path', via Old Fr.
Cf. the preceding entry.

eschew. 'Let him eschew evil, and do good; let him seek
peace, and ensue it' (*ensue* = 'to follow after and overtake', a
sense that has long been obsolete: Fr. *ensuivre*, from L. *in-
sequor*): 1 *Peter*, iii, 11.

To avoid; to escape (something dangerous): ca. 1370–1740.
Cf. Latimer, ca. 1550, 'In teaching evil doctrine all preachers
are to be eschewed, and in no wise to be hearkened unto'
(Wright).

From Old Fr. *eschever* or *eschiver*, the word is of the
Common Romanic stock (O.E.D.).

espouse. In *Matthew*, i 18, and *Luke*, i, 27 ('a virgin espoused
to a man whose name was Joseph'), and *Luke*, ii, 5 ('Mary his

espoused wife'), *espouse*='to betroth' in the first two passages; 'married' in the third.

In English, the earliest sense of *espouse* was 'to marry' (Caxton, 1475); the sense 'to betroth' occurs first in Camden, 1605, 'Two lovers who being espoused, died both before they were married'. From Old Fr. *espouser*, which corresponds to L. *sponsare* (from *spondere*, to betroth). O.E.D.

establish (*Hebrews*, xiii, 9). See the second quotation at **occupy.**

estate. 'And when a convenient day was come, that Herod on his birthday made a supper to his lords, high captains, and chief estates of Galilee' (*Mark*, vi, 21); 'As also the high priest doth bear me witness, and all the estate of the elders' (*Acts*, xxii, 5).

In the former, *estate* = 'a person of estate', i.e. of high estate: a sense that appears first in Langland, 1399, and was obsolete by the end of C. 17.

In the latter, *estate* = 'a class, rank, order': C. 16–17; cf. Shakespeare's 'Egally indeed to all estates' (*Richard III*, III, vii, 216). In C. 16–17, *estate* very generally meant 'state' or 'status'; thus in *Luke*, i, 48, 'the low estate of his handmaiden' is 'her humble condition'.

Via Old Fr. *estat* from L. *status*, 'state' (*stare*, to stand).

evangelist and **Evangelist.** The *Evangelists* are the writers of the four Gospel narratives, but *evangelist* is not so used in the N.T.

The term *evangelist* occurs thrice: 'We entered into the house of Philip the evangelist, which was one of the seven' (*Acts*, xxi, 8); 'And he gave some, apostles; and some, prophets; and some, evangelists' (*Ephesians*, iv, 11); 'But watch thou in all things, endure afflictions, do the work of an evangelist, make full proof of thy ministry' (2 *Timothy*, iv, 5). In these passages, *evangelist* is applied to those 'ministers of the Church who assisted the Apostles in spreading the Gospel, or Evangel, of our Lord Jesus Christ, and who were sent from place to place to execute such particular commissions as the Apostles thought fit to intrust to them. In some of the old writers, the [Greek] word is Englished into *Gospeller*, though this last word came afterwards to be applied to the person who read the "gospel" in the Communion Office' (Wright).

In the Gr. Test. the word is εὐαγγελιστής, which signifies 'a missionary': cf. εὐαγγέλιον, '*the good news* of the coming of the Messiah' (Souter), and εὐαγγελίζω (or—ίζομαι), 'I bring good news', whence the agent-noun derives and comes to us via L. *evangelista* and Fr. *évangéliste*.

The n. *evangelist* reached England ca. 1530, whereas *Evangelist* arrived late in C. 12.

even, adv., has in the N.T., three senses:—

1. 'Exactly, precisely'; *even so* = 'precisely so, just so', as in *John* xvii, 18, 'As thou hast sent me into the world, even so have I also sent them into the world'. Now an archaism.

2. 'Quite, fully', as in 2 *Corinthians*, x, 13. Now archaic.

3. 'Viz., namely; that is to say', as in 1 *Corinthians*, xv, 24, 'Then cometh the end, when he shall have delivered up the kingdom to God, even the Father'—cf. 2 *Corinthians*, i, 3; *Philippians*, ii, 8, 'He . . . became obedient unto death, even the death of the cross'. A C.16–17 sense of the word.

exceeding, adj. and adv. 'That in the ages to come he might shew the exceeding riches of his grace in his kindness toward us through Christ Jesus' (*Ephesians*, ii, 7); 'Men blasphemed God because of the plague of the hail; for the plague thereof was exceeding great' (*Revelation*, xvi, 21).

Respectively 'surpassing; very great' and 'extremely'. Both adj. (mid C. 16–20) and adv. (C. 16–20) are archaic: have, indeed, been archaic since mid C. 19.

The adv. derives directly (cf. *exceedingly*) from the adj., which is obviously participial from the v., *exceed* (via Fr. from L. *excedere*, 'to go out', hence 'to exceed').

excellency. 'I count all things but loss for the excellency of the knowledge of Christ Jesus my Lord' (*Philippians*, iii, 8).

Exceeding (or surpassing) eminence, worth, merit: C. 15–18: cf. Camden, 1605, 'Lady Jane Grey . . . for her excellency in the Greek tongue was called for'—i.e., called—'Greia, Graia'. Slightly later than *excellence*, *excellency* = that n. + *ency*, and it comes from L. *excellentia*, which was formed from the present participle of *excellere*, 'to excel' (O.E.D.).

exchanger (see quotation at **usury**) is 'an exchange-broker', hence (as here) 'a dealer in money, a banker'. The word belongs to C. 16–18. The King's Exchangers were 'officers appointed by the king to give coin in exchange for bullion or plate' (O.E.D.). From Old Fr. *eschangier*, itself from Late L. *excambiare*, 'to change or exchange'.

exorcist. 'Then certain of the vagabond Jews, exorcists, took upon them to call over them which had evil spirits the name of the Lord Jesus' (*Acts*, xix, 13).

'*Exorcists* were those who pretended to raise or cast out devils by adjuring, or commanding them in the Divine Name to come forth.

> Thou, like an exorcist, hast conjured up
> My mortified spirit.
> Shakespeare, *Julius Cæsar*, II, i, 323' (Wright).

In *Matthew*, xxvi, 63, the Gr. ἐξορκίζω σε is rendered 'I adjure thee', wherein we see the origin of the Gr. v. from ὅρκος, 'an oath'. *Exorcist* comes, via the L. transliteration *exorcista*, from the Gr. ἐξορκιστής, '*a caster out of evil spirits by the use of names or spells*' (Souter), itself from the v. ἐξορκίζειν, '*cast out by appeal to a god*' (id.).

expect. 'From henceforth expecting till his enemies be made his footstool' (*Hebrews*, x, 13).

Waiting: here *expect* means 'to defer action until some contingency arises' (O.E.D.). This mid C. 16–18 sense is well exemplified in 'A dog expects till his master has done picking of the bone' (Henry More, 1653), and the corresponding transitive sense, 'to wait for; await', occurs in Shakespeare's 'Let's in and there expect their coming' (*The Merchant of Venice*, v, i, 49).

L. *ex(s)pectare*, 'to look out for', on *spectare*, 'to look' (O.E.D.).

express. 'Who being the brightness of his glory, and the express image of his person . . .' (*Hebrews*, i, 3): Gr. Test., ὅς ὢν ἀπαύγασμα τῆς δόξης καὶ χαρακτὴρ τῆς ὑποστάσεως αὐτοῦ, 'who being a light flashing forth from his glory and a representation of his substance-reality': Vulgate, 'qui, cum sit splendor gloriæ et figura substantia ejus' (rendered by Verdunoy as 'qui, rayonnement de sa gloire et empreinte de son être').

Cf. Milton's 'He created thee, in the image of God | Express' (1667) and Reid's 'Language is the express image and picture of human thoughts' (1764), where, as in the N.T. passage, the sense is thus admirably defined by the O.E.D.: 'Of an image or likeness: Truly depicted, exactly resembling, exact. Now chiefly with reminiscence of *Heb.* i. 3.'

Via Fr. *expresse* (the feminine of *exprès*), from L. *expressus*, the passive participle of *exprimere*, 'to press out', hence 'to express', this adj. occurs earliest in Sir Thomas More's *Richard III*, 1513.

eye-service. 'Not with eyeservice, as menpleasers; but as the servants of Christ, doing the will of God from the heart' (*Ephesians*, vi, 6); cf. *Colossians*, iii, 22.

The Gr. Test. reads: μὴ κατ' ὀφθαλμοδουλείαν ὡς ἀνθρωπάρεσκοι, ἀλλ' ὡς δοῦλοι τοῦ Χριστοῦ ποιοῦντες τὸ θέλημα τοῦ Θεοῦ ἐκ ψυχῆς, 'not according to the enslavement to the eye . . .' (or, as Souter glosses that definition: 'the subjection that waits upon a glance of a master's eye'). The Vulgate: non ad oculum servientes ('non d'une obéissance à l'œil', Verdunoy).

This rare word, coined by Tyndale (1526) in his translation of this passage and used in reminiscence thereof, corresponds to *lip-service*.

F

faint. 'And he spake a parable unto them, to this end, that men ought always to pray, and not to faint (*Luke*, xviii, 1); 'For which cause we faint not; but though our outward man perish, yet the inward man is renewed day by day' (2 *Corinthians*, iv, 16); cf. verse 1 of the same chapter.

To lose courage; become afraid or depressed; to flag or yield: C. 14–mid 18, then archaic and, as an archaism, only in reminiscence of Biblical usage: cf. Shakespeare, 'But if you faint, as fearing to do so, | Stay and be secret, and myself will go' (*Richard II*, II, i, 297: Wright).

Immediately from the adj., which comes from Old Fr. *faint* or *feint*, 'sluggish, cowardly', from *faindre* or *feindre*: L. *fingere*, 'to form or mould', hence 'to feign': O.E.D.

faithless. 'Then Jesus answered and said, O faithless and perverse generation, how long shall I be with you?' (*Matthew*, xvii, 17); cf. *Mark*, ix, 19; 'Then said he to Thomas, Reach hither thy finger, and behold my hands; and reach thither thy hand, and thrust it into my side: and be not faithless, but believing' (*John*, xx, 27): καὶ μὴ γίνου ἄπιστος, ἀλλὰ πιστός: et noli esse incredulus, sed fidelis ('et ne sois pas incrédule, mais croyant', Verdunoy).

Unbelieving; without belief, trust, confidence: C. 14–20; archaic since ca. 1860. Cf. Shakespeare's 'She is issue to a faithless Jew' (*The Merchant of Venice*, II, iv, 38: Wright) and Tennyson's 'The faithless coldness of the times' (*In Memoriam*, 1850: O.E.D.).

fame, in its primary sense (now obsolete), 'news, tidings, report, public report'—L. *fama*, 'a report', from Gr. φήμη, 'a voice; a saying; a report'—occurs, or appears to occur, in *Luke*, iv, 14, 'And Jesus returned in the power of the Spirit into Galilee: and there went out a fame of him through all the region round about'; cf. v. 15; probably in *Matthew*, ix, 26; possibly in xiv, 1.

fan. 'Whose fan is in his hand, and he will thoroughly purge his floor, and gather his wheat into the garner' (*Matthew*, iii, 12); so too in *Luke*, iii, 17. The Vulgate has 'Cujus ventilabrum in manu sua'; the Gr. Test., οὗ τὸ πτύον ἐν τῇ χειρὶ αὐτοῦ.

A winnowing fan, 'a basket of special form . . . used for separating the corn from the chaff by throwing it into the air' (O.E.D.): C. 14–20; but archaic since ca. 1750. But in the passages belonging to C. 9–13, as in the Gr., the *fan* is nothing more than 'a sort of wooden shovel' (O.E.D.) or, more probably, 'a simple wooden pitchfork' (Souter). Shakespeare metaphorizes it in:

> Distinction, with a broad and powerful fan,
> Puffing at all, winnows the light away.
> *Troilus and Cressida*, I, iii, 27.

Via O.E. *fann*, from L. *vannus* (which, in Fr., became *van*).

far spent. 'And when the day was now far spent, his disciples came unto him, and said, This is a desert place, and now the time is far passed' (*Mark*, vi, 35); 'Abide with us: for it is toward evening, and the day is far spent' (*Luke*, xxiv, 29); 'The night is far spent, the day is at hand' (*Romans*, xiii, 12).

Gr. Test., καὶ ἤδη ὥρας πολλῆς γενομένης, it being already an advanced period (of the day): et cum jam hora multa fieret ('comme l'heure était déjà avancée', Verdunoy); κέκλινεν ἤδη ἡ ἡμέρα, the day has already approached its end: inclinata est jam dies ('le jour est déjà sur son déclin'); ἡ νὺξ προέκοψε, the night has advanced: nox praecessit ('la nuit s'est avancée').

I.e., 'far passed': mid C. 16–20; archaic since ca. 1850. Its lit. meaning is 'far consumed' (consumed to a very great extent), for the basic meaning of *spend* is 'to consume'.

fashion. 'And as he prayed, the fashion of his countenance

was altered, and his raiment was white and glistening'
(*Luke*, ix, 29); 'And being found in fashion as a man, he
humbled himself, and became obedient unto death, even the
death of the cross' (*Philippians*, ii, 8).

Gr. Test., καὶ ἐγένετο . . . αὐτὸν τὸ εἶδος τοῦ προσώπου
αὐτοῦ ἕτερον, and the very appearance (or shape) of his face
became different; καὶ σχήματι εὑρεθεὶς ὡς ἄνθρωπος, and
being found a man as to outward form.

'Make, build, shape. Hence, in wider sense, visible charac-
teristics, appearance' (O.E.D.): C. 14–20, but archaic since
C. 18. 'By heaven, I will, | Or let me lose the fashion of a
man!' and 'This something-settled matter in his heart, |
Whereon his brains still beating puts him thus | From fashion
of himself': Shakespeare, *Henry VIII* and *Hamlet*. From L.
factio (accusative *factionem*), n. of action from *facere*, 'to do or
make', the word comes to us via Old Norman Fr. *fachon*.

fearful. ('And, behold, there arose a great tempest in the
sea. . . . And his disciples came . . ., saying, Lord, save us:
we perish.) And he saith unto them, Why are ye fearful, O
ye of little faith?' *Matthew*, viii, 26; cf. *Mark*, iv, 40; 'But the
fearful, and unbelieving, and the abominable, and murderers . . . shall have their part in the lake which burneth with
fire and brimstone: which is the second death' (*Revelation*,
xxi, 8).

Here, the sense is *fear-full*, 'full of fear; timorous or faint-
hearted'; a sense that is virtually obsolete; since ca. 1820,
the dominant sense has been 'causing fear'.

feast of charity. See **charity.**

fervent. 'But the day of the Lord will come as a thief in the
night; in the which the heavens shall pass away with a great
noise, and the elements shall melt with fervent heat, the earth
also and the works that are therein shall be burned up'
(2 *Peter*, iii, 10, as also in 12).

The Gr. of 'the elements shall melt with fervent heat' is
στοιχεῖα δὲ καυσούμενα λυθήσεται, where στοιχεῖα ('ele-

ments') = 'the heavenly bodies' and is merely synonymous
with the οὐρανοί of the preceding clause. (Souter.)

Fervent is 'burning' or 'glowing': from L. *fervére*, 'to be
boiling or glowing'.

figure, in a. 'Accounting that God was able to raise him
[Isaac] up, even from the dead; from whence also he [Abra-
ham] received him in a figure' (*Hebrews*, xi, 19).

The Gr. is ὅθεν αὐτὸν καὶ ἐν παραβολῇ ἐκομίσατο; Abraham
received Isaac 'from the dead' *as in a figure*, i.e. fig. or
parabolically (see **parable**); '*In a figure*, i.e. as a figure, either
of the future general resurrection of all men, or of Christ
offered up to God and raised again from the dead', as it is
glossed in Thayer's revision of Wilke's *Clavis Novi Testamenti*;
Thayer himself, however, prefers to interpret ἐν παραβολῇ as
'in risking him, i.e. at the very moment "when he exposed his
son to mortal peril" '.

filthy lucre. See **lucre.**

floor, in the quotation at **fan,** = threshing-floor.

flux. 'And it came to pass, that the father of Publius lay sick
of a fever and of a bloody flux' (*Acts*, xxviii, 8): ἐγένετο δὲ τὸν
πατέρα τοῦ Ποπλίου πυρετοῖς καὶ δυσεντερίᾳ συνεχόμενον
κατακεῖσθαι , 'and it happened that Publius's father lay in bed
afflicted with fever and dysentery'.

Flux, 'dysentery', has been in use since ca. 1370, but in C. 20
it is (except as a medical term) archaic; also called *bloody flux*,
i.e., a bloody flowing.

L. *fluxus* (*fluere*, to flow), via Fr.

for all. 'Simon Peter went up, and drew the net to land full
of great fishes, an hundred and fifty and three: and for all there
were so many, yet was not the net broken' (*John*, xxi, 11); i.e.,
and although there were so many. . . .

For all and *for all that* as conjunctions, meaning 'although;
notwithstanding that', are obsolete. The sense, here, of *for*
is 'in despite of'.

for that. Because; inasmuch as.

See the quotation at **enable.** Like the preceding conjunction, it is obsolete.

forbear. 'With all lowliness and meekness, with longsuffering, forbearing one another in love' (*Ephesians*, iv, 2); 'Forbearing one another, and forgiving one another, if any man have a quarrel against any' (*Colossians*, iii, 13).

Cf. the Gr. Test., ἀνεχόμενοι ἀλλήλων ἐν ἀγάπῃ, 'enduring one another in love' (Vulgate, 'supportantes invicem in caritate': 'vous supportant les uns les autres avec charité', Verdunoy); so too for the *Colossians* passage.

To bear with, put up with, tolerate; to have patience with: late C. 9–18. 'With the little godliness I have, I did full hard'—with great difficulty—'forbear him', Shakespeare, *Othello*, I, ii, 10. The predominant current sense is 'to refrain from' ('He forbears to reproach her'). The word is of Common Germanic stock.

foreknow; foreknowledge. 'For whom he did foreknow, he also did predestinate to be conformed to the image of his Son, that he might be the firstborn among many brethren' (*Romans*, viii, 29); 'Him, being delivered by the determinate counsel and foreknowledge of God, ye have taken, and by wicked hands have crucified and slain' (*Acts*, ii, 23); 'Elect according to the foreknowledge of God the Father, through sanctification of the Spirit' (1 *Peter*, i, 2).

To know beforehand; previous knowledge.

forepart and **foreship.** 'And falling into a place where two seas met, they ran the ship aground; and the forepart stuck fast, and remained unmoveable' (*Acts*, xxvii, 41); '. . . cast anchors out of the foreship' (*ibid.*, nine verses before).

The bow of the ship, in each passage. *Forepart* was common only in C. 16–early 18; since then, it has been archaic. But *foreship* has been current since late C. 10.

forerunner. 'Whither the forerunner is for us entered, even

Jesus' (*Hebrews*, vi, 20): ὅπου πρόδρομος ὑπὲρ ἡμῶν εἰσῆλθεν
Ἰησοῦς: where πρόδρομος is 'forerunner' in its lit. sense,
'one who runs in front' (to announce another person's arrival).

fornicator. See the quotation at **effeminate.** The word
occurs on four other occasions in the N.T., which affords no
example of the v. *fornicate*, but numerous examples of *fornication*, used—as Cruden shows—in four senses: 1, sexual indulgence between unmarried persons (1 *Corinthians*, vii, 2)—the
usual sense; 2, adultery (*Matthew*, v, 32); 3, incest (1 *Corinthians*, v, 1); 4, metaphorically for idolatry ('infidelity to,
and forsaking of, the true God for false gods', as in *Revelation*,
xix, 2)—generally called *spiritual fornication*.

The English *fornicator* comes, not from the v. *fornicate*, but
as a direct adoption of L. *fornicator*, the agent formed from
fornicari ('to commit fornication—to have sexual intercourse'),
itself formed from *fornix*, 'a brothel', lit., 'a vaulted chamber',
the primary sense of L. *fornix* being 'an arch' (O.E.D.).

forsomuch as. 'And Jesus said unto him, This day is salva-
tion come to this house, forsomuch as he also is a son of
Abraham' (*Luke*, xix, 9): Gr. Test., κάθοτι ('because', Souter):
Vulgate, 'eo quod' ('parce que', Verdunoy).

I.e., inasmuch as, in that; because.

Forsomuch as is obsolete, having been current only ca. 1450–
1660; its variant *forasmuch as*, used since late C.13, is archaic.

forwardness. 'I speak not by commandment, but by occasion of the forwardness of others, and to prove the sincerity of
your love' (2 *Corinthians*, viii, 8); 'For I know the forwardness
of your mind, for which I boast of you to them of Macedonia,
that Achaia was ready a year ago' (*ibid.*, ix, 2).

In the former, the nuance is 'earnestness, or zeal'; in the
latter, 'readiness, or eagerness': nuances that are obsolescent.

frankly and **freely.** 'And when they had nothing to pay'
—i.e., no money with which to pay their debts—'he frankly
forgave them both' (*Luke*, vii, 42)—'Heal the sick, cleanse the
lepers, raise the dead, cast out devils: freely ye have received,

freely give' (*Matthew*, x, 8); 'And the Spirit and the bride say, Come. And let him that heareth say, Come. And whosoever will, let him take the water of life freely' (*Revelation*, xxii, 17).

With this example of *frankly*, 'unreservedly', cf. that in Shakespeare, *Henry VIII*, ii, i, 81:

> I do beseech your grace, for charity,
> If ever any malice in your heart
> Were hid against me, now to forgive me frankly.

Freely, in the passage from *Matthew*, signifies 'unstintedly'; so too in that from *Revelation*.

froward. 'Servants, be subject to your masters with all fear; not only to the good and gentle, but also to the froward' (1 *Peter*, ii, 18).

Perverse, hard to satisfy or please. The opposite of the obsolete adj. *toward*, *froward* has been a literary word since C. 18. The semantic idea is: disposed to turn *from* that which is proposed; 'turning off from the truth' (Souter).

fruits. See at **bestow.**

fuller. 'And his raiment became shining, exceeding white as snow; so as no fuller on earth can white them' (*Mark*, ix, 3): καὶ τὰ ἱμάτια αὐτοῦ ἐγένετο στίλβοντα, λευκὰ λίαν, οἷα γραφεὺς ἐπὶ τῆς γῆς οὐ δύναται οὕτω λευκᾶναι, and his (long, flowing) outer garment became a-gleam, exceedingly white, such as the fuller cannot thus whiten upon the ground (cf. 'The fuller treads upon that cloth which he means to whiten', Bishop Hall, 1645): Et vestimentia ejus facta sunt splendentia, et candida nimis velut nix, qualia fullo non potest super terram candida facere.

A *fuller* of cloth is, in O.E., *fullere*: which represents L. *fullo* (a fuller) + agential -*er*, the English v. *full* (to tread or beat cloth in order to cleanse and thicken it) arising many centuries later and coming from Old Fr. *fuler* (now *fouler*), 'to tread under foot'.

G

Gadarene swine. 'If you take my advice, you'll avert your skirts from the question of the Gadarene swine and the problem of whether their keepers were breaking the local laws or not', writes a witty and by no means irreverent friend of the lexicographer's.

The evil spirits driven from the Legion-possessed man's were permitted to enter the bodies of 'a great herd of swine' feeding 'nigh unto the mountains in 'the country of the Gadarenes' (*Mark*, v, 1–17): it is difficult not to sympathize with the owners; but that is an aspect beyond my province.

Gadarene signifies 'walled, surrounded' (Cruden). 'Into the country of the Gadarenes' is, in the Gr. Test., εἰς τὴν χώραν τῶν Γερασηνῶν, into the district of the *Gerasenes*, the inhabitants of Gerasa, a town on the East of Lake Tiberias: 'Wherever this people is mentioned the variants Γαδαρηνός and Γεργεσηνος occur': the third is the best, the first a by-form, the second a conscious alteration (Souter).

gain a loss. 'But after long abstinence Paul stood forth in the midst of them, and said, Sirs, ye should have hearkened unto me, and not have loosed'—i.e., weighed anchor, set sail (cf. *Acts*, xiii, 13)—'from Crete, and to have gained this harm and loss' (*Acts*, xxvii, 21): κερδῆσαί τε τὴν ὕβριν ταύτην καὶ τὴν ζημίαν.

'The Greek is here literally translated; but the English phrase conveys an erroneous idea, as if it meant to *incur* danger, whereas it can be proved by numerous examples to mean *escape* or *avoid* danger. The Geneva version . . . adds in a note, "that is, ye should have saved the loss by avoiding the danger" ' (Wright).

Souter translates κερδαίνω ὕβριν καὶ ζημίαν as 'I gain injury and loss', and adds, '*I.e.*, I gain by shunning injury and loss, I do not suffer (I am spared) injury and loss'.

See also the paragraph in the O.E.D. at *gain*, v., sense 1.

gainsay; gainsayer; gainsaying. 'For I will give you a mouth and wisdom, which all your adversaries shall not be able to gainsay nor resist' (*Luke*, xxi, 15).—'Holding fast the faithful word as he hath been taught, that he may be able by sound doctrine both to exhort and to convince the gainsayers' (*Titus*, i, 8).—(As adj.) 'But to Israel he saith, All day long I have stretched forth my hands unto a disobedient and gainsaying people' (*Romans*, x, 21); as noun, in two passages, 'Therefore came I unto you without gainsaying, as soon as I was sent for' (*Acts*, x, 29), and 'Woe unto them! for they have gone in the way of Cain, and ran greedily after the error of Balaam for reward, and perished in the gainsaying of Core' (*Jude*, 11).

To *gainsay* is 'to contradict, to resist in speech'; a *gainsayer* is a verbal opponent; as adj., *gainsaying* means 'contumacious, disputatious'—what used to be called 'contradictious'; and as n., it means 'questioning, cavil'.

In all these words, *gain-* signifies 'against'; and in all there is a connotation of refractoriness.

Galatians. *The Epistle of Paul the Apostle to the Galatians* is a formal letter to the inhabitants of the large Roman province Galatia in central Asia Minor: it included the districts of Paphlagonia, Pisidia, Isaurica, Lycaonia Galatica, Phrygia Galatica, Pontus Galaticus, and Galatia (the *district*, not province): cf. *Acts*, xvi, 6, where *the region of Galatia* is the province Galatia (which was racially Phrygian).

Galatian, n. and adj., is from a regular L. *-anus* formation on *Galatia*, 'the land of milk' (Gr. γάλα, milk).

garner, n. '. . . Gather his wheat into the garner' (*Matthew*, iii, 12); with which, cf. *Luke*, iii, 17.

A granary: C. 12–20; but in C. 19–20 only poetic and/or rhetorical. The derivative 'to *garner*' has survived, as a metaphor. Chaucer, 'Wel cowde [could] he kepe a garner and a bynne'; Shakespeare, 'Earth's increase, foison plenty, | Barns and garners never empty'; Landor, 'All the garners of Surrey'.

Via Old Fr. *garn(i)er*, 'a storehouse, a garret', by metathesis from L. *granarium* (a granary), which holds *grana*, 'grains', as a *salarium* holds *sal*, 'salt'.

(Wright; O.E.D.)

garnish. 'And when he is come, he findeth it empty, swept, and garnished' (*Matthew*, xii, 44), cf. *Luke*, xi, 25; 'Woe unto you, scribes and Pharisees, hypocrites! because ye built the tombs of the prophets, and garnish the sepulchres of the righteous' (*Matthew*, xxiii, 29); 'And the foundations of the wall of the city were garnished with all manner of precious stones' (*Revelation*, xxi, 19).

In the first passage, *empty* must = 'emptied of rubbish', for here, as in the other passages, to *garnish* = 'to ornament, decorate, embellish'; except in reference to *Matthew*, xii, 44, this sense is archaic.

From Old Fr. *garnir* (with stem *garniss-* in certain parts of the v.), 'to provide, to prepare', probably from some Germanic word. Both the Fr. word and the Eng. word had also the basic sense, 'to fortify or defend': to defend oneself, one must *furnish* oneself with requisites.

gazing-stock. 'Partly, whilst ye were made a gazingstock both by reproaches and afflictions' (*Hebrews*, ix, 33).

That at which many persons gaze, precisely as the slightly earlier *laughing-stock* is an object of general laughter and as the still, though slightly, earlier *mocking-stock* (very common in C. 16–17, but obsolete since ca. 1850) signifies a person (or a thing) that incurs a widespread mockery; archaic since ca. 1850.

[**Gehenna** does not occur in the N.T., where Gr. γέεννα is translated 'hell'; the ecclesiastical L. form of this Gr. word (a transliteration of post-Biblical Heb.—i.e., Aramaic—*gehinnom* or rather, *ge ben hinnom*, 'place of fiery torment for the dead') is *gehenna*. See esp. the O.E.D., Hastings, Leclercq.]

gender, v. 'But foolish and unlearned questions avoid, knowing that they do gender strifes' (2 *Timothy*, ii, 23). [*Unlearned* = ignorant.]

To engender (fig., from the lit. sense, 'to beget'); to produce, to bring about, give rise to; to occasion: mid C. 15–mid 19, then archaic, the usual C. 19–20 form being *engender* (itself literary and rhetorical).

Via Old Fr. *gendrer* from L. *generare*, 'to beget, to breed', itself formed from *genus*, 'a breed; a race' (O.E.D.).

generation. 'But when he saw many of the Pharisees and Sadducees come to his baptism, he said unto them, O generation of vipers, who hath warned you to flee from the wrath to come?' (*Matthew*, iii, 7, cf. *Luke*, iii, 7): Gr. Test., γεννήματα ἐχιδνῶν, which is plural ('children of vipers'): Vulgate, 'progenies viperarum'.

Progeny: a sense current ca. 1380–1700. Shakespeare, 'The barbarous Scythian, | Or he that makes his generation messes | To gorge his appetite', *Lear*, I, i, 119 (adduced by Wright). Directly ex the lit. sense, '(a) procreation'; from L. *generatio*, an active n. formed on *generare*, 'to beget or generate', cf. **gender.**

Gentile; Gentiles. 'Why compellest thou the Gentiles to live as do the Jews?' (*Galatians*, ii, 14); St. Paul, by the way, generally called them Greeks ('To the Jew first, and also to the Greek', *Romans*, i, 16—cf. ii, 9–10; iii, 9; x, 12).

In the quoted passage, the Gr. Test. has πῶς τὰ ἔθνη ἀναγκάζεις Ἰουδαΐζειν; which= 'why do you force the *gentes*, or nations outside Judaism, to live as Jews?': to which the corresponding Vulgate is 'quomodo gentes cogis judaizare?' ('comment peux-tu contraindre les Gentils a judaïser?', Verdunoy).

The n. *Gentile* comes immediately from the adj. *Gentile*, which represents (not necessarily by way of Fr. *gentil*) L. *gentilis*, 'belonging to a *gens* or nation'. *Gentile* soon became equivalent to 'a pagan, a heathen'—a sense archaic since C. 18, obsolete since ca. 1914.

Gethsemane. 'Then cometh Jesus with them unto a place called Gethsemane' (*Matthew*, xxvi, 36); cf. *Mark*, xiv, 32,

'And they came to a place which was named Gethsemane'. Gr. Test., εἰς χωρίον λεγόμενον Γεθσημανῆ and εἰς χωρίον οὖ τὸ ὄνομα Γεθσημανῆ.

Gethsemani is 'a small place between the brook Kidron and the Mount of Olives near Jerusalem' (Souter) and etymologically it means 'a fertile valley' (or perhaps 'the valley of oil'), or, according to others, 'an oil-press'.—For an informative short account, see *The Encyclopædia Britannica*.

Ghost, the Holy. The Holy Spirit.

(For the etymology, etc., of the adjective, see **holy**.)

'I shall be greatly indebted to you if you will explain the precise significance of "the Holy Ghost" . . . ; also the "sin against the Holy Ghost" (which is sometimes supposed to be the act of attributing to the Devil the works of Christ); and also the precise grounds which led the translators to use the word "Ghost" instead of "Spirit". If you will clear up these matters in words easily understood by non-theologians, it will certainly be of service to one reader': thus an inquiring friend.

The Holy Ghost has no precise significance: to different theologians, it has different connotations; but the general acceptation is 'the Divine Spirit; the Third Person of the Godhead' (the third member of the Trinity).

Whereas *spirit* comes from the L. *spiritus*, 'breathing' or 'breath' ('The earlier English uses of the word are mainly derived from passages in the Vulgate, in which *spiritus* is employed to render Gr. πνεῦμα PNEUMA ', O.E.D.),—see Gr. quotation at **comfort**,—*ghost*, in the dim pre-Teutonic past, seems to have meant 'anger' or 'fury' and, in O.E. texts of ca. 900–1000 A.D., meant 'the soul, as the principle of life', a sense surviving in *give up the ghost* (earlier *yield up* or *give the ghost*), 'to breathe one's last [breath], to die', as in 'Jesus, when he had cried again with a loud voice, yielded up the ghost' (*Matthew*, xxvii, 50). *Ghost*, in the sense 'the spirit of God', is obsolete, except in *the Holy Ghost*, which is itself confined to the language of dogma and liturgy. The translators of the A.V. may have changed *spirit* to *ghost* in their effort to be 'Anglo-Saxon' rather than Latin in their language.

In the N.T., *ghost* (by itself) is used of the higher nature, the moral nature, of man: of the spirit as opposed to the flesh. The prevailing current sense is 'the soul of a deceased person, spoken of as appearing in a visible form, or otherwise manifesting its presence, to the living' (O.E.D.).

glass. 'For now we see through a glass, darkly; but then face to face; now I know in part; but then shall I know even as also I am known' (1 *Corinthians*, xiii, 12); 'But we all, with open face beholding as in a glass the glory of God, are changed into the same image from glory to glory, even as by the Spirit of the Lord' (2 *Corinthians*, iii, 18); 'For if any be a hearer of the word, and not a doer, he is like unto a man beholding his natural face in a glass' (*James*, i, 23).

In these passages, *glass = looking-glass* or *mirror*. The earliest mirrors were made of metal. The word *mirror* arose in the 13th, *glass* in the 14th, and *looking-glass* not until the 16th Century.

glister. 'And as he prayed, the fashion of his countenance was altered, and his raiment was white and glistering' (*Luke*, ix, 29): where we would say 'shining'.

Glister, 'to glisten', has been superseded by *glitter*; both of these verbs arose in the 14th Century. The proverb, 'All that glitters is not gold' was originally 'All that glisters . . .' (O.E.D.).

go about. 'For they being ignorant of God's righteousness, and going about to establish their own righteousness, have not submitted themselves unto the righteousness of God' (*Romans*, x, 3).

'Going about to establish their own righteousness' translates the Gr. τὴν ἰδίαν [δικαιοσύνην] ζητοῦντες στῆσαι, where ζητοῦντες is 'seeking'.

This sense of *go about* occurs often enough in 16th–17th Century writers; e.g., Latimer, 'I go about to make my fold: you go about to break the same'.

76

go beyond. 'That no man go beyond and defraud his brother in any matter' (1 *Thessalonians*, iv, 6).

To overreach, to trick. Cf.:

> 'The king has gone beyond me: all my glories
> In that one woman I have lost for ever.'
>   (Shakespeare, *Henry VIII*, III, ii, 409–10: quoted
>   by Wright.)

God speed. 'If there come any unto you, and bring not this doctrine, receive him not into your house, neither bid him God speed: For he that biddeth him God speed is partaker of' —sharer in—'his evil deeds' (2 *John*, 10–11). The relevant Gr. is μὴ λαμβάνετε αὐτὸν εἰς οἰκίαν, καὶ χαίρειν αὐτῷ μὴ λέγετε· ὁ γὰρ λέγων αὐτῷ χαίρειν; the relevant Latin in the Vulgate, 'nec Ave ei dixeritis. Qui enim dicit illi Ave'. The N.T. χαίρειν is an imperatival infinitive and means 'rejoice!', i.e., 'farewell!'

To *bid* (a person) *God-speed* is to utter the words *God speed* (*you*), 'God cause you to prosper', esp. on your journey or in an adventure or enterprise.

Golgotha. 'A place called Golgotha, that is to say, a place of a skull' (*Matthew*, xxvii, 33; Gr. Test., τόπον λεγόμενον Γολγοθᾶ, ὅς ἐστι λεγόμενος Κρανίου τόπος; Vulgate, 'locum qui dicitur Golgotha, quod est Calvariæ locus'; Verdunoy, 'lieu appelé Golgotha, ce qui signifie lieu du crâne'); cf. *Mark*, xv, 22, and esp. *John*, xix, 17, 'He bearing his cross went forth into a place called the place of a skull, which is called in the Hebrew Golgotha' (ὃ λέγεται Ἑβραϊστὶ Γολγοθᾶ) (see also **Calvary.**).

Golgotha is 'a knoll outside the wall of Jerusalem' (Souter). The Gr. Γολγοθᾶ is a transliteration of the Aramaic form of the Heb. word meaning 'skull'. (For the witty University pun on *Golgotha*, see my *Dictionary of Slang*.)

goodman. 'And when they had received it, they murmured against the goodman of the house' (*Matthew*, xx, 11); 'But know this, that if the goodman of the house had known in what watch the thief would come, he would have watched, and would not have suffered his house to be broken up' [i.e. broken into, here = burgled; cf. *Mark*, ii, 4], *ibid.*, xxiv, 43 (so too in *Luke*, xii, 39).

Goodman of the house is 'master of the house'. By itself, *good-man* bore this sense as early as the 14th Century. Undoubtedly *good* (adj.) + *man*. *Goodwife* arose at the same period and in the same way: in the eyes of the rest of the household (family, dependants, servants), master and mistress were, in some sense or other, the *good* man and the *good* woman.

good Samaritan. See **Samaritan**.

good works. For an instance, see at **provoke** (second quotation); 'Now there was at Joppa a certain disciple named Tabitha, which by interpretation is called Dorcas: this woman was full of good works and almsdeeds which she did' (*Acts*, ix, 36); 'In all things shewing thyself a pattern of good works' (*Titus*, ii, 7); 'A peculiar people, zealous of good works' (*ibid.*, ii, 14); and elsewhere.

Good works are the good one *does*, in opposition to the good one merely professes; esp. such acts of piety as are done in accordance with divine law or are prompted by faith or godliness. The corresponding Gr. is ἀγαθά ἔργα or καλά ἔργα; the Vulgate has 'opera bona' or 'bona opera'.

gospel; Gospels, the. The term *Gospel* 'is taken for an historical narration of what *Christ* did and spake, of his life, miracles, death, resurrection, and doctrine; as the Gospel according to *Matthew, Mark, &c.*'; *The Gospel according to St Mark* opens thus, 'The beginning of the gospel of Jesus Christ'. In *Romans*, i, 9, 'For God is my witness, whom I serve with my spirit in the gospel of his Son, that without ceasing I make mention of you always in my prayers', it = 'the preaching and publication of the gospel' (Cruden). In the quotation from *Mark* and in the phrase from Cruden, we should rather use a capital G for what is, or is virtually, a Proper Noun.

The common n. is *gospel*, and *gospel* is employed to

translate the Gr. εὐαγγέλιον, 'good news' or 'glad tidings', with especial reference to the coming of the Messiah; 'The genitive after it expresses sometimes the giver (God), sometimes the subject (the Messiah), sometimes the human transmitter (an apostle)', as Souter has discriminatingly remarked.

The term *gospel* is O.E. *godspel*, i.e. *god spel*, 'good tidings'; not *God-spell*, 'a story or discourse of or about God', as is sometimes supposed.

Cf. the entry at **evangelist.**

governor. 'Behold, we put bits in the horses' mouths, that they may obey us; and we turn about their whole body. | Behold also the ships, which though they be so great, and are driven of fierce winds, yet they are turned about with a very small helm, whithersoever the governor listeth' or wishes (*James*, iii, 3–4).

Here, the *governor* is the pilot: L. *gubernator*, via Old Fr. *governeur* (Modern Fr. *gouverneur*). This sense, 'steersman', was current in the 14th–early 17th Centuries.

In *Galatians*, iv, 2, '(The heir, so long as he is a child,) is under tutors and governors until the time appointed of the father', it = 'a guardian': so that 'tutors and governors' is a tautological phrase, for *tutor* also = 'a guardian'.

In *John*, ii, 8–9, 'governor of the *feast*' and 'ruler of the feast' are translations of the Gr. ἀρχιτρίκλινος, which Souter renders as 'master of ceremonies (at a dinner), master of the feast'; cf. L. *arbiter bibendi.*

graff. 'And if some of the branches be broken off, and thou, being a wild olive tree, wert graffed in among them, and partakest of the root and fatness of the olive tree; | Boast not against the branches' (*Romans*, xi, 17–18); cf. verses 23–4.

To *graft*, which it precedes by a century; Langland, 1377, has 'To graffe ympes'. In C. 16–17, both forms were used freely: Udall, in his translation, 1548, of Erasmus's commentary on the N.T., has *grafted* and *graffed* on the same page.

Graff, v., derives immediately from the n., which comes

from Old Fr. *grafe* (or *graffe*), Late L. *graphium*, Gr. γϱαφεῖον, 'a stylus'; 'the transferred sense of "scion, graft" was suggested by the similarity of shape' (O.E.D.).

Grecians. 'And in those days, when the number of the disciples was multiplied, there arose a murmuring of the Grecians against the Hebrews, because their widows were neglected in the daily ministration' (*Acts*, vi, 1; cf. ix, 29, and xi, 20).

Grecians, for *Greeks* (natives or inhabitants of Greece), has been archaic since C. 18, and virtually obsolete since ca. 1890. *Grecian* is an adj. used substantivally: L. *Græcianus*. The English corresponding to the L. n. *Græcus* is *Greek*, which, indeed, was used in England some centuries before *Grecian* (whether n. or adj.).

The Græci were the Γϱαιϰοί, 'said by Aristotle . . . to have been the prehistoric name of the Hellenes in their original seats in Epirus' (O.E.D.). The usual. Gr. word (Classical and N.T.) for a Greek is ῞Ελλην, adj. ῾Ελληνιϰός: our *Hellene* and *Hellenic*.

guest-chamber. 'The Master saith, Where is the guest-chamber, where I shall eat the passover with my disciples?' (*Mark*, xiv, 14; cf. *Luke*, xxii, 11).

Not a bed-room for guests, but a reception-room for them —a room in which they may be entertained. Farrar, in his *St Paul*, speaks of 'the guest-chambers which were attached to Jewish synagogues'.

The Gr. is ϰατάλυμα, which, however, has generally the sense, 'an inn, lodging' (Souter).

guilty of. 'What think ye? They answered and said, He is guilty of death' (*Matthew*, xxvi, 66); 'Ye have heard the blasphemy: what think ye? And they all condemned him to be guilty of death' (*Mark*, xiv, 64).

I.e., guilty to the extent of being worthy to be condemned to death. Here, *guilty of* = '(legally) deserving of': *guilty of death* imitates the *reus mortis* of the Vulgate. The Gr. is ἔνοχον θανάτου: ἔνοχος (cf. L. *obnoxius*) = 'involved in', hence 'liable to' (with either the dative or, as here, the genitive of the punishment), as Souter points out.

Cf. 'Whosoever shall eat this bread, and drink this cup of the Lord, unworthily, shall be guilty of the body and blood of the Lord' (1 *Corinthians*, xi, 27), where *guilty of* = 'guilty against', perhaps with the connotation 'guilty even against'.

H

had. 'I have brought him forth before you, and specially before thee, O king Agrippa, that, after examination had, I might have somewhat to write' (*Acts*, xxv, 26), where *had* = 'held', and *after examination had* (a L. construction: *post quæstionem habitam*) = 'after the holding of an examination'.

'Then stood up there one in the council, a Pharisee, named Gamaliel, a doctor of the law, had in reputation among all the people, and commanded to put the apostles forth a little space' (*Acts*, v, 34), where *had in reputation*, an adjectival phrase agreeing with 'Gamaliel', = 'held in reputation', i.e., esteemed, well reputed.

hail! 'And forthwith he [Judas Iscariot] came to Jesus, and said, Hail, master; and kissed him' (*Matthew*, xxvi, 49)—to which the corresponding O.E. text is 'Hál beo thú, láreow'; 'And they bowed the knee before him, and mocked him, saying, Hail, King of the Jews!' (*ibid.*, xxvii, 29), the O.E. being 'Hál waes thú, Judea cyning', as Wright points out.

Cf. 'All hail, Macbeth, hail to thee, thane of Glamis!' in Shakespeare's *Macbeth* (I, iii, 48).

Hail!, a common salutation obsolete since the 17th Century, is an exclamatory use of the adj. *hail* (cf. the variant *hail be thou*), which means 'unhurt; safe; healthy'. The O.E. *hál* comes from Old Norse *heill*, 'hale; sound; whole'.

halt, adj. 'If thy hand or thy foot offend thee, cut them off, and cast them from thee: it is better for thee to enter into life halt or maimed, rather than having two hands or two feet to be cast into everlasting fire' (*Matthew*, xviii, 8; cf. *Mark*, ix, 45); 'Go out quickly into the streets and lanes of the city, and bring in hither the poor, and the maimed, and the halt, and the blind' (*Luke*, xiv, 21); 'A great number of impotent folk, of blind, halt, withered' (*John*, v, 3).

Halt, 'lame, or merely limping; crippled (as to the feet)', is an adj. common to the Germanic languages; possibly cognate with the old past participle of *hold*, in the sense 'constrained, or restrained'.

haply. 'And seeing a fig tree afar off having leaves, he came, if haply he might find anything thereon' (*Mark*, xi, 13).

I.e., by chance, perchance; perhaps.

Haply (since ca. 1870, an archaism—except in poetry, where, however, it is now held to be a poetic counter, to be avoided by any self-respecting poet) = *hap*, 'luck, lot; a chance; a happening', + the adverbial suffix -*ly*.

hardly; hardness. 'Then said Jesus unto his disciples, Verily I say unto you, That a rich man shall hardly enter into the kingdom of heaven' (*Matthew*, xix, 23).—'Thou therefore endure hardness, as a good soldier of Jesus Christ' (2 *Timothy*, ii, 3).

The Gr. Test. has δυσκόλως πλούσιος εἰσελεύσεται εἰς τὴν βασιλείαν τῶν οὐρανῶν, with difficulty shall a rich man enter into the kingdom of the skies: dives difficile intrabit, 'un riche entrera difficilement' (Verdunoy).—Labora sicut bonus miles Christi Jesu, 'prends ta part d'épreuves comme un bon soldat du Christ Jésus' (Verdunoy): συγκακοπάθησον ὡς καλὸς στρατιώτης Χριστοῦ Ἰησοῦ, 'take your share of suffering like a good soldier of Christ Jesus' (see an excellent gloss in Souter).

Hardly = with difficulty (C. 16–mid 19); *hardness* = hardship (obsolete since C. 18).

harlot. The word occurs in 1 *Corinthians*, vi, 15, 16; *Hebrews*, xi, 31; *James*, ii, 25; and the plural on four occasions in the N.T.

'Very frequent in 16th Century *Bible* versions, where Wyclif had *hoore*, whore; probably as a less offensive word' (O.E.D.). In the sense 'prostitute' it arose in C. 15; in C. 20, somewhat archaic and, in C. 19–20, rather literary: Tennyson, 1859, *Vivien*, 'Tho' harlots paint their talk as well as face, | With colours of the heart that are not theirs'. Earliest in English as 'a vagabond or beggar, rogue or villain, knave or low fellow' (C. 13–17)—in C. 16–17, sometimes 'a fornicator'.

From Old Fr. *herlot* or (*h*)*arlot*, 'a base fellow, a vagabond': cf. Old Spanish *arlote*, by metathesis from the synonymous *alrote*, 'lazy'—cf. Old Portuguese *alrotar*, 'to go about begging' (perhaps ultimately from L. *rogare*, 'to ask'): O.E.D.

harp, v. 'How shall it be known what is piped or harped?' (I *Corinthians*, xiv, 7); 'I heard the voice of harpers harping with their harps' (*Revelation*, xiv, 2).

Harp, 'to play on the harp', is obsolete, except in the figurative phrase, 'to *harp* on (or upon) a thing'.

have, to hold; **have in reputation.** See **had.**

heady. See **high-minded,** third quotation.

heathen as adj. occurs only in *Matthew*, xviii, 17; *the heathen* (collective) in *Matthew*, vi, 7—2 *Corinthians*, xi, 26—*Galatians*, i, 16, ii, 9, and iii, 8.

The corresponding Gr. Test. and Vulgate original and translation are respectively ἔστω σοι ὥσπερ ὁ ἐθνικός ('let him be unto you as an heathen man', as a non-Jew) and *sit tibi sicut ethnicus* ('qu'il soit pour toi comme un païen', Verdunoy); προσευχόμενοι δὲ μὴ βαττολογήσετε, ὥσπερ οἱ ἐθνικοί ('use not vain repetitions, as the heathen do', praying, you will not be long-winded, as [are] the non-Jews) and *orantes autem nolite multum loqui sicut ethnici* ('en priant ne multipliez pas les paroles comme les païens', Verdunoy); κινδύνοις ἐξ ἐθνῶν ('in perils by the heathen', . . . by the Gentiles) and *periculis ex gentibus* ('dangers venant des païens', Verdunoy); ἵνα εὐαγγελίζωμαι αὐτὸν ἐν τοῖς ἔθνεσι ('that I might preach him among the heathen') and *ut evangelizarem illum in gentibus* ('que je le prêche parmi les Gentils'); etc., etc.

In Gr. Test., ἐθνικός = 'non-Jewish', precisely as τὰ ἔθνη = 'the nations outside Judaism': the corresponding L. is *gentilis* and *gentes*, lit. 'of the *gens* or nation' and 'the nations', i.e. *Gentile* and *the Gentiles*. (See **Gentile.**)

Heathen probably comes from an Armenian word meaning 'a nation' and deriving from Gr. ἔθνος, but there may, in the Germanic languages, have been assimilation with Gothic *haithi*, 'a heath': thus the old 'dweller on the heath' etymology is not 'mere folk-etymology' (O.E.D.).

Heaven and **Hell.** Etymologically, *heaven* is obscure; it belongs to the common West Germanic stock; its earliest sense, as Skeat suggests, may have been 'cover' or 'canopy'. If that is so, then it is analogous to *hell*, which seems to have originally meant 'the hider, the coverer-up'. The oldest use of *heaven* is 'the firmament'; of *hell*, 'the abode of the dead'; the usual modern sense of *heaven*, 'the abode of God and his angels, and the receptacle of the good', arose ca. 1000, whereas *hell* in its predominant modern sense, 'the infernal regions as the place of torment, the place (hence the state) of the post-mortem punishment of the wicked', is recorded ca. 888.

In the N.T., *heaven* renders the Gr. οὐρανός or the plural, οὐρανοί, but *hell* renders(*a*) Gr. ᾅδης, '*Hades, the unseen world*, into which the spirits of all persons pass at death' (Souter), ten times out of eleven, the exception being 1 *Corinthians*, xv, 55, where the text has 'grave' and the marginal gloss is 'hell'; in all eleven cases, the R.V. substitutes *Hades* for *hell*.

(*b*) Gr. γέεννα, on twelve occasions (e.g., *Matthew*, v, 22 and 29; x, 28); in these passages, the R.V. puts 'Gehenna' in the margin. See **Gehenna.**

(*c*) In 2 *Peter*, ii, 4, 'Cast them down to hell' renders Gr. ταρταρώσας, lit., 'having sent [them] to Tartarus', 'Tartarus being in the Gr. view a place of punishment under the earth' (Souter).

In the O.T., *hell* is, in 31 out of 65 occurrences of the Heb.

84

word, the A.V. rendering of Heb. *sheol*, which is 'restored' in
the R.V.; in the other 34 instances, 'grave' or 'pit' is used.
Sheol is the Heb. underworld of the dead and of departed
spirits, the Gr. *Hades*; its etymology is uncertain, but probably
it = 'the hollow place'.

heavy. Sorrowful, sad.
See the first quotation at **amazed.**
This sense of *heavy* is virtually obsolete; it is now, at best, a
literarism—some critical persons would call it an affectation.
Cf. the extant *heavy-hearted* and the obsolescent *heaviness*, 'sadness, sorrow; mental or emotional depression': 'Great heaviness and continual sorrow' (*Romans*, ix, 2); 'Joy turned into
heaviness' (*James*, iv, 9).

Hebrews. *The Epistle of Paul the Apostle to the Hebrews:* ἡ πρὸς
Ἑβραίους ἐπιστολή Παυλοῦ.
'An Hebrew of the Hebrews' (*Philippians*, iii, 5): Ἑβραῖος
ἐξ Ἑβραίων, 'a Hebrew descended from the Hebrews' (Souter):
Hebræus ex Hebræis, 'Hébreu fils d'Hébreux' (Verdunoy).
M.E. *Ebreu*, from Old Fr. *Ebr(i)eu*, from Medieval L.
Ebreus, from Classical L. *Hebræus*, from Gr. Ἑβραῖος, a trans-
literation of an Aramaic word for 'one from the other side (of
the river)', ultimately from a Hebrew v., 'to cross over'. At
the Renaissance, the initial *H* was resumed in deference to
Gr. and to Classical L. (O.E.D.)

Hell. See **Heaven.**

helps. 'And God hath set some in the church, first apostles,
secondarily'—we should say, 'secondly'—'prophets, thirdly
teachers, after that miracles, then gifts of healing, helps,
governments, diversities of tongues' (1 *Corinthians*, xii, 28).
Helps = (acts of) assistance: C. 14–18. Bacon writes, 'Em-
brace, and invite helps, and advices, touching the execution of
thy place'. The Gr. Test. original is ἀντιλήψεις, of which the
singular means 'a lending a hand, a helping' (Souter): the
Vulgate has *opitulationes*, 'aids'.

high-minded. 'Well; because of unbelief they [branches] were broken off, and thou standest by faith. Be not high-minded, but fear: for if God spared not the natural branches, take heed lest he also spare not thee' (*Romans*, xi, 20–1); 'Charge them that are rich in this world, that they be not high-minded, nor trust in uncertain riches, but in the living God' (1 *Timothy*, vi, 17); 'Traitors, heady, highminded, lovers of pleasure more than lovers of God' (2 *Timothy*, iii, 4), where *heady* = headstrong.

Haughty: a sense common in C. 16–18, then archaic. 'Poor in spirit . . . free from pride . . . not high-minded' (Blackall, ca. 1716). *High*, 'haughty', belongs to C. 13–mid 19 (O.E.D.).

him for *himself* occurs in *Matthew*, ix, 22 ('But Jesus turned him about, and when he saw her, he said . . .'); and **himself** for *he himself* in *Matthew*, viii, 17 ('Himself took our infirmities, and bare our sicknesses').

hitherto, used for *hither*. See at **let.**

hoise. 'And when they had taken up the anchors, they committed themselves unto the sea, and loosed the rudder bands, and hoised up the mainsail to the wind, and made toward shore' (*Acts*, xxvii, 40): cf. 'He, mistrusting them, | Hoised sail and made away for Brittany' (Shakespeare, *Richard III*).

An early form (since early C. 19, obsolete except in dialect) of 'to *hoist*', it occurs in 1509; but the original of *hoise* is *hyse* or *hysse*, occurring in 1490 and perhaps as early as 1450. It is of West Germanic stock: Swedish *hissa*, Danish *hisse*, Low Ger. *hiesen* or *hissen* (O.E.D.).

hold. 'All hold John as a prophet' (*Matthew*, xxi, 26).

We should omit 'as' and prefer 'All hold John to be a prophet', i.e. 'All think that John is a prophet'.

hold to. 'No man can serve two masters: for either he will hate the one, and love the other; or else he will hold to the one, and despise the other' (*Matthew*, vi, 24; cf. *Luke*, xvi, 13).

Hold to = cling to (in affection): a sense that has fallen into disuse.

holden. 'Jesus himself drew near, and went with'—mingled with—'them. But their eyes were holden that they should not know him' (*Luke*, xxiv, 16).

I.e., 'so holden that . . .', which = 'so held that . . .' They turned their eyes away.

This form of the past participle has long been obsolete, except in *beholden*.

holy comes from an O.E. word that is a derivative either of O.E. *hal*, 'free from injury, hale, whole' or of the Old Norse *heill*, 'health, good luck, omen, auspice'. As the O.E.D. remarks, 'we cannot in O.E. get behind Christian senses in which *holy* is equated with L. *sanctus* ["sacred" or "inviolable"], *sacer* ["consecrated to a deity" or divinity: Lewis & S.]'. The O.E.D. says that 'the primitive pre-Christian meaning is uncertain, although it is with some probability assumed to have been "inviolate, inviolable, that must be preserved *whole* or intact, that cannot be injured with impunity" . . . ; hence the adj. would naturally be applied to the gods, and all things pertaining to them; and, with the introduction of Christianity, it would be a ready word to render L. *sanctus*, *sacer*. But it might also start from *hail-* in the sense "health, good luck, well-being", or be connected with the sense "good omen, auspice, augury", as if "of good augury": cf. . . . O.E. *hálsian*, to HALSE, augur, divine, exorcise, etc.' 'In Christian use', continues the O.E.D., it means 'free from all contamination of sin and evil, morally and spiritually perfect and unsullied, possessing the infinite moral perfection which Christianity attributes to the Divine character'; hence, of persons, 'sinless' or 'saintly'.

Holy Ghost, the. See **Ghost, the Holy.**

honest; honesty. In *Romans*, xii, 17 ('Provide things honest in the sight of all men'), 2 *Corinthians*, xiii, 7 ('Now I pray to God that ye do no evil; not that we should appear approved, but that ye should do that which is honest'), and *Philippians*, iv, 8 ('Whatsoever things are true, whatsoever things are honest, whatsoever things are just'), *honest* is used in its original sense, as in L. *honestus*: 'honourable, fitting, seemly': cf. the contrast in Fr. between 'un homme honnête' and 'un honnête homme'.

In 1 *Timothy*, ii, 2, 'A quiet and peaceable life in all godliness and honesty', *honesty* means 'respectability' (true respectability) or 'seemly deportment or behaviour'.

honourable. 'When thou art bidden of any man to a wedding, sit not down in the highest room'—i.e., place, seat—'lest a more honourable man than thou be bidden of him; and he that bid thee and him come and say to thee, Give this man place; and thou begin with shame to take the lowest room' or place (*Luke*, xiv, 9–10).

'More honourable' = 'of higher rank'.

This sense of *honourable* is obsolete except in the title *the Honorable*; cf. the legal form of address, *your Honour*.

how = the archaic *how that*, the modern *that*, in 'When therefore the Lord knew how the Pharisees had heard that Jesus made and baptized more disciples than John . . .' (*John*, iv, 1).

howbeit. See at **conscience** and at **convince** (2nd quotation).

husbandry. 'For we are labouring together with God: ye are God's husbandry, ye are God's building' (1 *Corinthians*, iii, 9): 'Dei agricultura estis, Dei ædificatio estis' (neatly rendered by Verdunoy as 'vous êtes le champ de Dieu, sa maison en construction').

Here we have the old sense of *husbandry*—that of 'tillage' or 'cultivation'.

Cf. Shakespeare's

'And all her husbandry doth lie on heaps [= in heaps],
Corrupting [= rotting] in its own fertility'.
                                                    (*Henry V*, v, ii, 40.)

I

if so be (that) is an obsolete elaboration of *if*, as in
'. . . Whom he raised not up, if so be that the dead rise not'
(1 *Corinthians*, xv, 15).

illuminate. 'But call to remembrance the former days, in
which, after ye were illuminated, ye endured a great fight of
afflictions' (*Hebrews*, x, 32).

Here, to *illuminate* is to enlighten; this sense of *illuminate* is
obsolete. The A.V. follows the Vulgate (*in quibus illuminati*),
whereas the Geneva Version of *The Bible* (1560) had the more
intelligible '. . . after ye had received light', as Wright points
out. The Gr. is ἐν αἷς φωτισθέντες, which Souter translates
as 'having received enlightenment' and glosses as 'having had
experience of God's grace in conversion'; note that 'those
who were once enlightened' (*Hebrews*, vi, 4) renders the Gr.
τοὺς ἅπαξ φωτισθέντας, and cf. 2 *Corinthians*, iv, 4, where
φωτισμός is 'enlightening', and *ibid.*, iv, 6, where it is passive,
'enlightenment'.

impart. 'He answereth and saith unto them, He that hath
two coats, let him impart to him that hath none; and he that
hath meat, let him do likewise' (*Luke*, iii, 11).

I.e., let him that hath two coats give one to him that hath
not; and let the possessor of meat give some to him that hath
none. The Gr. is μεταδότω, 'share' (*impart to* = share with).

Impart in this concrete sense (cf. Shakespeare's 'Some certain
special honours it pleaseth his greatness to impart to Armado',
Love's Labour's Lost, v, i, 113) has given way to 'a metaphorical sense, as in imparting knowledge or information'
(Wright).

implead. 'The law is open . . . : let them implead one
another' (*Acts*, xix, 38).

I.e., to sue in a court of justice. This sense, like the derivative one 'to accuse', is now archaic.

From the Anglo-Fr. *empleder* = Old Fr. *emple(i)dier*; the origin of the Fr. is Medieval L. *placitare*, 'to litigate'. The Fr. *plaider* is our *plead*.

impotent. 'In these lay a great multitude of impotent folk, of blind, halt, withered, waiting for the moving of the water' and 'The impotent man answered . . . saying, Sir, I have no man . . . to put me into the pool' (*John*, v, 3 and 7); 'The good deed done to the impotent man, by what means he is made whole' (*Acts*, iv, 9); 'A certain man, impotent in his feet, being a cripple . . . who had never walked' (*ibid.*, xiv, 8).

Lit., 'powerless' or 'strengthless'; hence, 'invalid' or 'weak'. This general sense is obsolete: *impotent* survives in two connexions: *impotent rage* is 'helpless rage'; *an impotent man* is either one that cannot impregnate a woman, or one that is wholly deficient in sexual power.

incontinent. 'Truce-breakers, false accusers, incontinent, fierce, despisers of those that are good' (2 *Timothy*, iii, 3).

'Wanting in self-restraint: chiefly with reference to sexual appetite' (O.E.D.): a sense now somewhat archaic. The prevalent sense is 'unable to retain one's urine or, less generally, one's urea'.

L. *incontinens* (*incontinentem*), probably via Fr. The L. *continere* is 'to contain, hence to restrain'.

inhabiter. 'And I beheld, and heard an angel flying through the midst of heaven, saying with a loud voice, Woe, woe, woe, to the inhabiters of the earth' (*Revelation*, viii, 13); 'Therefore rejoice, ye heavens, and ye that dwell in them. Woe to the inhabiters of the earth and of the sea! for the devil is come down unto you, having great wrath, because he knoweth that he hath but a short time' (*ibid.*, xii, 12).

Inhabitant: late C. 14–20, but now archaic.

injurious. 'Who was before a blasphemer, and a persecutor, and injurious: but I obtained mercy, because I did it ignorantly in unbelief' (1 *Timothy*, i, 13): πρότερον ὄντα βλάσφημον καὶ διώκτην καὶ ὑβριστήν: qui prius blasphemus fui, et persecutor, et contumeliosus.

Not quite 'insolent', as Wright glosses it, but rather 'insulting; contumelious; calumnious': cf. Shakespeare's 'Injurious Duke, that threatest where's no cause' (2 Henry VI) and 'Call me their traitor! thou injurious tribune' (Coriolanus): late C. 15–20; but since C. 17, only of speech or words. Via Fr. injurieux from L. injuriosus (injuria, 'a wrong, detriment': the opposite of jus, 'right'). O.E.D.

insomuch. See at **blase.**

instant; instantly. 'And they were instant [ἐπέκειντο] with loud voices, requiring that he might be crucified' (Luke, xxiii, 23); 'Rejoicing in hope; patient in tribulation; continuing instant [προσκαρτεροῦντες] in prayer' (Romans, xii, 12·); 'Preach the word; be instant [ἐπίστηθι] in season, out of season' (2 Timothy, iv, 2).—'And when they came to Jesus, they besought him instantly, saying, That he was worthy for whom he should do this' (Luke, vii, 4); 'Unto which promise our twelve tribes, instantly serving God day and night, hope to come' (Acts, xxvi, 7).

Importunate or urgent: from ca. 1470; in C. 20, archaic.— The adv. = 'urgently' in the first, 'unceasingly' in the second passage. Via Fr., from L. instare, 'to be at hand', hence 'to urge'.

insult upon, in Romans, xi, heading ('The Gentiles may not insult upon them'), = insult over, i.e. to exult over, behave insultingly towards. Ex L. insultare, 'to leap at (or on)', hence 'to insult'.

intent. 'Now no man at the table knew for what intent he spake this unto him' (John, xiii, 28). Cf. Shakespeare's 'And, if I fail not in my deep intent, | Clarence hath not another day to live' (Richard III, I, i, 149).

This earlier form of intention is obsolete. In the two passages quoted above, the sense is 'purpose'. Ex L. intentus, 'a stretching out' (in Late L., 'intention').

Israel; Israelites. Etymologically, these two words have not much interest. The latter is formed regularly on the former. In the Vulgate, it is *Israel*; in the Gr. Test., Ἰσραήλ, from Heb. *'yisrael*, lit. "he that striveth with God", symbolic proper name conferred upon Jacob, *Genesis*, xxxii, 28' (O.E.D.).—*Israelite* is L. *Israelita*, Gr. Ἰσραηλίτης, and it arose some four centuries later than *Israel* (ca. 1000).

issue (of blood) is a discharge of blood in *Luke*, viii, 43–4: 'A woman having an issue of blood twelve years . . . came behind him [Jesus], and touched the border of his garment: and immediately her issue of blood stanched', i.e. was stanched.
An obsolete sense.

J

jacinth. See the quotation at **chrysolite.**
Jacinth is a contraction of *hyacinth*, from Gr. ὑάκινθος (cf. Hyacinth, that youth who, in Gr. myth, was beloved by Apollo), the gem and the flower; in modern use, *hyacinth* is the sole form for the flower, whereas both *hyacinth* and *jacinth* are the names of the gem. *Hyacinth* or *jacinth* is, anciently, a blue-coloured stone (prob. the sapphire, says the O.E.D.); but, in modern use, it is, usually, understood to be a reddish-orange variety of zircon, though it is, esp. in the form *hyacinth*, applied also to varieties of topaz and garnet of similar colour.
Hyacinth, the precious stone, formed one of the twelve foundations of the new Jerusalem; it 'seems to correspond with the Hebrew word rendered "ligure" (*Exodus*, xxviii, 19), which was one of the stones of the high priest's "breast-plate". The "ligure" has been identified with rubellite, a red variety of tourmaline, but there is great uncertainty about it' (Wright, 1884). Souter renders ὑάκινθος as 'a sapphire of dusky red colour like the martagon lily'.

In *Revelation*, ix, 17, the colour, not the stone, is referred to: the Gr. is θώρακας . . . ὑακινθίνους: 'of the colour of the martagon lily . . . dusky red' (Souter).

James. 'The Hebrew Jacob was'—via Gr. *Ἰάκωβος*—'latinized as Jacobus, whence French Jacques, and gave in a way puzzling to phoneticians the Spanish dialect Jaime, which appears in Chaucer—"I thanke yow by God and by Saint Jame" . . . In Gaelic, James became Hamish, now sometimes given to English children, while Ireland spells it Seumas (Shamus). No apostolic name, except Peter and John, has been so widely spread in Europe. As patron saint of Spain, St James the Great was one of the Seven Champions of Christendom' (*Jack and Jill*). Note that English *James* comes immediately from Old Fr. *James* (or *Gemmes*) and that the Spanish *Jaime* is cognate with Italian *Giacomo*, representing a postulated Low L. *Jacomus* for Classical L. *Jacobus*: which goes to show how extraordinarily convenient these postulated, these presumed, these invented forms can be to philologists in difficulties.

jangling. '[Faith unfeigned:] From which some having swerved have turned aside unto vain jangling' (1 *Timothy*, i, 6): ὧν τινὲς ἀστοχήσαντες ἐξετράπησαν εἰς ματαιολογίαν, from which some, making a false aim, have wandered, or turned aside, to foolish talking (or vain speech): a quibus quidam aberrantes, conversi sunt in vaniloquium, 'desquels quelques-uns s'étant écartés se sont égarés en de vains discours' (Verdunoy).

Verbal n. from *jangle*, 'to talk excessively; to babble': C. 14–18. From Old Fr. *jangler* (in same sense), which is probably echoic (cf. English *jingle*).

jasper. See the quotation at **chrysolite.**

From Old Fr. *jaspre*, a variant of *jaspe*, which comes from L. *jaspis*, a transliteration of Gr. ἴασπις, itself an approximation to Heb. *yaspeh* (with cognates in Assyrian, Persian, Arabic), *jasper* was, among the ancients, 'any bright-coloured chalcedony except carnelian, the most esteemed being of a green colour' (O.E.D.); it occurs in English as early as the early C. 14. 'In modern use, an opaque cryptocrystalline variety of quartz' (O.E.D.). 'The Jasper', remarked Randle Holme in 1688, 'is somewhat green, yet specked with bloody spots' (caused by an admixture of iron oxide).

jeopardy. '. . . There came down a storm of wind on the lake; and they were filled with water, and were in jeopardy' (*Luke*, viii, 23); 'And why stand we in jeopardy every hour?' (1 *Corinthians*, xv, 30).

In danger: from ca. 1370. From the sense, 'a dangerous position in a game, esp. chess', the etymological origin being Old Fr. *iu* (later *geu*, modern Fr. *jeu*) *parti*, lit. 'a divided or even game', hence 'uncertainty': cf. Medieval L. *jocus partitus* (O.E.D.).

'Were in danger' is a rendering of Gr. ἐκινδύνευον, which the Vulgate translates as *periclitabantur*; 'stand we in jeopardy' represents Gr. κινδυνεύομεν, which the Vulgate translates as *periclitamur* ('et nous, à quoi bon courir les dangers à toute heure?', Verdunoy).

Jerusalem. E.g., 'Ye have filled Jerusalem with your doctrine' (*Acts*, v, 28): πεπληρώκατε τὴν Ἰερουσαλὴμ τῆς διδαχῆς ὑμῶν: et ecce replestis Jerusalem doctrina vestra, 'et voici que vous avez rempli Jérusalem de votre enseignement' (Verdunoy).

The English *Jerusalem* (in C. 16–18, often *Hierusalem*) comes either direct from L. or via Fr.; the Gr. Ἰερουσαλήμ is a transliteration of the Aramaic form of the Heb. name. According to Cruden it means 'the vision—or, the possession —of peace'; at first it was called *Salem*; *the new Jerusalem* (*Revelation*, iii, 12) symbolizes the church triumphant. In *Galatians*, iv, 25, *Jerusalem* stands for 'Judaism', whereas in the next verse it allegorizes 'Christendom, the Christian Church' (Souter).

See esp. Hastings and Leclercq.

Jesus Christ. L. *Jesus* (in the Vulgate, *Jesu*), from Gr.
Ἰησοῦς, an approximation to an Aramaic (or perhaps a late
Heb.) word that yields *Jeshua*, for earlier *Joshua* or *Jehoshua*
('Jah'—Jahveh, Jehovah—'is salvation'). 'A frequent Jewish
personal name' (O.E.D.), this 'the human name of our
Saviour' (Souter).

In O.E., *Crist* (so, too, usually in M.E., the *Ch-* spelling
becoming general only in C. 16): from L. *Christus*, a transliteration of Gr. Χριστός, used to translate the Aramaic
m'shiax (Messiah), 'anointed'—in full, *m'shiax yahweh*, 'the
anointed of Jahweh' (Jehovah), 'the Lord's Anointed'
(O.E.D.). Χριστός is ὁ χριστός 'the anointed one', from
χρίειν, 'to anoint'. 'Anointing being the outward sign of
. . . appointment to kingship', ὁ χριστός is *the* expected *king*
of Israel, to be appointed by God as his vicegerent. In the N.T.
this epithet is, therefore, attached (either prefixed or affixed
[Christ Jesus or Jesus Christ]) to (ὁ) Ἰησοῦς, *Jesus*, recognized by his followers as the expected Messiah. The epithet
with or without article [ὁ: the] is also found alone referring
to Jesus; gradually it tends to lose the meaning it already had
and to become merely a proper name, *Christ*. (By many
the curious word was [formerly] confused with χρηστός,
"good" . . .)', Souter.

For a list of the names and titles given to Jesus Christ, see
Cruden.

The true Life of Christ has yet to be written. Meanwhile,
see esp. Hastings and Leclercq. For a poetic conception of
Christ as the great hunter of souls, Francis Thompson's *The
Hound of Heaven* is unequalled. And for a Jewish interpretation, read Sholem Asch's powerful and sympathetic historical
novel, *The Nazarene*, 1939.

Jews; Judæa (or Judea); Judah.
'Unto the Jews I became as a Jew, that I might gain the
Jews' (1 *Corinthians*, ix, 20): ἐγενόμην τοῖς Ἰουδαίοις ὡς
Ἰουδαῖος, ἵνα Ἰουδαίους κερδήσω: *factus sum Judæis tanquam
Judæus, ut Judæos lucrarer* ('je suis devenu comme Juif pour
les Juifs afin de gagner les Juifs', Verdunoy).

'Ye, brethren, became followers of the churches of God which in Judæa are in Christ Jesus' (1 *Thessalonians*, ii, 14): ὑμεῖς μιμηταὶ ἐγενήθητε, ἀδελφοί, τῶν ἐκκλησιῶν τοῦ Θεοῦ τῶν οὐσῶν ἐν τῃ Ἰουδαίᾳ ἐν Χριστῷ Ἰησοῦ: *vos imitatores facti estis, fratres, ecclesiarum Dei quæ sunt in Judæa in Christo Jesu* ('. . . qui sont en Judée . . .').

'And thou, Bethlehem, in the land of Juda' (*Matthew*, ii, 6): Ἐν Βηθλεὲμ τῆς Ἰουδαίας: *et tu Bethlehem, terra Juda.*

Originally a *Jew* (Heb. *γ'hudhi* > Aramaic *γ'hudai* > Gr. Ἰουδαῖος > L. *Judæus* > Old Fr. *Jui(e)u* and later *Giu(e)* > M.E. *Gyu* or *Giu* or *Ieu(e)*) was an inhabitant of *Juda(h)*, *Judah* representing Heb. *γ'hudhah*, the patriarch, hence the tribe descended from him, hence the land occupied by the tribe; but later, *Jew* was extended to include all descendants of Abraham, and, in the process, *Juda* became *Judea* (O.T.) or *Judæa* (N.T.): note that in both the second and third quotations the Gr. word is Ἰουδαῖα (*Ioudaia*). 'As most of the Israelites returning from the captivity belonged to the tribe of Judah, they came to be called Jews and their land Judæa [afterwards a Roman province: capital Jerusalem]', *The International Standard Bible Encyclopædia*. In the N.T., *Jews* is co-extensive and synonymous with *Israelites*, and the religion of the Jews (*Galatians*, i, 13–14) is Ἰουδαϊσμός (Judaism).

John comes from Old Fr. *Jehan* (Modern Fr. *Jean*), from L. *Joannes* (later *Johannes*), a transliteration of Gr. Ἰωάννης (Hebraistic: Ἰωάνης), which represents Heb. *γοχanan*, short for *γ'hoχanan*, 'Johanan' or 'Jehohanan', meaning 'Jah (= Jahveh = Jehovah) is gracious' or 'God is kind'. (Souter; O.E.D.)

'John, whether in honour of the Baptist or of the "beloved disciple", was easily the favourite [apostolic name] and finally it overhauled William which had reigned supreme for more than a century [after the Norman Conquest, 1066]. It has spread everywhere; cf. Fr. Jean, Ger. Johann (whence Hans), Sc. Ian, Ir. Shane, Welsh Evan, Sp. Juan, It. Giovanni, Russ.

Ivan, and even Basque Iban, whence the surname Ibañez. Equally popular was its feminine Joanna or Joan' (*Jack and Jill*). 'Taking the European languages as a whole, the dominant name is *John*' (Weekley, *Words and Names*). 'Its brevity and strength have contributed to make it, in the minds of the majority, the finest of all male given names' (Partridge).

John the Baptist (as a name). See **John** and **baptist.**

jot. 'For verily I say unto you, Till heaven and earth pass, one jot or one tittle shall in no wise pass'—i.e., be excised, abrogated—'from the law, till all be fulfilled' (*Matthew*, v, 18): ἰῶτα ἓν ἢ μία κεραία οὐ μὴ παρέλθῃ ἀπὸ τοῦ νόμου, not one iota nor one apostrophe shall disappear from the law: iota unum aut unus apex non præteribit a lege, 'un seul iota on un seul trait [stroke] de lettre ne passera de la loi' (Verdunoy).

The iota (ι) is the smallest letter in the Gr. alphabet; its L. form *iota* was in C. 16 read as *jota*; hence our *jot*, by curtailment. Tyndale, 1526, was the first to use it.

It should, however, be remembered that the reference is to *yod*, the smallest letter of the Aramaic alphabet: ἰῶτα is, therefore, less a translation than an equivalent.

joy, v. To rejoice, as in 'Therefore we were comforted in your comfort: yea, and exceedingly the more joyed we for the joy of Titus, because his spirit was refreshed by you all' (2 *Corinthians*, vii, 13).

As v.i., *joy* is archaic; as v.t., it is archaic in the sense 'to gladden', obsolete in the sense 'to enjoy'.

Judah; Judæa. See **Jews . . .**

Judas Iscariot. For Judas, see **Jude.**

Iscariot: L. *Iscariota* (perhaps via Fr.), from Gr. Ἰσκαριώτης, 'understood to be . . . Heb. *ish-q'riyoth*, man of Kerioth (a place in Palestine)'; the surname of Christ's betrayer; hence, in C. 17–20 English, 'an accursed traitor' (O.E.D.).

'Orion' (R. H.) Horne wrote a fine play on the subjective tragedy in the life of Judas Iscariot: see his *Bible Plays*, 1881.

Jude. 'Jude, the servant of Jesus Christ, and brother of James [the Less]': Ἰούδας Ἰησοῦ Χριστοῦ δοῦλος ἀδελφὸς δὲ Ἰακώβου: Judas, Jesu Christi servus, frater autem Jacobi ('Jude, esclave de Jésus-Christ et frère de Jacques', Verdunoy).

Judas and *Judah* are variants of a Heb. name that signifies 'the praise of the Lord': *Jude* comes from the latter, via the Fr. (where L. *-a* normally becomes *e*). '*Judah* was besmirched by *Judas*, the traitor; even the nobility of Judas Maccabæus and the eloquent apostolate and gallant death of St Jude ... have not freed the name of all stigma; nevertheless, *Jude* lingers in rural England and is green in literary memory because of ... Hardy's *Jude the Obscure* ... 1895' (Partridge).

judge in 'Out of thine own mouth will I judge thee, thou wicked servant' (*Luke*, xix, 22) = 'to condemn, to pronounce sentence against', a sense that has been obsolete since ca. 1700.

The Gr. Test. has κρινῶ σε (I judge you); the Vulgate, *te judico.*

K

keep, 'to remember': see at **ponder.**

keep silence, in 1 *Corinthians*, xiv, 28, 'If there be no interpreter, let him keep silence in the church; and let him speak to himself, and to God', and in verse 34, 'Let your women keep silence in the churches', the phrase means no more than 'be silent' (cf. Fr. *garder le silence*) and has been in common use— in C. 20, rather literary—since C. 14. Earlier was *hold silence* (C. 13–15).

know. 'Therefore to him that knoweth to do good, and doeth it not, to him it is sin' (*James*, iv, 17).

The earlier versions have 'knoweth how to do good': which is the sense of 'knoweth to do good'.

Cf. the French construction after *savoir*; the Gr. is εἰδότι οὖν καλὸν ποιεῖν, καὶ μὴ ποιοῦντι, ἁμαρτία αὐτῷ ἐστιν. In English, *know to* (do something) for 'know how to . . .' has, since the 17th Century been poetic, as in 'Tell them we know to tread the crimson plain' (Barlow, 1808: O.E.D.); and since ca. 1840, it has been archaic even in poetry.

knowledge, have; take knowledge. 'And when the men of that place had knowledge of him, they sent out into all that country round about, and brought unto him all that were diseased' (*Matthew*, xiv, 35); 'But when the Jews of Thessalonica had knowledge that the word of God was preached of [= by] Paul at Berea, they came thither also, and stirred up the people' (*Acts*, xvii, 13).—'Now when they saw the boldness of Peter and John, and perceived that they were unlearned and ignorant men, they marvelled; and they took knowledge of them, that they had been with Jesus' (*Acts*, iv, 13); 'By examining of whom thyself mayest take knowledge of all these things, whereof we accuse him' (*ibid.*, xxiv, 8).

To have knowledge, here, is 'to be informed', now not only archaic but stiffly formal; *to take knowledge* is 'to take notice; hence, to know, to recognize', nuances that have been obsolete since ca. 1700 and that had been archaic for half a century before that.

L

latchet. 'There cometh one mightier than I after me, the latchet of whose shoes I am not worthy to stoop down and unloose' (*Mark*, i, 7).

Generally defined as 'a shoe-lace'; more accurately (so far as concerns the N.T.) to be defined as 'a thong used to fasten a shoe' (O.E.D.). Dating, in this sense, from ca. 1430, it has, except in dialect, been archaic since mid C. 19.

From Old Fr. *lachet*, a dialectal variant of *lacet*; ultimately from L. *laqueum*, 'a noose' (cf. the word's earliest sense in English: 'a loop').

laud, v. 'Praise the Lord, all ye Gentiles; and laud him, all ye people' (*Romans*, xv, 11): αἰνεῖτε, πάντα τὰ ἔθνη, τὸν Κύριον, καὶ ἐπαινέσατε αὐτὸν πάντες οἱ λαοί, praise the ruler, all the non-Jewish nations, and commend him, all the Jews: laudate, omnes gentes, Dominum; et magnificate eum, omnes populi, 'louez le Seigneur, vous tous, les Gentils, et que tous les peuples le célèbrent' (Verdunoy).

'Originally implying an act of worship', *laud* here = 'to speak, chant, or sing the praises of': 1377, Langland; Caxton; Tyndale; Walton; in C. 18, literary; in C. 19–20, except in Biblical allusion, an elegancy. From L. *laudare*, 'to praise'. (Wright; O.E.D.)

leave. 'When they saw the chief captain and the soldiers they left beating of Paul' (*Acts*, xxi, 32).

I.e., left off beating—ceased to beat—Paul.

An obsolete use (common in C. 16–18).

legion, my name is. *Mark*, v, bears the heading, 'Christ delivering the possessed [= a man possessed] of the legion of devils, they enter into the swine', and verses 8–9 run, 'For he [Christ] said, Come out of the man, thou unclean spirit. And he asked him, What is thy name? And he answered, saying, My name is Legion: for we are many.'

In this passage, *legion* is used in the derivative sense, a vast host or multitude (of persons or things); the primary sense is that of the L. *legio*, which may, approximately, be rendered as 'a brigade of infantry' with—usually—a complement of cavalry. *Legio* is itself formed from *legere*, 'to choose', hence 'to levy' (an army).

My name is Legion has given rise to the vaguely allusive but somewhat inaccurate cliché, *their name is Legion*, which = they are innumerable.

let is used in its archaic sense, 'to hinder'—cf. the noun in the repetitious intensive, *without let or hindrance*—in *Romans* i, 13, 'Now I would not have you ignorant, brethren, that oftentimes I purposed to come unto you (but was let hitherto), that I might have some fruit'—preach successfully—'among

you also', *let hitherto* being 'prevented [from coming] hither';
as also in 2 *Thessalonians*, ii, 7, 'For the mystery of iniquity
doth already work: only he who now letteth will let, until
he be taken out of the way'.

Let be = 'cease' in *Matthew*, xxvii, 49, 'The rest said, Let
be, let us see whether Elias will come to save him'; cf. *Mark*,
xv, 36.

Levite. From the L. *levita*, transliterating Gr. λευίτης (or
λευείτης), a descendant of *Levi* (Λευί), the Heb. proper name
that signifies '(one) who is held and associated'.

In *Luke*, x, 32, 'And likewise a Levite . . . came and looked
on him, and passed by on the other side'—*Acts*, iv, 36,
'Barnabas . . . a Levite . . . of the country of Cyprus'—
John, i, 19, '. . . The Jews sent priests and Levites from Jerusalem to ask him, Who art thou?', we have the derivative
sense, 'one of that portion of the tribe who acted as assistants
to the priests in the temple-worship' (O.E.D.).

Ca. 1640–1730, *Levite* was employed allusively for a
clergyman.

lewd; lewdness. 'But the Jews which believed not, moved
with envy, took unto them certain lewd fellows of the baser
sort, and gathered a company, and set all the city on an
uproar' (*Acts*, xvii, 5).—'Gallio said unto the Jews, If it were
a matter of wrong or wicked lewdness, . . . reason would
that I should bear with you' (*ibid.*, xviii, 14).

In the former passage, *lewd* = 'unlearned, ignorant', as
often in Middle and Early Modern English; from O.E.
læwed, 'lay' as opposed to 'clerical'. The Gr. ἀγοραῖος has the
connotation of 'agitator' (Souter).

In the latter passage, *lewdness* represents the Gr. ῥαδιούργημα,
which Souter renders as 'a moral wrong, a crime'. The
phrase 'a matter of wrong or wicked lewdness' is slightly
ambiguous, for there are two nouns— 'a matter of wrong'
and 'wicked lewdness' (ῥαδιούργημα πονηρόν), 'a matter of
wrong' translating the one Gr. word ἀδίκημα.

In Middle English and (very) Early Modern English,

lewdness generally = 'ignorance' or 'rusticity'; in the 18th–20th Centuries, it has meant 'sexual excess, proneness to sexual indulgence, habitual desire for sexual intercourse'.

lie on. 'No small tempest lay on us' (*Acts*, xxvii, 20) is merely 'We were exposed to a considerable storm'. The Gr. is χειμῶνός τε οὐκ ὀλίγου ἐπικειμένου, genitive absolute, 'a not little storm pressing hard'; the Vulgate has 'tempestate non exigua imminente' ('la tempête était si forte . . .', Verdunoy).

limit, v. 'Again, he limited a certain day, saying . . . To day if ye will hear his voice, harden not your hearts' (*Hebrews*, iv, 7): τινὰ ὁρίζει ἡμέραν: terminat diem quemdam ('il fixe un jour', Verdunoy).

'To put a limit to', hence 'to fix definitely', 'to appoint' (a day or a date): common in C. 15–18; thereafter, rare except as a legal term.

Via Fr. *limiter*, from L. *limitare*, 'to establish the boundaries of' (*limes*, a boundary).

lineage. 'He was of the house and lineage of David' (*Luke*, ii, 4): ἐξ οἴκου καὶ πατριᾶς Δαβίδ, of the household and family (or tribe) of David: de domo et familia David, 'de la maison et de la famille de David' (Verdunoy).

Here, *lineage* is in the late C. 14–mid 17 sense, 'a family or race viewed with reference to its descent' (O.E.D.), as in Sir Thomas More, 'Descended of the worthy linage of themperoure'—the emperor—'Constantyne', and in E. Grimstone, 'From him sprang two families or linages'.

From Old Fr. *lignage*, ultimately L. *linea*, a line.

list and **lust.** 'They know him not, but have done unto him whatsoever they listed' (*Matthew*, xvii, 12; cf. *Mark*, ix, 13); 'The wind bloweth where it listeth' (*John*, iii, 8); 'Behold also the ships, which though they be so great, and are driven of fierce winds, yet are they turned about with a very small helm, whithersoever the governor [steersman] listeth' (*James* iii, 4).—'For all that is in the world, the lust of the flesh, and the lust of the eyes, and the pride of life, is not of the Father,

but is of the world. And the world passeth away, and the
lust thereof: but he that doeth the will of God abideth for
ever' (1 *John*, ii, 16–17).

List, 'to wish or desire', was common in mid C. 14–17,
then archaic. Originally it was impersonal: e.g., *me list* (or
lyst) is 'I choose'—hence 'wish'—to do something: C. 10–17,
then archaic. Of West Germanic stock.—*Lust* is the corresponding n.: in the quoted passage, it means 'a sensuous
desire or appetite' (not necessarily 'an illicit or immoral
desire'—a Biblical (from ca. 1000) and, in C. 19–20, theological sense. In the fourth quotation, the Gr. Test. has
ἐπιθυμία, 'eager (or passionate) desire'; the Vulgate has the
exaggerated *concupiscentia*, which is skilfully rendered by
Verdunoy as 'convoitise'.

living. 'She of her want did cast in all that she had, even all
her living' (*Mark*, xii, 44); 'A woman ... which had spent
all her living upon physicians, neither could be healed of any'
(*Luke*, viii, 43); also *ibid.*, xv, 12 and 30, and xxi, 4.

The Gr. Test. has ὅλον τὸν βίον (αὐτῆς), 'her entire livelihood': Vulgate, *totum victum suum*, 'tout ce qu'elle avait pour
vivre' (Verdunoy).

Livelihood, or means of living: from C. 14. The derivative
sense 'an income' is obsolete.

loft. 'He ... fell down from the third loft, and was taken
up dead' (*Acts*, xx, 9): here, *loft* is an upper room of a house
(not, as it would now connote, of an outhouse): lit., that
which is *aloft*, up in the air, *loft* being a C. 11–16 word for
'air' or 'sky' and cognate with the much-longer-lived
synonymous *lift*.

loose, v. See at **gain a loss**.

lucre. 'Not given to wine, no striker [q.v.], not greedy of
filthy lucre' (1 *Timothy*, iii, 3; cf. iii, 8); 'Whose mouths must
be stopped, who subvert whole houses, teaching things which
they ought not, for filthy lucre's sake' (*Titus*, i, 11): αἰσχροῦ

κέρδους χάριν: *turpis lucri gratia* ('pour un gain honteux', Verdunoy).

Lucre is 'gain or profit', especially 'pecuniary advantage or profit'; Wyclif introduced it, ca. 1380, perhaps via Fr. *lucre* but probably direct from the synonymous L. *lucrum* (with which Gr. ἀπολαύειν, 'to enjoy', and Ger. *Lohn*, 'wages, reward', are cognate).

Hence, *filthy lucre* is 'sordid gain', 'base or degrading profit': a phrase that has been grossly overworked (see my *A Dictionary of Clichés*).

Luke. 'Only Luke is with me. Take Mark, and bring him with thee: for he is profitable to me for the ministry' (*2 Timothy*, iv, 11): Λουκᾶς ἐστι μόνος μετ᾽ ἐμοῦ. Μάρκον ἀναλαβὼν ἄγε μετὰ σεαυτοῦ· ἔστι γάρ μοι εὔχρηστος εἰς διακονίαν: Lucas est mecum solus. Marcum assume et adduc tecum; est enim mihi utilis in ministerium ('Luc est seul avec moi. Prends Marc et emmère-le avec toi . . .', Verdunoy).

From the Fr. form of the name rather than direct—as its variant *Lucas* is direct—from the L. derivative or the Gr. original, which is a pet-form of Λουκανός ('as the Old Latin Bible gave in the title of the Third Gospel') or perhaps of Λούκιος: Professor Weekley inclines to the former in his cautious '? Of Lucania'; certain early theologians derived *Lucanus* (Gr. Λουκανός) from *lucus*, 'a grove', and identified *Luke* with Silas by deriving the latter name from *silva*, 'a wood' (*Jack and Jill*, 68). This Christian physician ('Luke, the beloved physician, and Demas, greet you', *Colossians*, iv, 14), and evangelist wrote not only the Gospel bearing his name but also *The Acts of the Apostles*.

lunatick, adj. 'Lord, have mercy on my son: for he is lunatick, and sore vexed: for ofttimes he falleth into the fire, and oft into the water' (*Matthew*, xvii, 15; cf. iv, 24): Κύριε, ἐλέησόν μου τὸν υἱόν, ὅτι σεληνιάζεται καὶ κακῶς πάσχει: Domine, miserere filio meo, quia lunaticus est et male patitur ('Seigneur, aie pitié de mon fils, qui est lunatique et souffre beaucoup', Verdunoy).

The Gr. original (σεληνιάζεται) of 'he is lunatick' is significant: lit., 'he is brought under the influence of the moon' (he is moonstruck), it here means 'he is epileptic': for, as Souter has remarked, the epileptic state used to be attributed to the moon. And the Gr. for 'moon' is σελήνη, the L. is *luna*, whence *lunaticus*, 'moony'. Therefore, 'he is lunatick, and sore vexed' does not mean 'he is mad and much troubled (or very angry!)', but 'he is epileptic, and has much suffering'.

lust. See at **list.**

M

make. 'And they drew nigh unto the village, whither they went: and he made as though he would have gone further' (*Luke*, xxiv, 28): 'acted as though he wished to go further', 'pretended to be desirous of going further'.

This construction is obsolete, though it has a very close analogue in the archaic and literary *make as if to* ('He made as if to stumble', he pretended to stumble).

make-bate, in the marginal gloss to 2 *Timothy*, iii, 3, is a causer or breeder of strife or trouble, a trouble-maker.

Since ca. 1740, the term has been archaic; and since ca. 1840, it has been virtually obsolete.

By itself, *bate* = 'strife, contention'; apparently it is a shortening of *debate*.

malice. 'Therefore let us keep the feast, not with old leaven, neither with the leaven of malice and wickedness: but with the unleavened bread of sincerity and truth' (1 *Corinthians*, v, 8); 'Let all bitterness, and wrath, and anger, and clamour, and evil speaking, be put away from you, with'—i.e., along with—'all malice' (*Ephesians*, iv, 31).

'Wickedness or vice in the wider sense, not merely malevolence, which is the more usual acceptation of the word.

See Bishop [Samuel] Hinds, *Scripture and the Authorized Version of Scripture* [2nd ed., 1853]', W. Aldis Wright.

The Gr. of the former passage is κακίας καὶ πονηρίας; of the latter, σὺν πάσῃ κακίᾳ; Souter renders κακία as 'evil'.

man of war in 'Herod with his men of war set him at nought, and mocked him' (*Luke*, xxiii, 11) is a warrior or soldier. This sense has long been archaic: to use it nowadays would be pedantic and, usually, confusing.

man-pleaser. 'Not with eyeservice, as menpleasers; but as the servants of Christ, doing the will of God from the heart' (*Ephesians*, vi, 6); 'Servants, obey in all things your masters . . . ; not with eyeservice, as menpleasers, but in singleness of heart, fearing God' (*Colossians*, iii, 22).

Introduced by Tyndale, perhaps on the analogy of *man-queller*, 'a murderer'; by 1800, it was obsolete. Swift, in 1727, has 'A man-pleaser, at the expence of all honour, conscience, and truth', which is virtually a definition. The Gr. word is ἀνθρωπάρεσκος, defined by Souter as '*a man-pleaser, a renderer of service to human beings* (as opposed to God)'; the Vulgate has *quasi hominibus placentes* ('comme des gens qui veulent plaire—*or*, cherchent à plaire—aux hommes', Verdunoy).

man-slayer. 'Knowing this, that the law is not made for a righteous man, but for the lawless and disobedient, for the ungodly and for sinners, for unholy and profane, for murderers of fathers and murderers of mothers, for man-slayers' (1 *Timothy*, i, 9): ἀνδροφόνοις: *homicidis*.

A *homicide*, by which it has been displaced: current in C. 14–17, then archaic. It was contemporaneous with the synonymous *man-queller*.

manifold. 'Verily I say unto you, There is no man that hath left house, or parents, or brethren, or wife, or children, for the kingdom of God's sake, | Who shall not receive manifold more in this present time, and in the world to come life everlasting' (*Luke*, xviii, 29–30).

The adj. used as adv.: 'manifold more' is 'many times

more', according to Wright; 'proportionately more' is perhaps closer. As adv., *manifold* has been obsolete since ca. 1660.

manner. In 'all manner vessels of ivory, and all manner vessels of most precious woods' (*Revelation*, xviii, 12), the *of* ('all manner of') has been omitted, according to a common practice of the 14th–early 17th Centuries; here, 'all manner' = all sorts or kinds. Cf. Shakespeare's 'What manner of man is he?'—'An old man.'

In *John*, xix, 40, 'Then took they the body of Jesus, and wound it in linen clothes with the spices, as the manner of the Jews is to bury', *manner* = custom. This sense of *manner* has been literary since the late 18th Century; archaic since ca. 1870.

mansions. 'In my father's house are many mansions' (*John*, xiv, 2). 'Like the *mansiones* of the Vulgate, which our translators followed, this word is used in its primary meaning of "dwelling places", "resting places" (Gr. μοναί); especially applied to halting places on a journey, or quarters for the night' (Wright). The prevalent sense in the 19th–20th Centuries is that of a house 'with some pretensions to magnificence'.

The Biblical sense above-mentioned is found in, e.g., Shakespeare's 'Timon hath made his everlasting mansion | Upon the beached verge of the salt flood'; cf. Bacon's 'And the pirates have a receptacle [a place of retirement; a shelter], and mansion, in Algiers'. *Mansio* is the n. formed from L. *manere*, 'to remain, to stay'.

Mark. See the quotation at **Luke.**

Either from Gr. Μᾶρκος or, via Fr. *Marc*, from L. *Marcus*, which may possibly have an origin independent of that of the Gr. word and, deriving from *Mavors* (later *Mars*), be cognate with *Martin*. According to Cruden, however, the name signifies 'polite' or 'shining'.

'Mark was not very popular with us until recent times, perhaps owing to the association of the evangelist's Latin name with the unrelated Celtic name of Isold's husband. . . . The Latin form Marcus came into use with us in the 19th Century' (*Jack and Jill*). 'The church has . . . done much to spread the name in Europe and, hence, in England; uncomparably, yet not negligibly, so has Marc Antony' (Partridge).

martyr. 'When the blood of thy martyr Stephen was shed, I [Paul] also was standing by' (*Acts*, xxii, 20); 'Antipas was my faithful martyr, who was slain among you' (*Revelation*, ii, 13); 'I saw the woman [Babylon personified] drunken with the blood of the saints, and with the blood of the martyrs of Jesus' (*ibid.*, xvii, 6).

The corresponding Gr. is μάρτυς, 'a witness' (whether by eye or by ear); in the passages quoted above, 'it approaches the ecclesiastical sense of *martyr*, i.e. one who gives public testimony to his faith before a tribunal, and suffers the penalty' (Souter); cf. μαρτυρέω, 'I bear witness or give evidence', and μαρτύριον, 'evidence'. But the English word probably comes from *martyr*, the Ecclesiastical L. equivalent of the Gr. term; note, however, that the Vulgate has *testis* in the *Acts* and *Revelation*, ii, passages, *martyr* only in the third.

See esp. Hastings—the International Commentaries—and Leclercq.

master-builder. 'According to the grace of God which is given unto me, as a wise master-builder, I have laid the foundation, and another buildeth thereon' (1 *Corinthians*, iii, 10).

A *master builder* is an architect, as in Ibsen's play, *The Master Builder* (1892). The term was in common use, ca. 1550–1660; from ca. 1660 until ca. 1900, it was confined to rhetorical contexts; in C. 20, it has been obsolete.

matter. 'The tongue is a little member, and boasteth great things. Behold, how great a matter a little fire kindleth!' (*James*, iii, 5). The subject in the second sentence is 'fire': ἰδού, ἡλίκον πῦρ ἡλίκην ὕλην ἀνάπτει, 'behold, how small a fire kindles how much brushwood', i.e., how small is the flame necessary to set fire to a great amount of fuel.

Matter is from L. *materia*, 'material' (hence 'fuel').

Matthew. 'The Heb. *Mattaniah*, "gift of the Lord" [or rather *Mattithiah*, "gift of Jehovah"], became, in Gr., Ματθαῖος (Mat-thaios) and Ματθίας (Mat-thias), L. *Matthæus* and *Matthias*: *Matthew* and *Matthias* are doublets, but it is more precise to derive the former from L. *Matthæus*, the latter from L. *Mathias* . . . *Matthew* (contrast *John*, *Mark*, *Peter*) is fast losing ground in the British Empire' (Partridge).

mean. 'But Paul said, I am a man which am a Jew of Tarsus, a city in Cilicia, a citizen of no mean city' (*Acts*, xxi, 39).— Cf. the marginal gloss to *Romans*, xii, 16.

No *mean*='no contemptible'; it is a eulogistic phrase applied to persons ('no mean foes') or to things; cf. Shakespeare's 'It is no mean happiness therefore to be seated in the mean', which occurs in a play staged in 1596.

The phrase (*a citizen of*) *no mean city* has become a cliché; *No Mean City*, by MacArthur & Long, 1935, is an account of the Glasgow gangsters.

measure. 'Are they ministers of Christ? (I speak as a fool) I am more; in labours more abundant, in stripes [lashes of the whip] above measure, in prisons more frequent, in deaths oft' (2 *Corinthians*, xi, 23).—'For ye have heard of my conversation in time past in the Jews' religion, how that beyond measure I persecuted the church of God, and wasted it', i.e., ravaged or damaged it (*Galatians*, i, 13).

Both *above measure* and *beyond measure* = 'excessively'; they represent L. *supra modum*. Variants are *above all measure* and *beyond all measure*. All four are obsolete.

meat, in the A.V., is used in the sense, 'food', which is obsolete except in the cliché, '(something is) meat and drink (to somebody)'. As Wright has observed, 'in no passage of the A.V. has this word the exclusive meaning of "flesh", to which it is restricted in modern usage. It denoted all kinds of victuals except bread and drink.' In *Hebrews*, xiii, 9 (see at **occupy**), the pl. *meats* is generic for 'food'.

Meat, which occurs in O.E., belongs to the common Germanic stock.

merchantman. 'Again, the kingdom of heaven is like unto a merchant man, seeking goodly pearls' (*Matthew*, xiii, 45).

Clearly, not a merchant ship (the modern sense) but a merchant. The sense 'merchant' arose in the 15th Century, whereas the sense 'vessel of the mercantile marine' did not arise until the 17th; but the latter sense had ousted the former by—if not before—the end of the 18th Century.

Messiah and **Messias.** *Messiah* is not to be found in the N.T. For the latter form, see the quotation at **pose**; it occurs also in *John*, i, 41, and iv, 25, respectively: 'We have found the Messias, which is, being interpreted, the Christ' and 'I know that Messias cometh, which is called Christ'. (For the use and non-use of 'the' before *Messias*, cf. its use and non-use before *Christ*.)

The Gr. Test. has Μεσσίας, which, in the Vulgate, is the same. (In Fr. it is *Messie*.) Μεσσίας represents the Aramaic *meshiha* (Heb. *mashiah*, 'the anointed one'), and *Messiah* is the Gr. word modified by analogy to the Aramaic and Heb. forms. The usual Gr. translation of the Aramaic is Χριστός; the usual A.V. one is *Christ* (q.v. at **Jesus Christ**). 'It is to be noted that "Messiah" as a special title is never applied in the O.T. to the unique king of the future'—except perhaps in *Daniel*, ix, 25. 'It was the . . . Jews of the post-prophetic period who . . . first used the term in a technical sense' (*The International Standard Bible Encyclopædia*).

mete. 'With what judgment ye judge ye shall be judged; and with what measure ye mete, it shall be measured to you again' (*Matthew*, vii, 2).

To *mete* is 'to measure'; this sense is archaic. The verb survives in the literary *mete out*, 'to allot by measure, to allot proportionately', applied especially to praise or blame, reward or punishment. The synonymous Gr. μετρεῖν and L. *metiri* are rather cognates than originals; *mete* belongs to the common Germanic stock, the O.E. form being *metan*.

mind, n. and v.; **minded.** In *Philemon*, 14, 'But without thy mind would I do nothing; that thy benefit should not be as it were of necessity, but willingly', *mind* = 'consent' or 'approval', according to Wright; but as it translates Gr. γνώμη, the sense is more likely to be either 'opinion' or 'counsel' (as Souter renders it).

In *Acts*, xx, 13, 'And we went before to ship [to embark], and sailed unto Assos, there intending to take in Paul: for so had he appointed, minding himself to go afoot', *minding* = 'intending', a sense often found in writings of the 16th–17th Centuries. The corresponding Gr. is μέλλων αὐτὸς πεζεύειν.

In *Matthew*, i, 19, 'Then Joseph her husband, being a just man, and not willing to make her a publick example, was minded to put her away privily', *minded* = 'determined' or perhaps merely 'inclined'. (The Gr. corresponding to 'was minded' is ἐβουλήθη.) Cf. 'I have a mind to do something'.

minister, n. and v. In 'And he closed the book, and he gave it again to the minister, and sat down. And the eyes of all them that were in the synagogue were fastened on him' (*Luke*, iv, 20), *minister* denotes that 'attendant in the synagogue who had the charge of the sacred books' (Wright); the Gr. word is ὑπηρέτης, 'a servant, an attendant' (Souter). In *Hebrews*, viii, 2, Christ is spoken of as 'a minister of the sanctuary': on which phrase, see Cruden. In *Romans*, xiii, 6, 'For this cause pay ye tribute also: for they are God's ministers', the reference is to magistrates, God's representatives on earth (see Cruden). And in 1 *Corinthians*, iv, 1 ('. . . us, the ministers of Christ, and stewards of the mysteries of God'), the application is to 'such as are appointed to attend the service of God in his church, to dispense and give forth, faithfully and wisely, the word, sacraments, and other holy things' (Cruden): whence derives the modern sense of *minister*, 'a minister of religion' (priest or clergyman), the other modern sense being 'a minister of the Crown' (he who is at the head of a Ministry). *Minister* comes direct and unchanged from L., where its primary sense is 'an attendant, a servant', perhaps from *manus*, 'the hand' (one who hands things to a superior).

The v. *minister*, in 2 *Corinthians*, ix, 10 ('He that minister-eth seed to the sower') = 'to supply, to furnish', as does L. *ministrare*.

misdeem '[Christ] was . . . born of the Virgin Mary when she was espoused to Joseph. The angel satisfieth the misdeem-ing thoughts of Joseph' (*Matthew*, i, heading).

Misdeeming = 'mistaken' or 'suspecting evil'; lit. 'misjudg-ing', i.e., 'wrongly judging'. *Misdeem* is a combination of *mis*, the prefix meaning 'amiss' or 'wrongly', and *deem*, 'to judge', 'to think'; the word has, since ca. 1840, been archaic except in poetry—but even poets have frowned on it since ca. 1918.

mite. 'And there came a certain poor widow, and she threw in two mites, which make a farthing' (*Mark*, xii, 42); 'I tell thee, that thou shalt not depart thence, till thou hast paid the very last mite' (Luke, xii, last verse).

From the *Mark* context has come the cliché, 'the widow's mite'. The word *mite* has come from Dutch (perhaps via Fr.); the corresponding term in the Vulgate is *minutum* (lit., a minished—hence, minute—thing); in the Gr. Test. the word is λεπτόν, which is the half of a κοδράντης. See esp. the O.E.D. and Souter.

mock. 'Then Herod, when he saw that he was mocked of the wise men, was exceeding wroth' (*Matthew*, ii, 16); 'Be not deceived; God is not mocked: for whatsoever a man soweth, that shall he also reap' (*Galatians*, vi, 7).

In all other N.T. passages, 'to *mock*' = 'to deride', 'to laugh at', 'to scoff at'; but in the two passages quoted above, *mock* = 'to beguile (with words), to delude'.

From the Fr. *se moquer de*, 'to mock at'.

more, adj., means 'greater' in *Acts*, xix, 32, 'Some therefore cried one thing, and some another: for the assembly was con-fused; and the more part'—the majority—'knew not wherefore they were come together'; so too in xxvii, 12, 'And because the haven was not commodious to winter in, the more part advised to depart thence'.

Cf. the modern phrase, *the more fool you!*

mortify. 'For if ye live after the flesh, ye shall die: but if ye through the spirit do mortify the deeds of the body, ye shall live' (*Romans*, viii, 13); 'Mortify therefore your members which are upon the earth; fornication, uncleanness, inordinate affection, evil concupiscence, and covetousness, which is idolatry' (*Colossians*, iii, 5).

In the former passage, the sense is 'cancel'; to 'mortify the deeds of the body' is to 'mortify the body'. To *mortify one's body*, to *mortify one's limbs*, is to kill them in a fig. sense, to vanquish them, to reduce them to powerlessness, to stupefy them. From L. *mortificare*, primarily 'to kill', derivatively 'to render powerless'.

mote. 'And why beholdest thou the mote that is in thy brother's eye, but considerest not the beam that is in thine own eye?' (*Matthew*, vii, 3; cf. verses 4, 5):

τί δὲ βλέπεις τὸ κάρφος τὸ ἐν τῷ ὀφθαλμῷ τοῦ ἀδελφοῦ σου . . . 'why do you see the wood-chip in your brother's eye . . . ?'

Quid autem vides festucam in oculo fratris tui . . . ?: 'Pourquoi vois-tu la paille qui est dans l'œil de ton frère . . . ?' (Verdunoy).

Mote, 'a particle of dust', is of West Germanic stock. *A mote in the eye* has come to be used fig. for 'a relatively trifling fault observed in another person by one who ignores a greater fault of his own' (O.E.D.).

motions. 'When we were in the flesh, the motions of sins, which were by the law, did work in our members to bring forth fruit unto death' (*Romans*, vii, 5).

Cf. Latimer's 'I withstand these ill motions, I follow the ensample of that godly young man, Joseph'.

Wright defines *motions* as 'emotions, impulses': but that is to be euphemistic and unhelpfully vague. *By the law* = in accordance with the law, the reference being to the sins of the flesh, esp. to sexual intercourse as practised by married couples. The Gr. is τὰ παθήματα τῶν ἁμαρτιῶν τὰ διὰ τοῦ νόμου, lit. 'those experiences'—probably, 'evil experiences'—'of the sins (which are) accordant with the law', *accordant* agreeing, not with 'sins' but with 'experiences'.

muse. 'All men mused in their hearts of John, whether he were the Christ, or not' (*Luke*, iii, 15).

They meditated about John, or wondered concerning him: both nuances date from C. 14; the latter is archaic. The Gr. Test. has διαλογιζομένων πάντων ἐν ταῖς καρδίαις περὶ τοῦ Ἰωάννου, 'all men debating in their hearts concerning John'; the Vulgate, cogitantibus omnibus in cordibus suis de Joanne, 'tous se demandaient dans leurs cœurs si Jean n'était pas le Christ' (Verdunoy).

Of difficult etymology, *muse* probably derives, via Fr. *muser*, from the Romance words for (a dog's) 'nose' held up as the animal sniffs the air inquiringly.

N

napkin. 'And another came, saying, Lord, behold here is thy pound, which I have kept laid up in a napkin' (*Luke*, xix, 20); 'His face was bound about with a napkin' (*John*, xi, 44); 'Then cometh Simon Peter following him, and went into the sepulchre, and seeth the linen clothes lie, | And the napkin, that was about his head, not lying with the linen clothes, but wrapped together in a place by itself' (*ibid.*, xx, 6–7).

In the *Luke* passage, *napkin* = a piece of cloth (e.g., linen) or, less probably, a handkerchief; in the two *John* passages, it is used to translate the Gr. σουδάριον, L. *sudarium* (lit., a sweat-cloth, i.e.), a handkerchief.

Either from M.E. *nape*, a table-cloth (cf. *napery*, table linen),
+ the diminutive suffix *-kin* (as in *lambkin*, a little lamb), or
direct from Fr. *nappe*, a cloth, + *-kin*.

nard occurs as a marginal gloss on *spikenard* in *Mark*, xiv, 3
('An alabaster box of ointment of spikenard very precious').

In the Gr. Test. the term is *νάρδος*; the corresponding L.
is *nardus*; the Heb. is *nêrd* ('borrowed into Persian and
Sanscrit', Souter). Nard is an aromatic plant.

See also **spikenard.**

naughtiness. 'Wherefore lay apart'—i.e., lay aside—'all
filthiness and superfluity of naughtiness, and receive with
meekness the engrafting word, which is able to save your
souls' (*James*, i, 21).

Here, *naughtiness* = 'wickedness', a sense it bore in the
16th–17th Centuries; this, indeed, was the original sense of
naughtiness. The sense prevalent in the 19th–20th Centuries—
that of 'waywardness' or 'disobedience'—did not arise until
the 18th Century.

Cf. 'like a good deed in a naughty world', i.e., a wicked
world.

Nazareth and **Nazarenes.** A Nazarene is a native of
Nazareth, as in 'He came and dwelt in a city called Nazareth:
that it might be fulfilled which was spoken by the prophets,
He shall be called a Nazarene' (*Matthew*, ii, 23):

ἐλθὼν κατῴκησεν εἰς πόλιν λεγομένην Ναζαρέτ· ὅπως
πληρωθῇ τὸ ῥηθὲν διὰ τῶν προφητῶν, ὅτι Ναζαραῖος
κληθήσεται :

Veniens habitavit in civitate quæ vocatur Nazareth, ut
adimpleretur quod dictum est per prophetas, quoniam
Nazaræus vocabitur.

Nazarene, adj. become n., represents either the Gr.
Ναζαρηνός, adj. and n. (of Nazareth; a Nazarene), or perhaps
rather the L. transliteration *Nazarenus*. In Heb., *Nazareth* =
'the separated or the sanctified (place)'. *Ναζαρέτ* is Hebraistic
Gr. (and undeclinable), whereas the true Gr. form is *Ναζαρά*
(declinable): it is the former which has prevailed.

Nazarenes came to mean 'the followers of Jesus of Nazareth' (*the Nazarene*), hence—esp. among Jews and Mohammedans —'Christians' (O.E.D.).

necessity, of. 'Every high priest is ordained to offer gifts and sacrifices: wherefore it is of necessity that this man have somewhat'—something—'also to offer' (*Hebrews*, viii, 3).

Of necessity = necessary; the corresponding Gr. is ἀναγκαῖον (necessary, essential).

The phrase *of necessity* is extant, but only as an adverb, as in ' "Do you think that he understands what has happened?" "Of necessity he understands" '; and it is formal and literary.

neither . . . neither. 'Whosoever speaketh against the Holy Ghost, it shall not be forgiven him, neither in this world, neither in the world to come' (*Matthew*, xii, 32).

This variation of *neither . . . nor* was current only in the 16th–mid 17th Century; the earliest form was *neither . . . ne* (13th–15th Centuries); *neither . . . nor* arose in the 14th Century.

neither yet. 'And being not weak in faith, he considered not his own body now dead,'—i.e., impotent—'when he was about an hundred years old, neither yet the deadness'— barrenness—'of Sarah's womb' (*Romans*, iv, 19).

Neither yet = *nor yet*, an intensive form of *nor*.—Cf. the preceding entry.

nephew. 'But if any widow have children or nephews, let them learn first to show piety at home, and to requite'— repay; make return to (a person) for some kindness or service —'their parents: for that is good and acceptable before God' (1 *Timothy*, v, 4).

Here (as in *Judges*, xii, 14—*Job*, xviii, 19—*Isaiah*, xiv, 22), *nephew* = a grandson. 'In *Genesis*, xxi, 23, the same Heb. word, which in *Isaiah* and *Job* is rendered "nephew", is translated "son's son". The usage of the word in this sense is common in old English' (Wright). It comes, via Fr. *neveu*, from L. *nepos* (genitive *nepotis*). The L. word meant, originally, 'a grandson', later 'a nephew'; in 17th Century literary French, *neveu* was 'a grandson', but in ordinary Modern Fr. of the 18th–20th Centuries it is 'a nephew'.

news. 'He blesseth God for his manifold spiritual graces: shewing that the salvation in Christ is no news, but a thing prophesied of old: and exhorteth them accordingly to a godly conversation, forasmuch as they are now born anew by the word of God' (1 *Peter*, i, heading).

No news = no new things; no novelties. *News* is a plural n., formed from the adj. *new*, on the analogy of the Fr. *novelles* (Modern Fr. *nouvelles*). As 'novelties', *news* belongs to the 14th–early 17th Centuries. In More's *Utopia*, as translated by Robinson (1551), we find the illuminating sentence, 'But as for monsters, bycause they be no newes, of them we were nothyng inquisitive'.

no not. 'To whom we gave place by subjection, no, not for an hour' (*Galatians*, ii, 5): οἷς οὐδὲ πρὸς ὥραν εἴξαμεν τῇ ὑποταγῇ, not even for a little time.

No not = 'not even'—a strong negative; obsolete except in rhetorical or Bible-reminiscent passages.

noise. 'And again he entered into Capernaum after some days; and it was noised that he was in the house' (*Mark*, ii, 1): ἠκούσθε ὅτι εἰς οἶκόν ἐστι: *auditum est* . . .

To *noise* is 'to report; to spread a rumour; to proclaim'; *it was noised* = 'there was a rumour'. The modern form (dating from the 16th Century) is *noise abroad*, now slightly obsolescent and either affected or literary; cf.

> My office is
> To noise abroad that Harry Monmouth fell
> Under the wrath of noble Hotspur's sword.
> (Shakespeare, 2 *Henry IV*, Induction).

This v. derives directly from the n. *noise* in its obsolete sense 'common talk; rumour, report'; cf. the history of *report*, n. and v.

none effect, of. Of no effect.

In *Matthew*, xv, 6; *Mark*, vii, 13; *Romans*, iv, 14, and ix, 6; 1 *Corinthians*, i, 17; and *Galatians*, v, 4.

The attributive use of *none*, adj. (preceding its n.), has long been obsolete; *none* is now only predicative.

none other. No other. 'None other name', *Acts*, iv, 12.— Cf. the preceding entry.

not = *not only* in 'He therefore that despiseth, despiseth not man, but God' (1 *Thessalonians*, iv, 8).

not ... nor ... neither = *neither ... nor ... nor* in *Luke*, xiv, 12, and *John*, i, 25. (Wright.)

notable. 1. 'And they had then a notable prisoner, called Barabbas' (*Matthew*, xxvii, 16): here, *notable* = 'notorious' rather than 'remarkable'.

2. 'The sun shall be turned into darkness, and the moon into blood, before that great and notable day of the Lord come' (*Acts*, ii, 20): here, it = 'glorious' or 'dazzling', according to Wright; 'terrible', according to Cruden.

3. 'What shall we do to these men? for that indeed a notable miracle hath been done by them is manifest to all them that dwell in Jerusalem' (*ibid.*, iv, 16): here, it = 'well known' (Wright) or—more probably—'apparent' (Cruden).

Notable comes, via Fr. *notable*, from L. *notabilis*, 'deserving to be noted or marked' (*nota*, a mark).

nothing, adv. 'Every creature of God is good, and nothing to be refused' (1 *Timothy*, iv, 4); 'Let him ask in faith, nothing wavering' (*James*, i, 6).

In no respect; in no way.

This usage survives, but only as a literary archaism; cf. *something*, 'in some respect, way, or degree', as in 'He was something anxious about his fate'.

novice. Concerning the appointment and qualifications of a bishop, we read, in 1 *Timothy*, iii, 6, that he should be 'not a novice, lest being lifted up with pride he fall into the condemnation of the devil'.

Not, as in Roman Catholicism, a probationer (one who has not yet taken the final vows), but either 'a newly converted person' (O.E.D.) or 'one newly admitted into the church' (Wright). Via Old Fr. *novisse*, from L. *novicius* (a n. formed from *novus*, 'new'); the corresponding Gr. is νεόφυτος, lit., 'newly planted', hence 'newly converted (to Christianity)'.

number of the beast, the. 'Here is wisdom. Let him that hath understanding count the number of the beast: for it is the number of a man; and his number is Six hundred threescore and six' (*Revelation*, xiii—which deals with 'a beast . . . having seven heads and ten horns'—18).

Many attempts have been made to fit the number 666 to the names of various historical personages: for some account of these attempts, see Brewer, *Phrase and Fable*, p. 901, and esp. Theodor Zahn, *Einleitung in das Neue Testament* (2 parts), 1897, 1899, at II, 622 ff., and, of course, Hastings, *Encyclopædia of Religion and Ethics*. Among these names are *Lateinos* (the Roman Empire), *Nero Cæsar*, *Trajan Hadrianus*, *Caligula*, *Apostates*, *Benedictos*, *Diocletian*, *Evanthas*, *Julian*, *Lampetis*, *Lutheranos* (Luther), *Maometis* (Mahomet), *Mysterium*, *Napoleon I*, *Niketes*, *Paul V*, *Silvester II*. As a friend of mine has remarked, 'Some of these require the variant 616, but this alteration is easily taken in the stride of certain ecclesiastics. Personally I'm inclined to favour *Nero*, even though it gives 616 and then only by the omission of a Heb. consonant. I have not bothered to try *Adolf* or *Hitler*, wishing to leave you the honour of identifying him with Antichrist if he will fit'; I fear that *Adolf* does not fit, though *Hitler* does, according to the following ingenious 'key' supplied by one of the members of the teaching staff of the Queen's University, Belfast:—

Put A = 100, B = 101, C = 102, etc., and you get

$$H = 107$$
$$I = 108$$
$$T = 119$$
$$L = 111$$
$$E = 104$$
$$R = 117$$
$$\overline{}$$
$$666$$

For *the Beast* as Antichrist, see esp. Hastings.

nurture. 'And, ye fathers, provoke not your children to wrath: but bring them up in the nurture and admonition of the Lord' (*Ephesians*, vi, 4).

The corresponding Gr. is ἐν παιδείᾳ καὶ νουθεσίᾳ Κυρίου, where παιδεία is the word here rendered as 'nurture': now, παιδεία = 'discipline'. *Nurture* is a much weaker word than it was in 1611. Trench, *Synonyms of the New Testament*, 7th edition (revised and enlarged), 1871, writes:—' "Discipline" might be substituted with advantage—the laws and ordinances of the Christian household, the transgression of which will induce correction.' In the 16th–early 17th Centuries, *nurture*, whether n. or v., was a powerful word: cf. Coverdale's rendering of 1 *Kings*, xii, 11, 'I wyl nourtoure you with scorpions': as Wright points out.

Here, *nurture* might well be glossed as 'training', '(careful) upbringing; education', with a connotation of morality; these nuances were current only in the 14th–17th Centuries.

Nurture comes from Old Fr. *nourture*, a variant of *nour(r)eture*, derived from Late L. *nutritura*, itself derived from Classical L. *nutrire*, 'to nourish'.

O

observe. 'Herod feared John, knowing that he was a just man and an holy, and observed him; and when he heard him, he did many things, and heard him gladly' (*Mark*, vi, 20).

For *observed*, all the earlier English versions except Wyclif's and the Rheims have, as Wright points out, 'gave him reverence'. This *observe* corresponds to and derives from the L. *observare*, the sense being 'to respect; to treat with reverence; to behave ceremoniously towards, treat with ceremonious respect; to honour'. The Gr. is συνετήρει αὐτόν, 'kept him safe'.

Observe, in these nuances, was current in the late 16th–mid 18th Century; rather a literarism than a general word.

occupy. 'He called his ten servants, and delivered them ten pounds, and said unto them, Occupy till I come' (*Luke*, xix, 13); 'Be not carried about with divers and strange doctrines. For it is a good thing that the heart be established'—be given calmness or steadiness (a 15th–17th Century usage)—'with grace; not with meats [i.e., food], which have not profited them that have been occupied therein' (*Hebrews*, xiii, 9).

In the *Luke* passage, the sense is 'trade with [them]'; in the *Hebrews* passage, 'traded therein' or 'employed them', although the best gloss is perhaps 'trafficked therein (or therewith)'. The Gr. is, respectively, πραγματεύσασθε ἕως ἔρχομαι, 'do business till I come', and οἱ περιπατήσαντες, 'those who have conducted their life [therewith]'—almost '. . . subsisted thereon'.

Occupy is 'from L. *occupare*; literally, to lay hold of; then, to use, employ, trade with; and, in a neuter [i.e., intransitive] sense, to trade' (Wright).

of, in the N.T., often = *by*, as in the quotation at **certify.**

often, adj.; **ofttimes.** 'Use a little wine for thy stomach's sake and thine often infirmities' (1 *Timothy*, v, 23); cf. 'The sundry contemplation of my travels, in which my often rumination wraps me in a most humorous sadness' (Shakespeare, *As You Like It*, IV, i, 19). *Often*, 'frequent', fell into disuse early in the 18th Century.

'Lord, have mercy on my son: . . . for ofttimes he falleth into the fire, and oft into the water' (*Matthew*, xvii, 15): as 'often', *ofttimes* was very common in the 14th–17th Centuries; since ca. 1730, it has been mainly poetic; in the 20th Century, it is archaic.

on this wise = *in this wise*, 'thus'. See, e.g., the first quotation at **sojourn**. *On this wise* arose in C. 9 and was already archaic by 1611.

open, v. 'Paul . . . reasoned with them out of the scriptures, | Opening and alleging, that Christ must needs have suffered, and risen again from the dead' (*Acts*, xvii, 2–3).

Here, to *open* is 'to expound, explain, make plain'—a sense that became obsolete in the 18th Century. On the title-page of W. Ames's *The Marrow of Faith*, 1642, are the amplificatory words, 'A table opening the hard words' (a *table* being a synoptical treatise).

Open belongs to the common Germanic stock.

other, in 'And there were also two other, malefactors, led with him to be put to death' (*Luke*, xxiii, 32), 'In lowliness of mind let each esteem other better than themselves' (*Philippians*, ii, 3), and 'I entreat thee also . . . help those women which laboured with me . . ., with Clement also, and with other my fellow-labourers' (*ibid.*, iv, 3), is the long obsolete plural of *other*; it = *others*; in the third passage, 'other my . . .' = 'others of my . . .'

other some. See at **babbler**.

ought; owe. In the edition of 1611, 'owed' was *ought* in *Matthew*, xviii, 24 and 28, and in *Luke*, vii, 41 ('There was a certain creditor which had two debtors: the one owed five hundred pence, and the other fifty'). *Ought* as the preterite of *owe* went out of general use in the late 16th Century; by 1620, it was archaic; by 1660, obsolete. From it, however, comes the obligatory v. in 'I *ought* to do something' (I should . . .).

outgo is 'to outstrip' in *Mark*, vi, 33, 'The people saw them departing, and many knew him, and ran afoot thither out of all cities, and outwent them, and came together unto him'; a sense that has been archaic since ca. 1810, and virtually obsolete since ca. 1860.

over = 'about' or 'concerning' (a sense now archaic except as a colloquialism) in 1 *Thessalonians*, iii, 7, 'Therefore, brethren, we were comforted over you in all our affliction and distress by your faith': cf. Gr. ὑπέρ, which, lit., = 'over', and by transference, = 'for (the sake of), in defence of', and, like περί, 'about, concerning'.

overcharge. 'Take heed to yourselves, lest at any time your hearts be overcharged with surfeiting, and drunkenness, and cares of this life, and so that day come upon you unawares' (*Luke*, xxi, 34); 'But if any have caused grief, he hath not grieved me, but in part: that I may not overcharge you all' (2 *Corinthians*, ii, 5).

The sense is 'to overburden' (cf. Fr. *surcharger*), esp. fig., with nuance 'to oppress' or 'to distress'; archaic since the mid-18th Century and obsolete since the end of that century.

The English *over* + Fr. *charger* (see **charge**), 'to load'.

owe. See **ought.**—In *Acts*, xxi, 11, in the edition of 1611, *owe* = 'to own'.

P

pained; painfulness. 'She being with child cried, travailing in birth, and pained to be delivered' (*Revelation*, xii, 2): in this rhetorically tautological verse, *pained* = 'in labour' or 'in pain, afflicted with pain'.

'In weariness and painfulness, in watchings often, in hunger and thirst, in fastings often, in cold and nakedness' (2 *Corinthians*, xi, 27): *painfulness* is 'hard work' or 'toil', from *painful*, 'laborious' or 'toilsome' (as in *Psalms*, lxxiii, 16)—a sense extended from that of 'full of pain or labour'. The corresponding Gr. is κόπῳ καὶ μόχθῳ, where μόχθος is 'hardship' —esp. the hardship involved in continued labour (Souter).

Palestine. Neither *Palestine* nor *Palestina* occurs in the N.T., but this place-name can hardly be omitted. *Palestina* in the O.T. is Philistia, the country of the Philistines ('those who dwell in villages'), and thus is *Palestine* used in Hudson's translation of Du Bartas's *Judith* and in Milton's *Paradise Lost*; to us, however, *Palestine* is the native land of the Jews. According to Cruden, the name signifies 'the watered (country)' or '(the country) tending to cause ruin'.

'The word properly means "Philistia", but appears to be first used in the extended sense, as meaning all the "Land of Israel" or "Holy Land" ... by Philo and by Ovid and by later Roman writers' (*The International Standard Bible Encyclopædia*); the original is a Heb. word that may be transliterated as *peleshteth*.

palsy. See the quotation at **cheer**; 'And his fame went throughout all Syria: and they brought unto him all sick people that were taken with divers diseases and torments, and those which were possessed with devils, and those which were lunatick, and those that had the palsy; and he healed them' (*Matthew*, iv, 24); 'And they come unto him, bringing one sick of the palsy, which was borne of four' (*Mark*, ii, 3,—cf. 4 and 9).

In Wyclif's version, the form is *palasie* or *palesie*, which are nearer to the Fr. *paralysie*; *palsy* is a contraction of *paralysie* ('paralysis'), which comes from Gr. παράλυσις; in the N.T., a paralytic person is παραλυτικός, a colloquial term, or παραλελυμένος, the medical term, which, lit., means 'one who has become loosened (unstrung)', hence 'one whose power of movement has gone' (Souter), παραλελυμένος being the passive participle of παραλύω (from λύω, 'I unloose or loosen').

pap. 'A certain woman of the company lifted up her voice, and said unto him, Blessed is the womb that bare thee, and the paps which thou hast sucked' (*Luke*, xi, 27); 'And in the midst of the seven candlesticks one like unto the son of man, clothed with a garment down to the foot, and girt about the paps with a golden girdle' (*Revelation*, i, 13).

Pap is a nipple of the breast, whether in woman or in man; cf. the L. *papilla*, though *pap* comes from Scandinavian. The Gr. in both passages is the plural of μαστός, 'a breast; esp. the nipple of a woman's breast' (Souter); perhaps cf. μαδάω, 'be moist'.

Pap is archaic (except in dialect) for the female breast or nipple, and both archaic and literary for the male breast or nipple (technically known as *mamilla*, the diminutive of L. *mamma*, 'a or the breast; a nipple').—Whence emerges the illuminating fact that both *mamma*, 'mother', and *papa*, 'father', are derived from the old words for the female breast, *papa* and *mamma* being childish echo-words of supplication or satisfaction; see esp. Ernest Weekley, *Adjectives and Other Words*, 1930, at the essay entitled 'Baby's Contribution to Speech'.

parable. In the N.T., *parable* (or *parables*) occurs some forty times; e.g. 'Hear ye therefore the parable of the sower' (*Matthew*, xiii, 18); 'And with many such parables [as that of the grain of mustard seed] spake he [Jesus] the word unto them, as they were able to hear it. | But without a parable spake he not unto them' (*Mark*, iv, 33–34).—For the Gr. ἐν παραβολῇ, see **figure.**

Via L. *parabola* and immediately from Fr. *parabole*, *parable* comes from Gr. παραβολή (itself from παραβάλλω, 'I cross over, or strike across'), lit., 'a placing side by side', hence 'a comparison or analogy', hence 'a parable' in our sense. The essence of the parable, as a literary form, is that it is a sustained emblematic allusion—an allegory on a small scale and in simple language.

For the history of this extremely interesting word, see the O.E.D. and Hastings; nor is the entry in Cruden to be neglected.

part, v. 'And sold their possessions and goods, and parted them to all men, as every man had need' (*Acts*, ii, 45).

I.e., distributed (or divided) them among all men. Dating from C. 14, this sense has been archaic since mid C. 19.

Pope, 1715, 'To part her time 'twixt reading and bohea' (tea); Dickens, 1840, 'Her friend parted his breakfast . . . with the child and her grandfather'. From Fr. *partir* in its obsolete sense, 'to divide', from L. *partiri*, 'to divide, to distribute' (*pars*, a part or portion). O.E.D.

particular, in. 'Now ye are the body of Christ, and members in particular' (1 *Corinthians*, xii, 27).

Severally: a C. 16–18 sense. The R.V. reads, 'severally members thereof': the Gr. Test., ὑμεῖς δέ ἐστε σῶμα Χριστοῦ, καὶ μέλη ἐκ μέρους. Cf.:—

particularly. 'When he had saluted them, he declared particularly what things God had wrought among the Gentiles by his ministry' (*Acts*, xxi, 19); 'And over it the cherubims of glory shadowing the mercy seat; of which we cannot now speak particularly' (*Hebrews*, ix, 5).

In the former passage, *particularly* = 'one by one'; in the latter, 'in detail'. The former is a late C. 14–19 sense (Prynne, 1630, 'They are all particularly redeemed by his death'); the latter, a late C. 15–20 sense (Chillingworth, 1638, 'Answering them more punctually and particularly').

The adj. *particular* comes, via Fr., from L. *particularis*, 'of or concerning a part' (*particula*, a little *pars* or part, i.e. a particle). O.E.D.

pass. 'And to know the love of Christ, which passeth knowledge, that ye might be filled with all the fulness of God' (*Ephesians*, iii, 19); 'And the peace of God, which passeth all understanding, shall keep your hearts and minds through Christ Jesus' (*Philippians*, iv, 7).

Wright glosses *pass* (in these two passages) as 'To surpass, exceed'. The corresponding Gr. phrases are τὴν ὑπερβάλλουσαν τῆς γνώσεως ἀγάπην τοῦ Χριστοῦ, lit., the knowledge-exceeding love of Christ' (felt *by* Christ), and ἡ εἰρήνη τοῦ Θεοῦ, ἡ ὑπερέχουσα πάντα νοῦν, lit., 'God's peace, the surpassing-the-reason [peace]'. Whence it appears that *pass* = to be beyond the compass of the human mind, beyond the range of human faculties; to transcend reason and perception.

passion and **Passion.** 'To whom also he shewed himself alive after his passion by many infallible proofs, being seen of them forty days, and speaking of the things pertaining to the kingdom of God' (*Acts*, i, 3): οἷς καὶ παρέστησεν ἑαυτὸν ζῶντα μετὰ τὸ παθεῖν.

With a small initial letter, *passion*, as in the quoted passage, means 'suffering': in 1 *Peter*, i, 11, the A.V., in reference to 'the Spirit of Christ', has '. . . it testified beforehand the sufferings of Christ . . .' (προμαρτυρόμενον τὰ εἰς Χριστὸν παθήματα, 'the sufferings destined for Messiah', Souter), whereas Tyndale has 'the passions that should come unto Christ'. (The plural is frequent in C. 16 writings.) Historically, theologically, and reverentially, *the Passion* (capital *P* obligatory) means, 'the sufferings of Jesus Christ on the Cross', and is often taken to include the Agony in Gethsemane; whence *instruments of the Passion*, the cross, the nails, the crown of thorns, the scourge, etc. Two significantly derivative senses are: 'the narrative of the sufferings of Christ from the Gospels' (or a musical version thereof), generally and preferably with capital *P*; 'martyrdom' (generic or particular), with a small *p* and, in C. 20, archaic.

From Old Fr. *passion* or *passiun*, itself from the accusative of *passio*, an action-noun from *pati*, 'to suffer'. In the Vulgate, *passio* renders Gr. πάθημα (or παθεῖν used substantively).— Cf.:—

passions. 'Elias was a man subject to like passions as we are' —i.e., to the same passions as to those to which we are subject—'and he prayed earnestly that it might not rain' (*Iames*, v, 17): Ἠλίας ἄνθρωπος ἦν ὁμοιοπαθὴς ἡμῖν, Elias was a man of like feelings with us, of a nature like ours: *Elias homo erat similis nobis passibilis*, which Verdunoy with admirable economy renders thus: 'Elie était un homme semblable à nous', Elias was a man like ourselves.—Cf. 'We also are men of like passions with you' (*Acts*, xiv, 15): καὶ ἡμεῖς ὁμοιοπαθεῖς ἐσμεν ὑμῖν ἄνθρωποι: *et nos mortales sumus, similes vobis* *homines*, which, as Verdunoy remarks, is a very inaccurate translation of the Gr. words.

Passion here = any mental feeling, any emotion; a sense introduced by Chaucer from Fr.; it corresponds to L. *passio*, used to render Gr. πάθος.

pastor. 'And he gave some, apostles; and some, prophets; and some, evangelists; and some, pastors and teachers' (*Ephesians*, iv, 11): Gr. Test., καὶ αὐτὸς ἔδωκε ... τοὺς δὲ ποιμένας καὶ διδασκάλους, where ποιμῆν is 'a shepherd', hence metaphorically 'a feeder, protector, ruler of a *flock* of men' (Souter): *alios autem pastores, et doctores* ('pasteurs et docteurs', Verdunoy).

In English, the senses 'shepherd of souls' and, lit., 'shepherd or herdsman' (now archaic) occur earliest in Langland's *Piers Plowman* in, respectively, 1362 and 1377. Via Anglo-Fr. from Old Fr. from L. *pastor* (lit., a giver of pasture, a feeder: *pascere*, to give pasture to).

pattern. 'It was therefore necessary that the patterns of things in the heavens should be purified with these; but the heavenly things themselves with better sacrifices than these' (*Hebrews*, ix, 23): ἀνάγκη οὖν τὰ μὲν ὑποδείγματα τῶν ἐν τοῖς οὐρανοῖς, 'signs (or images) of heavenly things', the same sense of ὑπόδειγμα occurring also in viii, 5: *necesse est ergo exemplaria quidem cælestium*, 'ainsi donc il est nécessaire que les images des choses célestes . . .', Verdunoy, who notes that 'les images des choses célestes' ('the patterns of things in the heavens') are, in effect, the Mosaic tabernacle and its furniture.

'In modern usage "pattern" commonly signifies that from which a copy is made, but in the time of the A.V. it denoted also the copy made from a model, as in the passage [quoted]', Wright. Never a common sense, this use was current only ca. 1550–1730: in 1570 in the form *pattern*; in 1557 in the form *patron* (the Geneva version of *Hebrews*, viii, 5). The M.E. form was *patron*, adopted direct from Fr. *patron*, 'which still means both "patron" and "pattern" ' (O.E.D.).

Paul comes, either via Old Fr. *Pol* (Modern Fr. *Paul*)—cf.
It. *Paolo* and Sp. *Pablo*—or direct from L. *Paulus*, a Latin
personal name (which in the Gr. Test. is Παῦλος): 'the
third part (cognomen) of the full Roman name of the Apostle,
the other two parts of which (Gaius Iulius?) are now unknown', Souter: Paul, 'the apostle of the Gentiles', whose
other name was Saul: *Acts*, xiii, 9, 'Then Saul, (who also is
called Paul,) . . .', Σαῦλος δέ, ὁ καὶ Παῦλος: Saulus autem, qui
est Paulus, 'Alors Saul, appelé aussi Paul', Verdunoy, whose
gloss is, 'Comme beaucoup d'autres Juifs, Paul avait, dès son
enfance, deux noms; Paul était le nom du citoyen romain,
celui que Luc emploiera désormais, à l'occasion de l'apostolat
paulien parmi les Gentils'.

Paulus, etymologically, is *paul(l)us*, 'little': 'the cognomen
. . . Paulus . . . originated with one of the Æmilian gens [or
clan], who was small in stature' (Charlotte M. Yonge). As a
given name, *Paul* has always been more popular on the Continent than in Britain. 'It is very prominent among the saints
(there were thirty-eight of them), among [European] kings
and princes, and in English literature' (Partridge).

peoples. 'And he said unto me, Thou must prophesy again
before many peoples, and nations, and tongues, and kings'
(*Revelation*, x, 11), where *tongues* = 'speakers of various
languages', almost 'foreigners',—cf. *Isaiah*, lxxi, 18, 'I will
come to gather all people and tonges' (Coverdale, 1535); 'And
he saith unto me, The waters which thou sawest, where the
whore sitteth, are peoples, and multitudes, and nations, and
tongues' (*Revelation*, xvii, 15).

Races; tribes.

'This plural form was avoided in C. 16 *Bible* versions, and
by many C. 17 and C. 18 writers' (O.E.D.).

Via Anglo-Fr. from Old Fr. *po(e)ple* from L. *populus*, 'the
people, the populace'.

perfectness. 'And above all these things put on charity,
which is the bond of perfectness' (*Colossians*, iii, 14): ὅ ἐστι

σύνδεσμος τῆς τελειότητος (moral completeness, i.e. perfection).

Concerning *perfectness* (C. 14–20; obsolescent), the O.E.D. remarks that it is 'in early use chiefly in the religious sense of a perfect life': so used by Hampole, Langland, Skelton, Latimer.

Perfect + *ness*; *perfect* being M.E. *parfit(e)*, which comes, via Old Fr., from *perfectus*, the passive participle of *perficere*, 'to accomplish, to complete' (*per*, 'thoroughly' + *facere*, 'to do or make').

persuade; persuasible. 'And he went into the synagogue and spake boldly for the space of three months, disputing and persuading the things concerning the kingdom of God' (*Acts*, xix, 8); '. . . To whom he expounded and testified'—proclaimed as something he knew or believed in—'the kingdom of God, persuading them concerning Jesus . . . from morning till evening' (*ibid.*, xxviii, 23).—*Persuasible* occurs in the marginal gloss to 1 *Corinthians*, ii, 4 ('And my speech and my preaching was not without enticing words').

Persuade, 'to use persuasion, be persuasive concerning; to advise concerning', or, as the O.E.D. defines this sense (ca. 1530–1700), 'to commend (a statement, opinion, etc.) to acceptance, to urge as credible or true; to inculcate'. (Perhaps via Fr.) from L. *persuadere*, 'to induce' (a person).

Persuasible = 'persuasive': a sense current only ca. 1380–1660; first used by Wyclif in the cited passage. From L. *persuasibilis* (likewise from *persuadere*).

Peter. 'It might be worth your while to get some professed Hebrew expert on to the subject of the text about Peter being the rock on which the Church was founded. It's an obvious pun in Greek; but then Jesus didn't speak in Greek; and it would be worth noting if the pun exists in Hebrew or if it was made by the author of the Greek version' (a University friend, in a letter of July 30, 1939, to the writer). That the earliest surviving version of the N.T. was written not in Heb. (Aramaic variety) but in Gr. (the L. and Syriac versions being later than the Gr.) does not affect the issue; for the Gr. Test. was written with reference to Aramaic oral and other records and memories.

The two Gr. words on which the pun is made are Πέτρος, *Petros* (our *Peter*), 'a Greek name meaning "rock", a translation of the Aramaic name Κηφᾶς given to Symeon (Simon) by our Lord' (Souter), this name being a personification of Aramaic *kefa* or *kepha*, 'a rock'; and πέτρα, 'rock, solid rock, native rock', applied in the ensuing quotation to 'such faith as Peter has just shown' (id.). This passage runs, 'And I [Jesus] say also unto thee, that thou art Peter, and upon this rock will I build my church; and the gates of hell shall not prevail against it' (*Matthew*, xvi, 18), glossed by Cruden thus, 'Christ . . . sustains and bears up his church, built upon him by faith, as a house upon a rock': κἀγὼ δέ σοι λέγω, ὅτι σὺ εἶ Πέτρος, καὶ ἐπὶ ταύτῃ τῇ πέτρᾳ οἰκοδομήσω μου τὴν ἐκκλησίαν, καὶ πύλαι ᾅδου οὐ κατισχύσουσιν αὐτῆς, '. . . thou art Peter, and upon this rock I shall build my church . . .': et ego dico tibi quia tu es Petrus, et super hanc petram ædificabo ecclesiam meam, 'et moi, je te dis que toi, tu es Pierre et que sur cette pierre je bâtirai mon Eglise' (Verdunoy).

L. *Petrus*, which merely transliterates Πέτρος, naturally becomes *Petre*, written *Peter*. It became, in various forms (Fr. *Pierre*, It. *Pietro*, Sp. *Pedro*), very popular as a European given name, though not at all general in England until C. 18; but in late C. 19–20, *Peter* has been an extremely, almost excessively, popular English name. (See *Jack and Jill*.)

Pharaoh occurs four times in the N.T.: *Acts*, vii, 13 and 21; *Romans*, ix, 17 ('For the scripture saith unto Pharaoh, Even for this same purpose have I raised thee up, that I might show my power in thee, and that my name might be declared throughout all the earth'); *Hebrews*, xi, 24.

Etymologically from an Egyptian word meaning 'great house' (hence used as a *dynastic* title), through Heb. into Gr. (where it is Φαραώ), thence into L. as *Pharao*; the final *h*, absent from Egyptian, Gr., L., Fr., and O.E. and M.E., arrived only in C. 17, through Heb. influence (O.E.D.). Though a dynastic title, '*the* Pharaoh', it was 'probably everywhere understood as a *Pharaoh*, a king of Egypt' (Souter).

Pharisee. See esp. the quotation at **platter,** and cf. 'Take heed and beware of the leaven of the Pharisees and of the Sadducees' (*Matthew*, xvi, 6).

A Pharisee belonged to 'an ancient Jewish sect distinguished by their strict observance of the traditional law, and by their pretensions to superior sanctity' (O.E.D.); it was a powerful sect. After the exile, the Pharisees or *Purists* constituted 'the strict religious legalistic party in Judaism' (Souter). In Heb. (and Aramaic), the name means 'separated or separatist': whence Gr. φαρισαῖος, whence L. *pharisæus*, whence the O.E. and Old Fr. forms of the word.

In English, from late C. 16, the word took on another, a derivative sense: a self-righteous formalist, a formalistic hypocrite.

Philemon, a Christian of Colossæ ('Paul . . . and Timothy . . . unto Philemon our dearly beloved, and fellow-labourer', *Philemon*, i, 1), is, in Gr., Φιλήμων or 'friendly', hence *Philemon* in L. and English, *Philémon* in Fr. As a given name, 'it has fallen, though not irretrievably, into disuse. Two Philemons were saints and martyrs (C. 1, C. 4), but to most cultured Englishmen the name evokes the pleasant figure of Philemon Holland, doctor-scholar and accurate, vivid translator of Livy, Pliny, Plutarch, and other Classics as well as . . . native, Latinizing Camden' (Partridge).

Philip, Fr. *Philippe*, L. *Philippus*, Gr. Φίλιππος, is a Gr. name, meaning, 'fond of horses, horse-lover' (cf. the synonymous Persian *Aspamistras*). It 'became general in the Near East colonized by Macedon, so many of whose kings and princes bore this name. The Apostle Philip and Philip the Deacon . . . ; French and Spanish kings; noblemen innumerable: they all contributed to spread *Philip* throughout Europe' (Partridge). And cf.:—

Philippians. *The Epistle of Paul the Apostle to the Philippians*: the Philippians were the natives or inhabitants of *Philippi* (Gr. *Φίλιπποι*), a large city in the Roman province Macedonia, north of Greece: in N.T. Gr., *Φιλιππήσιος*, a Philippian, corresponds to Classical Gr. *Φιλιππεύς* or *Φιλιππηνός*. (Cf. *Philip of Macedon*, the great general.)

piety. 'But if any widow have children or nephews, let them learn first to show piety at home, and to requite their parents: for that is good and acceptable before God' (1 *Timothy*, v, 4).

L. *pietas*, the origin (via Fr.) of *piety*, meant, esp., 'filial affection': Erasmus (*On the Creed*) speaks thus, 'To the love of God and to the love of our parents, is given one commune name in the Latyne . . . *pietas*. For *pietas* properly is called the affection or love towardes God and towardes our parentes, and towards our countrye, which is as it were a commune parent of many men, lykewyse as God is the father of all men' (adduced by Wright); cf. Virgil's *pius Æneas*.

pitiful. 'Behold, we count them happy which endure. Ye have heard of the patience of Job, and have seen the end of the Lord [the Lord's purpose]; that the Lord is very pitiful, and of tender mercy' (*James*, v, 11); 'Finally, be ye all of one mind, having compassion one of another, love as brethren, be pitiful, be courteous' (1 *Peter*, iii, 8).

Actively 'full of pity', i.e. either 'compassionate' or 'tender', 'merciful'. Tyndale's translation of the *James* passage is: 'The Lord is very pitiful and merciful.' The relevant Gr. passages are: *πολύσπλαγχνός ἐστιν ὁ Κύριος καὶ οἰκτίρμων*, 'the Lord is full of tender feeling and merciful', and *εὔσπλαγχνοι, ταπεινόφρονες*, 'tender-hearted, meek-minded'.

Pitiful = pity-full; pity, from M.E. *pite* (disyllabic), from Old Fr. *pitet, pitez, pité, pitié*, from L. *pietas* (O.E.D.): cf. **piety.**

place. 'The place of the scripture which he read was this, He was led as a sheep to the slaughter . . .' (*Acts*, viii, 32): *ἡ δὲ περιοχὴ τῆς γραφῆς ἣν ἀνεγίνωσκεν ἦν αὕτη*, 'the sentence (or short passage) of scripture which he read aloud was this': locus autem Scripturæ quam legebat, erat hic, 'le passage de l'Ecriture, qu'il lisait, était, celui-ci' (Verdunoy).

A. C. 16–mid 18 sense of *place* (ultimately, via L. *platea*, from Gr. πλατεῖα (ὁδός), 'a broad way': cf. Fr. *place*, 'a city square or open place').

plague. See at **press.** But *'the* plague' = bubonic.

plainness. 'Seeing then that we have such hope, we use great plainness of speech' (2 *Corinthians*, iii, 12).

Frankness; directness: cf. Sir Philip Sidney's 'Rudeness, which he interpreted plainness (though there be great difference between them)'. This is, in language, what *openness* or *straightforwardness* is in conduct: cf. Shakespeare's 'Whilst some with cunning gild their copper crowns, | With truth and plainness I do wear mine bare'.

Via Old Fr. from L. *planities*, 'a flat surface'; the earliest sense in English is 'flatness', 'levelness' (O.E.D.).

platter. 'Woe unto you, scribes and Pharisees, hypocrites! for ye make clean the outside of the cup and of the platter, but within they are full of extortion and excess. | Thou blind Pharisee, cleanse first that which is within the cup and platter, that the outside of them may be clean also' (*Matthew*, xxiii, 25–6), cf. *Luke*, xi, 39.

A flat dish.

Existing in English since ca. 1300, the word comes from Old Fr. *plater* (from *plat*, 'flat', hence 'a flat thing', prob. ultimately from Gr. πλατύς, 'broad' or 'flat'): O.E.D.

ponder. 'But Mary kept all these things' (kept them in her mind, remembered them), 'and pondered them in her heart' (*Luke*, ii, 19); the operative Gr. Test.word being συμβάλλουσα, 'pondering' or 'reflecting on' (them): in the Vulgate, *conferens*, 'reviewing' (them).

Here, *ponder* is used almost in its literal sense, 'to weigh', for it = 'to weigh mentally' (hence 'to think over'), a nuance introduced, ca. 1380, by Wyclif. The word comes, via Old Fr. *ponderer* (Modern Fr. *pondérer*), from L. *ponderare*, 'to weigh', (*pondus*—genitive *ponderis*—'weight').

porter. 'He that entereth in by the door is the shepherd of the sheep. | To him the porter openeth' (*John*, x, 3); 'For the Son of Man is as a man taking a far journey, who left his house, and gave authority to his servants, and to every man his work, and commanded the porter to watch' (*Mark*, xiii, 34).

The Gr. word is θυρωρός, 'a door-keeper', in both of these passages; to it correspond the Vulgate *ostiarius* ('le portier', Verdunoy) in *John* and the *janitor* ('portier', Verdunoy) in *Mark*. Dating from late C. 13, the word survives mainly in colleges, inns of court, and government institutes: from Old Fr. *portier*, from late L. *portiarius* (*porta*, a door). Not to be confused with a (railway) *porter*, 'one who carries things', from L. *portator* (*portare*, to carry).

pose. 'Christ . . . poseth the Pharisees about the Messias' (*Matthew*, xxii, heading).

Puzzles or perplexes; asks difficult questions of: 1593, Donne, 'A thing which would have pos'd Adam to name'; ca. 1677, Barlow (in a sermon), 'A question wherewith a learned Pharisee thought to pose or puzzle him'; 1856, Dove, 'We have thus posed the mathematician . . . and the historian'; in C. 20, slightly archaic (O.E.D.).

An aphetic (fore-shortened) form of *appose*, 'to put (something) before (a person)'; less probably a shortening of *oppose*.

prefer and **prelation.** 'John bare witness of him, and cried, saying, This was he of whom I spake, He that cometh after me is preferred before me: for he was before me' (*John*, i, 15; cf. i, 27).—'All gifts, however excellent soever, are nothing worth without charity. The praises thereof, and prelation before hope and faith' (1 *Corinthians*, xiii, heading).

The Gr. Test. verbal phrase is ἔμπροσθεν γέγονε, 'has (be)come in front of me', the Vulgate has *ante me factus est*, 'est passé devant moi' (Verdunoy). The sense is 'to promote or advance; give preference to', introduced by Wyclif in 1388. Via Fr. from L. *præferre*, 'to bear or put before; to advance (a person)'.

Prelation = 'preference' or 'exaltation': C. 15–20; archaic since ca. 1850. In M.E., *prelacioune*, from Old Fr. *prelacion*, from L. *prelatio*, 'a preferring' (*præferre*).

presently. 'Thinkest thou that I cannot now pray to my Father, and he shall presently give me more than twelve legions of angels' (*Matthew*, xxvi, 53): καὶ παραστήσει μοι ἄρτι, this ἄρτι relating to the present and signifying 'now' or 'just now' (colloquially 'right now'): *et exhibebit mihi modo* . . . , 'et il m'enverrait à l'instant' (Verdunoy).

The sense, therefore, is 'instantly': C. 15–20; archaic since ca. 1870. The adj. *present* + the adverbial suffix *-ly*. *Present*, adj., comes, via Fr., from L. *præsens*, 'being at hand', hence 'immediate' or 'prompt'.

press, v. and n. 'He had healed many; insomuch that they pressed upon him for to touch him, as many as had plagues' (*Mark*, iii, 10), where *plague* = 'any infectious disease'; 'Master, the multitude throng thee and press thee' (*Luke*, viii, 45); 'The kingdom of God is preached, and every man presseth into it' (*ibid.*, xvi, 16).—'. . . They could not come nigh unto him for the press' (*Mark*, ii, 4); 'When she had heard of Jesus, [she] came in the press behind, and touched his garment' (*ibid.*, v, 27—cf. 30); *Luke*, viii, 19, and xix, 3.

To crowd or throng; a crowd or throng.

Apparently, in English, the v. derives from the n.; the n., via Fr., comes ultimately from L. *premère* (supine *pressum*).

prevent. 'We which are alive and remain unto the coming of the Lord shall not prevent them which are asleep' (1 *Thessalonians*, iv, 15): ἡμεῖς . . . οὐ μὴ φθάσωμεν τοὺς κοιμηθέντας, 'we shall not precede those who have fallen asleep [in death]: *nos* . . . *non præveniemus eos qui dormierunt*', 'nous ne devancerons pas ceux qui sont morts' (Verdunoy).

Prevent is here used literally, 'to come before' (an exact rendering of the L. *prævenire*): earliest record, 1523; since C. 18, archaic (O.E.D.).

price. 'The kingdom of heaven is like unto a merchant man, seeking goodly pearls: who, when he had found one pearl of great price, went and sold all that he had, and bought it' (*Matthew*, xiii, 45–6): εὑρὼν δὲ ἕνα πολύτιμον μαργαρίτην, 'having found one precious pearl': *inventa autem una pretiosa margarita*, 'quand il eût trouvé une perle de grand prix' (Verdunoy).

Price, 'value, price', is of C. 13–20; archaic in C. 19–20. Via Old Fr. *pris*, from Late L. *precium*, which is Classical L. *pretium*, 'price or value'.

Note that it is usually misquoted as '*a* pearl of great price'; the misquoters may have reason on their side, for in O.E., M.E., and early Modern English, *one* = either *1* or *a*(*n*).

prick, n. and v. 'It is hard for thee to kick against the pricks' (*Acts*, ix, 5; cf. xxvi, 14).—'Now when they heard this, they were pricked in their heart, and said . . . , Men and brethren, what shall we do? | Then Peter said unto them, Repent' (*ibid.*, ii, 37–8).

A *prick* is a prickle, a thorn: since early C. 17, archaic; in C. 20, except in the phrase *to kick against the pricks*, it is obsolete. Of Low Germanic stock, and from the same radical as the v.; 'pricked in their heart' is 'heart-pierced as with a thorn'.

privy. 'But a certain man . . . sold a possession, | And kept back part of it, his wife also being privy to it' (*Acts*, v, 1–2): συνειδυίας καὶ τῆς γυναικός, 'the wife being also aware of it, or sharing his secret': *conscia uxore sua*, 'd'accord avec sa femme' (Verdunoy).

Privy, 'in the secret; privately cognizant', arose in late C. 14, the earliest English sense being 'private'. 'The clergy', wrote Buckle, ca. 1862, 'believed that they alone were privy to the counsels of the Almighty' (O.E.D.). The sense is now archaic —or, at best, literary.

From Fr. *privé*, itself from L. *privatus*, 'withdrawn from public life': thus *private*, direct from L., is a doublet (a later doublet) of *privy*.

profess. 'I will profess unto them, I never knew you' (*Matthew*, vii, 23); 'They profess that they know God; but in works they deny him, being abominable, and disobedient, and unto every good work reprobate' (*Titus*, i, 16), i.e., morally corrupt in respect of every good work.

To declare openly, to affirm, to announce: a sense dating from ca. 1520. 'I do profess | You speak not like yourself', Shakespeare, *Henry VIII*, ii, iv, 84; Scott, ' "I profess I thought I was doing you a pleasure" '. Before C. 16, the word was used only in an ecclesiastical sense (*to be professed*, to have become monk or nun).

From L. *profiteri* (preterite *professus sum*), to profess.

profit. 'For what shall it profit a man, if he shall gain the whole world, and lose his own soul?' (*Mark*, viii, 36); 'It is the spirit that quickeneth; the flesh profiteth nothing' (*John*, vi, 63); 'Behold, I Paul say unto you, that if ye be circumcised, Christ shall profit you nothing' (*Galatians*, v, 2).

The relevant Gr. Test. passages are:—τί γὰρ ὠφελεῖ ἄνθρωπον, 'in what way does it benefit a man?'; ἡ σάρξ οὐκ ὠφελεῖ, 'the flesh is not helpful'; Χριστὸς ὑμᾶς οὐδὲν ὠφελήσει, 'Christ will help you in no way'.

Profit, 'to benefit', is of C. 14–20; now only literary or archaic. In *Galatians*, i, 14, '[I] profited in the Jews' religion above many my equals' (προέκοπτον ἐν τῷ Ἰουδαϊσμῷ ὑπὲρ πολλοὺς συνηλικιώτας, 'I advanced in Judaism beyond many (of my) contemporaries'), *profit* = 'to progress' (C. 14–mid 17).

Either direct from the English n. or from Old Fr. The n. comes, via Old Fr., from L. *profectus*, 'an advance; progress; profit' (*proficere*, 'to make profit, to be useful'). O.E.D.

profiting, n. 'Meditate upon these things; give thyself wholly to them; that thy profiting may appear to all' (1 *Timothy*, iv, 15): ἵνα σου ἡ προκοπὴ φανερὰ ᾖ πᾶσι, 'in order that your progress may be clear to all'. For this sense, 'progress or advance', almost 'proficiency': cf. the verb in *Galatians*, i, 14 (see preceding entry).

proper. 'That field is called in their proper tongue, Acel-
dama, . . . the field of blood' (*Acts*, i, 19); 'Every man hath
his proper gift of God, one after this manner, and one after
that' (1 *Corinthians*, vii, 7).

In the former, *their proper* = 'their own'; in the latter, *his
proper gift of God*, 'from God a gift peculiar to himself'.

Via Fr. *propre*, it comes from L. *proprius*, 'owned or possessed by, or characteristic of oneself' (hence *property*, that
which is one's own).

prophesy. 'Every woman that prayeth or prophesieth with
her head uncovered dishonoureth her head: for that is even all
one'—i.e., the same—'as if she were shaven' (1 *Corinthians*,
xi, 5); 'He that speaketh in an unknown tongue speaketh not
unto men . . . : for no man understandeth him . . . | But he
that prophesieth speaketh unto men to edification, and ex-
hortation, and comfort. | He that speaketh in an unknown
tongue edifieth himself; but he that prophesieth edifieth the
church' (*ibid.*, xiv, 2–4; cf. verse 5).

In the first passage the sense appears to be 'to profess' (her
faith); but in the second, it is 'to expound'. There used to be a
practice of the Established Church, at least in certain parts of
England, a practice that consisted in a small number of clergy-
men dealing, in turn, with one and the same Biblical text
before a select gathering of gentlemen and men of leisure.
(Wright quotes an extremely apposite passage from Bacon's
The Edification and Pacification of the Church of England, 1604, a
tract reprinted in that selection of Bacon's works which was
entitled *Resuscitatio*, 1657 (see p. 247).

Prophesy derives from the n. *prophecy* (or, early, *prophesy*),
from Old Fr. *profecie*, itself from Late L. *prophetia*, which
comes from a Gr. word; cf. the next term.

prophet occurs so frequently in the N.T. (as in the Old), that
to quote examples were hopelessly invidious.

In M.E. *prophete* or *profete*, the word comes, perhaps via
Old Fr., from L. *propheta*, which, in the Vulgate, transliterates
to the exclusion of the variant *prophetes*, the Gr. προφήτης, 'an

intepreter or spokesman, esp. of the will of a deity' (προφητεύω,
'I declare', hence 'I prophesy'). 'By the Septuagint it was
adopted to render the Heb. *nabi*, in the O.T. applied indis-
criminately to the prophets of Jehovah, of Baal and other
heathen deities, and even to . . . reputed or pretended sooth-
sayers. In the N.T. it is used in the same senses as in the
Septuagint, but mainly applied to the Heb. prophets of
Jehovah, also to John the Baptist, as well as to certain persons
in the Early Church, who were recognized as possessing more
or less of the character of the old Hebrew prophets, or as
inspired to utter special revelations and predictions' (O.E.D.).
In the N.T., a prophet is 'a man specially endowed to *tell forth*
(declare) the will of God . . . , whether as touching the present
or as regards the future, *a prophet*. . . . Epimenides (in *Titus*,
i, 12) is so styled, perhaps as related to the Cretans in the same
way as the prophets of Israel were to Israel' (Souter).

prove. The N.T. use of this v. has four senses:—

1. To try and examine; to test, as in 2 *Corinthians*, xiii, 5,
'Examine yourselves, whether ye be in the faith; prove your
own selves'.

2. To make plain (or clear) by arguement, as in *Acts*, ix, 22,
'Proving that this is very Christ', and *Romans*, iii, 9, 'We have
before proved both Jews and Gentiles, that they are all under
sin'.

3. To make good, as in *Acts*, xxiv, 13, 'Neither can they
prove the things whereof they now accuse me'.

4. To discern, then approve, then conform to, as in *Romans*,
xii, 2, 'Be ye transformed by the renewing of your mind, that
ye may prove what is that . . . will [i.e., laws and commands]
of God.'

Prove comes, via Old Fr. *prover* (Modern Fr. *prouver*), from
L. *probare*, 'to test (a thing) in respect of its goodness or worth',
which is the basic sense of the English and Fr. words as well
as of the L. word.

providence. 'Tertullus began to accuse him [Paul], saying,
Seeing that by thee we enjoy great quietness, and that very

worthy deeds are done unto this nation by thy providence, |
We accept it . . . with all thankfulness' (*Acts*, xxiv, 2–3);
where 'by thy providence' (cf. the Vulgate *per tuam provi-
dentiam*) is rather pompous for the Gr. διὰ σοῦ, 'through you'
(or 'grâce à toi', as Verdunoy sensibly renders it).

Providence, here in the lit. sense 'foresight' (Wyclif, 1382),
comes via Fr. from an action-noun formed from L. *providere*,
'to foresee'.

provoke. 'I know the forwardness (i.e., eagerness) of your
mind . . . ; and your zeal hath provoked very many' (2 *Corinthians*, ix, 2); 'Let us consider one another to provoke unto
love and to good works' (*Hebrews*, x, 24).

Here, *provoke* signifies 'to excite' in the former; 'to incite (or
urge)' in the latter.

From Old Fr. *provoker* (Modern Fr. *provoquer*), from L.
provocare, 'to call—or summon—forth; to challenge; hence, to
excite' (O.E.D.).

publican. 'And if ye salute your brethren only, what do ye
more than others? do not even the publicans so?' (*Matthew*,
v, 47); 'John came unto you in the way of righteousness, and
ye believed him not: but the publicans and the harlots believed
him' (*ibid.*, xxi, 32); and in a score of other places.

A tax-gatherer: since C. 17, only historical. The publicans
(*publicani*) were those officials of the Roman Empire who
farmed the *public* taxes: L. *publicum*, 'the public revenue' (from
publicus, 'public'), gives *publicanus*, originally 'a farmer of
taxes', then 'a gatherer of taxes'. 'How like a fawning publican he looks!', says Shakespeare in *The Merchant of Venice*,
I, iii, 42.

publish.. See at **blase.**

purchase. 'They that have used the office of a deacon well
purchase to themselves a good degree [q.v.], and great boldness in the faith which is in Jesus Christ' (1 *Timothy*, iii, 13):
οἱ γὰρ καλῶς διακονήσαντες βαθμὸν ἑαυτοῖς καλὸν περιποιοῦνται, καὶ πολλὴν παρρησίαν ἐν πίστει τῇ ἐν Χριστῷ

Ἰησοῦ, 'those who have well deaconed acquire for themselves a fine position and much boldness in Jesus Christ's faith'.

Purchase here = 'to obtain; to win': late C. 13–mid 18. 'Then, as my gift and thine own acquisition | Worthily purchased, take my daughter' (Shakespeare, *The Tempest*, IV, i, 14).

Via Anglo-Fr. *purchacer* (Old Fr. *purchacier, pourchasser*, 'to seek to obtain': L. *pro*, 'for', + Low L. *captiare*, 'to hunt' (O.E.D.).

purge. 'Who being the brightness of his glory, and the express image of his person, and upholding all things by the word of his power, when he had by himself purged our sins, sat down on the right hand of the Majesty on high' (*Hebrews*, i, 3; concerning Christ in relation to God).

Purge, 'to remove by some cleansing operation or by some purifying process': C. 14–20; archaic since C. 18 except in the form *purge away* (less often *out*).

Via Old Fr. *purg(i)er* from L. *purgare* (earlier *purigare*, from *purus*, 'pure'), 'to cleanse' (O.E.D.).

put away, 'to divorce', occurs in *Matthew*, i, 19, 'Joseph . . . not willing to make her a publick example, was minded to put her away privily'; *ibid.*, v, 31; *Mark*, x, 2 and 12; 1 *Corinthians*, vii, 11.

This sense arose (as also did 'to *divorce*') in the 14th Century; but since ca. 1660 it has been archaic. The basic sense of *put away* is 'to set aside'.

Q

quarrel. 'Forbearing one another, and forgiving one another, if any man have a quarrel against any: even as Christ forgave you, so also do ye' (*Colossians*, iii, 13): ἀνεχόμενοι ἀλλήλων, καὶ χαριζόμενοι ἑαυτοῖς, ἐάν τις πρός τινα ἔχῃ μομφήν· καθὼς καὶ ὁ Κύριος ἐχαρίσατο ὑμῖν, οὕτω καὶ ὑμεῖς, 'enduring one another and forgiving one another, if anyone have any complaint [to make] . . .': supportantes invicem, et donantes vobismetipsis, si quis adversus aliquem habit querelam, 'vous supportant les uns les autres et vous pardonnant réciproquement, si quelqu'un a sujet de se plaindre d'un autre' (Verdunoy).

Whence it appears that the sense is 'a (ground or occasion of) complaint' against a person; esp. one that will—or may— produce ill-will or hostile action: C. 14–20; but archaic in C. 19–20. 'Against whom comest thou? and what's thy quarrel?' (Shakespeare, *Richard II*, I, iii, 33).

Via Fr. from L. *querela*, 'a plaintiff's action at law' (*queri*, 'to complain').

quaternion. 'And when he [Herod] had apprehended [i.e., arrested] him [Peter], he put him in prison, and delivered him to four quaternions of soldiers to keep him; intending after Easter to bring him forth to the people' (*Acts*, xii, 4).

The Gr. Test. word is τετράδιον; the Vulgate has *quaternio*, whence our *quaternion*: *quaternio* (via *quaterni*, 'four together') is a set of *quattuor* or four, i.e. a group, file, or squad of four soldiers. *Quaternion* was introduced into English by Wyclif, to translate this passage; taken up by Tyndale and Ben Jonson; rendered magnificent by Milton's

> 'Air, and ye elements the eldest birth
> Of nature's womb, that in quaternion run
> Perpetual circle, multiform; and mix
> And nourish all things' (*Paradise Lost*, v, 181–4);

and used in several technical senses,—yet it has never been more than a learned word.

question, n. and v. 'Foolish and unlearned questions avoid, knowing that they do gender strifes' (2 *Timothy*, ii, 23).— 'The Pharisees came forth, and began to question with him, seeking of him a sign from heaven, tempting him' (*Mark*, viii, 11); 'He [Jesus] asked the scribes, What question ye with them?' (*ibid.*, ix, 16).

A discussion or a subject of discussion: from C. 14.

To dispute or argue: mid C. 14–18.

The v. occurs in Shakespeare's *The Merchant of Venice*, IV, i, 70; the n. in *As You Like It*, III, iv, 39 and v, iv, 168.

The v. comes from Old Fr. *questionner*, the n. from Old Fr. *question* (or Anglo-Fr. *questiun*): both from L. *quæstio*, action-noun from *quærere*, 'to ask or inquire'.

quick. 1. The phrase *the quick and the dead*, 'the living and the dead', occurs not even once in the O.T.; thrice in the N.T. —*Acts*, x, 42; 2 *Timothy*, iv, 1; 1 *Peter*, iv, 5. This sense arose in the 9th Century and became archaic (except in the set phrase, and in dialect) early in the 18th Century. A witticism made, ca. 1934, by Vernon Rendall, is to the effect that, in this age of motor speed, 'There are only two kinds of pedestrians: the quick and the dead'.

2. In 'The word of God is quick, and powerful, and sharper than any two-edged sword' (*Hebrews*, iv, 12), the sense of quick seems to be 'lively' or, rather, 'vigorous'.

The basic sense of *quick* is 'endowed with life; living, alive'; and the word comes from the Common Germanic stock.

quicken. 'Thou fool, that which thou sowest is not quickened, except it die' (1 *Corinthians*, xv, 36); 'And you hath he quickened, who were dead in trespasses and sins' (*Ephesians*, ii, 2).

To invest with spiritual life; to give life and soul to, hence to *animate* in its lit. sense: C. 14–20; but since C. 17, only—or mostly—in Biblical reminiscence: cf. Shakespeare's 'The mistress which I serve quickens what's dead | And makes my labours pleasures' (*The Tempest*, III, i, 6).

The archaic adj. *quick*, 'alive', + the v. ending *-en*.

quit. 'Watch ye, stand fast in the faith, quit you like men, be strong' (1 *Corinthians*, xvi, 13).

To acquit oneself, i.e. to conduct or bear oneself (in some specified manner), to behave: 1386, Chaucer; Shakespeare, 'Now quit you well'; 1868, Browning, 'I . . . quitted me like a courtier'; archaic in C. 20.

Earliest sense is 'to set free, to release': perhaps from Medieval L. *quittare* (cf. Medieval L. *quitare*, *quietare*, 'to make *quietus* or quiet'). (O.E.D.)

R

raca. 'But I say unto you, That whosoever is angry with his brother without a cause shall be in danger of the judgment: and whosoever shall say to his brother, Raca, shall be in danger of the council: but whosoever shall say, Thou fool, shall be in danger of hell fire' (*Matthew*, v, 22),—whence it appears that *raca*, as a term of abuse, is weaker than *fool*.

The Gr. Test. has ῥακά; it merely transliterates the Aramaic word, instead of translating it; Souter notes the variant ῥαχά, and renders it 'empty; foolish'. In the 'International Critical Commentary' series, the Rev. Willoughby Allen, in *The Gospel according to S. Matthew* (1907), mentions that this 'term of contemptuous address' is 'not infrequently used in Jewish writings'; moreover, he points out that Gr. μωρέ (thou fool) may be simply a translation of ῥακά— which, in a rhetorical and stylistic view, is improbable. (It is not, however, for a layman to rush in where even Biblical commentators fear to tread; for this passage is a crux.)

rail on; railer; railing, adj. and n. 'They that passed by railed on him' (*Matthew*, xv, 29); 'One of the malefactors railed on him' (*Luke*, xxiii, 39).—'A fornicator, or covetous, or an idolater, or a railer, or a drunkard, or an extortioner' (1 *Corinthians*, v, 11).—*Railing accusation*: 2 *Peter*, ii, 11, and *Jude*, 9.—*Railing*, n.: 1 *Timothy*, vi, 4, 'He is proud, knowing nothing, but doting about questions and strifes of words, whereof cometh envy, strife, railings, evil surmisings'; 'Not rendering evil for evil, or railing for railing: but contrariwise blessing' (1 *Peter*, iii, 9).

To *rail*, v.i., is 'to utter abusive language'; hence, to *rail on* (now *at* or *against*) is to revile; to insult; from Fr. *railler*, 'to rally, to scoff at'. Whence come the agential *railer*, 'a scoffer', and the adjectival *railing*, 'insulting' or 'abusive' or 'vituperative', and the abstract *railing*, 'an insult' (particular) or 'insult' (generic), 'abuse' or 'abusing'. *Railer* is obsolete; *railing*, adj., is obsolete; *railing*, n., is archaic; and *rail against* (a person) or *at* (a thing) is now only literary.

ravening, n. *Ravening* is usually an adj., as in *Matthew*, vii, 25, 'Beware of false prophets, which come to you in sheep's clothing, but inwardly they are ravening wolves'. But it is a n. in *Luke*, xi, 39, 'Your inward part is full of ravening and wickedness', where *ravening* = 'plunder' (Wright) or 'robbery, robbing' (Souter's translation of the corresponding Gr. ἁρπαγή).

Ravening, n., corresponds to the n. *ravin* (robbery; plunder), but comes from the v. *raven*, 'to despoil or plunder; to devour voraciously', from Old Fr. *raviner*, 'to ravage', from a presumed L. v. *rapinare* (cf. the n. *rapina*), itself from *rapere*, 'to seize'.—The phrase *ravening wolves* = 'wolves that are prowling hungrily in search of prey'.

readiness, in a. 'Having in a readiness to revenge all disobedience, when your obedience is fulfilled' (2 *Corinthians*, x, 6).

Have in a readiness is obsolete for 'to have in a state of preparation; to have ready, have in readiness'. The grammatical object of *having* is 'to revenge all disobedience'; the general sense, therefore, is 'Being ready to revenge all disobedience' or, in the commentary of the Rev. Dr. Alfred Plummer, 'Being quite prepared to avenge all disobedience, whenever *your* obedience shall have been completed' (in the 'International Critical Commentary' series, 1915).

ready to be offered and **ready to die; ready to be revealed.** 'I am now ready to be offered, and the time of my departure is at hand' (2 *Timothy*, iv, 6); 'A certain centurion's servant . . . was sick, and ready to die' (*Luke*, vii, 2). In these two sentences, *ready to* = 'on the point of' (being offered; of dying), where *ready* connotes an objective preparedness (an external compulsion), whereas in 'Kept by the power of God through faith unto salvation ready to be revealed in the last time' (1 *Peter*, i, 5), *ready* is 'prepared'.

The word comes from the common Germanic stock.

reap down, in *James*, v, 4 ('. . . The labourers who have reaped down your fields'), is an obsolete tautology (current only in C. 16–17), with a reference to 'cut *down*'. The earliest recorded example occurs in Arthur Golding's *Cæsar* (1565).

reason, n. and v.; **reasoning.** 'Then the twelve called the multitude of the disciples unto them, and said, It is not reason that we should leave'—give up preaching—'the word of God, and serve tables' (*Acts*, vi, 2), where *it is not reason* is obsolete for 'it is not reasonable', *not* quite 'there is no reason (why)'; cf. *reason would*, 'it were reasonable', in *Acts*, xviii, 14.—'As he [Paul] reasoned of righteousness, temperance, and judgment to come, Felix trembled' (*ibid.*, xxiv, 25), where 'to *reason*' is 'to converse', or rather 'to discourse', a sense current in C. 15–17; cf. *reasoning*, 'talk; discussion', in *Luke*, ix, 46, 'There arose a reasoning among them, which of them should be greatest'.

The n. and v. *reason* come, via Fr., from L. *ratio*, 'reckoning; reasoning power', itself derived from *reri*, 'to think; to reckon'.

receipt. 'As Jesus passed forth from thence, he saw a man, named Matthew, sitting at the receipt of custom' (*Matthew*, ix, 9)—cf. *Mark*, ii, 14, and *Luke*, v, 27, where *sitting at the receipt of custom* recurs. (The phrase has become a cliché.)

In these passages, *receipt* means 'a place for receiving; a receiving-office'; the phrase = 'an office for the receipt of taxes' (see **custom**). This sense arose in C. 15 and fell into disuse in C. 19; but it survives historically in *the Receipt of* (*the King's*) *Exchequer*, the Revenue Office.

Immediately from Old Fr. *receit*(*e*), which comes from L. *recepta* (? *res recepta*, 'thing received'), L. *recipere*, 'to receive'.

recompense, v. 'Recompense to no man evil for evil'. (*Romans*, xii, 17); 'Vengeance belongeth unto me, I will recompense, saith the Lord. And again, The Lord shall judge his people' (*Hebrews*, x, 30).

To requite or repay—to make a return or requital for (something done or received)—whether favourably, neutrally, or unfavourably:

1530, Palsgrave; ca. 1550, Latimer; ca. 1586, the Countess of Pembroke, translating *Psalms*, ciii, 5, 'He doth not . . . recompence | Unto us each offence | With due revenge'; since ca. 1850, somewhat archaic.

Via Fr., from Late L. *recompensare* (Classical L. *compensare*, 'to compensate'). O.E.D.

record. In *bear record*, 'to bear witness, to testify' (*John*, i, 19 and 32; *Romans*, x, 2; 2 *Corinthians*, viii, 3; *Galatians*, iv, 15; *Colossians*, iv, 13; *Revelation*, i, 2; and elsewhere in the N.T.), the n. has a well-known sense; but in *Philippians*, i, 8, 'God is my record, how greatly I long after you all', and 2 *Corinthians*, i, 23, 'I call God for a record upon my soul, that to spare you I came not as yet unto Corinth', *record* is personal, 'a person that bears witness, one who testifies', the Gr. word being μάρτυς (whether 'an eye-witness' or 'an ear-witness', Souter).

The n. *record* is the substantivization of the English v. *record*, which comes from the Old Fr. *recorder* (used in most of the senses of the English v.), which comes from Low L. *recordare* (Classical L. *recordari*), i.e., the prefix *re* ('back' or 'again') + *cor*, 'heart' + the v.-ending, *are* (or *ari*).

reduce. 'We ought . . . to reduce a straying brother to the truth' (*James*, v, heading).

In the lit. sense, 'to lead back' (L. *reducere*); common in C. 16–17, this sense arose ca. 1390 and became obsolete ca. 1750.

refresh; times of refreshing. 'They [Stephanas, Fortunatus, Achaicus] have refreshed my spirit and yours' (2 *Corinthians*, xvi, 18), i.e., 'made fresh again', i.e., 'revived'.— 'Repent ye therefore, and be converted, that your sins may be blotted out, when the times of refreshing shall come from the presence of the Lord' (*Acts*, iii, 19), where *refreshing* = 'a cool-ing comfort', in opposition to, and as a release from, afflictions ('called a fiery trial', Cruden).

Refreshing is the verbal n. formed from 'to *refresh*', which comes from the Old Fr. *refresch(i)er* (cf. Medieval L. *refrescare*), formed from Old Fr. *freis* (fem. *fresche*), 'fresh', itself probably a derivative from Romance *fresco*, itself an adoption of a common-stock Germanic adjective (e.g., Old High Ger. *frisc*), as the O.E.D. tends to show.

reject. 'For his oath's sake, and for their sakes which sat with him [i.e., for the sake of those who sat . . .], he [Herodias] would not reject her [Salome]' (*Mark*, vi, 26).

'We now commonly speak of refusing a request and reject-ing a person', says Wright in 1884: but C. 20 usage admits 'to *refuse*' a person (the sense, in this passage, of *reject*) or a gift, an offer, and 'to *reject*' a request or supplication, an offer or some-thing offered, and also to repel, rebuff, refuse to listen to a person.

Lit., 'to throw (or cast) back': L. *re(j)icere*, supine *rejectum*.

rejoice of is a C. 15–17 form of *rejoice at* or *in* or *over*; prob-ably on the analogy of Fr. *se réjouir de*. 'He rejoiceth more of that sheep (lost but then found) than of the ninety and nine which went not astray' (*Matthew*, xviii, 13).

religion; religious. *Religion* occurs at *Acts*, xxvi, 5; *Galatians*, i, 13 and 14; *James*, i, 26 and 27 (Cruden's interpreta-tion of verse 27 is erroneous).—*Religious*, at *Acts*, xiii, 43, and *James*, i, 26.

Before passing to the N.T. use of these two words, we should remember their etymology. *Religious* comes either directly or indirectly (via Anglo-Fr. *religius* from Old Fr. *religeus* or *-ious*) from L. *religiosus*, 'concerned with religion'. *Religion* comes either directly or indirectly (via Anglo-Fr. *religiun*) from L. *religio* (genitive *religionis*), which is, approxi-mately, religion. *Religio* is, according to Cicero, from *relegere*, 'to read over again'; but, according to prevalent C. 20 opinion, from *religare*, 'to bind (again)': a binding to God.

In the Vulgate, the n. is *religio*, the adj. is *religiosus*: which fact does not help us much. In the Gr. Test., the relevant passages for the n. are:—'After the most straitest sect of our religion' (*Acts*, xxvi, 5): κατὰ τὴν ἀκριβεστάτην αἵρεσιν τῆς ἡμετέρας θρησκείας, 'according to the most precise sect of our religion' ('*worship* as expressed in ritual acts', Souter).—'In the Jews' religion' (*Galatians*, i, 13, and again in 14): ἐν τῷ Ἰουδαϊσμῷ, 'in Judaism'.—

'If any man among you seem to be religious, and bridleth not his tongue, but deceiveth his own heart, this man's religion is vain. Pure religion and undefiled before God and the Father is this, To visit the fatherless and widows, and to keep himself unspotted from the world' (*James*, i, 26–27): εἴ τις δοκεῖ θρῆσκος εἶναι, μὴ χαλιναγωγῶν γλῶσσαν αὐτοῦ ἀλλ᾽ ἀπατῶν καρδίαν αὐτοῦ, τούτου μάταιος ἡ θρησκεία. θρησκεία καθαρὰ καὶ ἀμίαντος παρὰ τῷ Θεῷ καὶ πατρὶ αὕτη ἐστίν, ἐπισκέπτεσθαι ὀρφανοὺς καὶ χήρας ἐν τῇ θλίψει αὐτῶν, ἄσπιλον ἑαυτὸν τηρεῖν ἀπὸ τοῦ κόσμου.

For the adj., both the preceding passage and *Acts*, xiii, 43, 'Many of the Jews and religious proselytes followed Paul and Barnabas': πολλοὶ τῶν Ἰουδαίων καὶ τῶν σεβομένων προσηλύτων τῷ Παύλῳ καὶ τῷ βαρνάβᾳ.

The two Gr. adjj., therefore, for the one English (*religious*) are θρῆσκος, 'carefully observant of religious rules, and restrictions', 'professing religion in the outward form' (Wright), and σεβόμενος, 'reverent'. But for *religion*, in these passages, only θρησκεία is the original, the translated term. Θρησκεία (= 'cultus', or perhaps more strictly, 'cultus *exterior*') is predominantly the ceremonial service of religion, . . . "mother of form and fear",—the external framework or body, of which εὐσέβεια [piety towards God; godliness] is the informing soul. . . . [In *James*, i, 26–7] the apostle claims for the new dispensation a superiority over the old, in that its very θρησκεία consists in acts of mercy, of love, of holiness . . . ; herein how much nobler than that old, whose θφησκεία was at best merely ceremonial and formal, whatever inner truth they might embody' (R. C. Trench, *Synonyms of the New Testament*, 7th ed., 1871; glossing Coleridge's *Aids to Reflection*, 1825, p. 15).

Whence it appears that in the passages quoted above, *religious* is the adj. of *religion* in its sense, 'ceremonial observance', 'ritual', 'the exercise of rites': a sense virtually obsolete since C. 18.

remembrance, put in. 'Wherefore I will not be negligent to put you always in remembrance of these things, though ye know them' (2 *Peter*, i, 12).

I.e., to remind you of these things. *To put* (a person) *in remembrance of* (something) was current in C. 15–17; contrast *put* (something) *in remembrance*, which, current only in C. 15–16, = to put it on record.

report. 'Men of honest report' (*Acts*, vi, 3); 'Cornelius the centurion, a just man, and one that feareth God, and of good report among all the nation of the Jews' (*ibid.*, x, 22); 'By it' —by faith—'the elders obtained a good report' (*Hebrews*, xi, 2); the famous 'Whatsoever things are true, . . . whatsoever things are lovely, whatsoever things are of good report' (*Philippians*, iv, 8); and elsewhere.

I.e., 'reputation', a sense that, elsewhere archaic, is extant in literary English. *Report* in this sense arose early in C. 16; as 'rumour', in C. 14. It comes from Old Fr. *raport* (Modern Fr. *rapport*), ultimately from L. *reportare*, 'to carry back (news)'.

reprobate in *Titus*, i, 16. See **profess,** second quotation, and cf. *Jeremiah*, vi, 30, 'Reprobate silver shall men call them' (*Argentum reprobum vocate eos, quia Dominus projecit illos*: Vulgate), silver that is adulterated and unable to stand the test (see Cruden).

requite. See at **nephew.**

resemble. 'Unto what is the kingdom of God like? and whereunto [= to what] shall I resemble it?' (*Luke*, xiii, 18).

To liken, to compare: mid C. 14–19; now so archaic as to be virtually obsolete. 'It was a great injustice in Plato . . . to esteem of rhetoric but as a voluptuary art, resembling it to cookery' (*Advancement of Learning*, II, xviii, 3); 'Yea, he allowed no other library than a full stored cellar, resembling the butts to folios, barrels to quartos, smaller runlets to less [= smaller] volumes', Fuller, *The Profane State* (both passages adduced by Wright).

From Old Fr. *resembler* (Modern Fr. *ressembler*), from *similare*, from *similis*, 'like, similar'.

resolve. 'Christ . . . resolveth a rich man how he may inherit life everlasting' (*Mark*, x, heading); '[Christ] resolveth the scribe, who questioned of the first commandment' (*ibid.*, xii, heading).

To solve the difficulties of (a person): a mid C. 16–mid 18 usage, as in

> 'I doubt not but you can resolve
> Me of a question that I shall demand'
>   Greene, *Alphonsus*;

> 'My lord the emperor, resolve me this:
> Was it well done of rash Virginius
> To slay his daughter with his own right hand?'
>   Shakespeare, *Titus Andronicus*, v, iii.

From L. *solvere*, 'to loosen'.

revelation and **Revelation** (not, by the way, *Revelations*). 'The day of wrath and revelation of the righteous judgment of God' (*Romans*, ii, 5); 'The revelation of the mystery' (*ibid.*, xvi, 25); 'What shall I profit you, except [= unless] I shall speak to you either by revelation, or by knowledge, or by prophesying, or by doctrine?' (1 *Corinthians*, xiv, 6; cf. 26); 'I will come to visions and revelations of the Lord' (2 *Corinthians*, xii, 1); 'Exalted above measure through the abundance of the revelations' (*ibid.*, verse 7); also *Galatians*, i, 12, and ii, 2; *Ephesians*, i, 17, and iii, 3; 1 *Peter*, i, 13; and *Revelation*, i, 1.

I have heard the short title of *The Revelation of St John the Divine* given, even by those who should know better, as *Revelations*. The Gr. Test. has, as the title Ἀποκάλυψις Ἰωάννου τοῦ Θεολόγου;* the Vulgate, in the Clementine version of 1915 (a lovely piece of printing), has *Apocalypsis Beati Joannis Apostoli*; Verdunoy's *Bible Latine-Française* (vol. III, 1935) has simply *Apocalypse*.

Whereas *apocalypse* is, lit., 'an uncovering', *revelation* is 'a drawing-*back* of the *veil*' (L. *revelatio*: from *velum*, 'a veil').

revive. 'To this end Christ both died, and rose, and revived, that he might be Lord both of the dead and living' (*Romans*, xiv, 9).

Here, *revive* is intransitive and used in its lit. sense, 'to come to life again'. In *Romans*, vii, 9, 'For I was alive without the law once: but when the commandment came, sin revived, and I died', it is also intransitive but the sense is rather 'sin arose again, or prevailed again'.

From Fr. *revivre*, itself from post-Classical L. *revivere*, 'to live again'.

reward. 'Alexander the coppersmith did me much evil: the Lord reward him according to his works' (2 *Timothy*, iv, 14): cf. *Revelation*, xviii, 6.

I.e., 'recompense' or 'requite' him: as Wright says, 'without reference to good or evil'. The corresponding Gr. in the *Timothy* passage is ἀποδώσει αὐτῷ ὁ Κύριος κατὰ τὰ ἔργα αὐτοῦ, where ἀποδίδωμι (also in *Revelation*, xviii, 6) is 'I render (as due'); the Vulgate has *reddet illi Dominus secundum opera ejus*, which Verdunoy (*Bible Latine-Française*, vol. III, 1935) translates as 'le Seigneur lui rendra selon ses œuvres'.

*The general relevant sense of θεολόγος is 'one versed in sacred knowledge'; in the Biblical title, however, it may bear the meaning, 'publisher and interpreter of divine oracles', according to Thayer's translation and recension (1886) of Grimm's edition of Wilke's *Clavis Novi Testamenti*.

Reward, in this sense, was common in C. 16–17. It comes from Old Norman Fr. *rewarder*, which corresponds to Fr. *regarder*, English *regard* (in sense, 'to take notice of'), as the O.E.D. shows.

riches. 'Your riches are corrupted, and your garments are motheaten' (*James*, v, 2); here *riches* = 'valuable possessions'. —'In one hour so great riches is come to nought' (*Revelation*, xviii, 17); here *riches* is still, as it was originally, a singular n., this construction being current in C. 14–17.

Riches, whose transition from singular to plural was aided by L. *divitiæ* (occurring in the Vulgate version of *James*, v, 2, and *Revelation*, xviii, 17, and of other passages), derives from the much older, since C. 17 obsolete, *richesse*. Now, *richesse* comes from Old Fr. *richeise*, formed on *riche*, an adoption from common Germanic stock (O.E.D.).

riot, n. and v.; **rioting; riotous.** 'They that count it pleasure to riot in the day time' (2 *Peter*, ii, 13)—Vulgate, *voluptatem existimantes diei delicias*—Gr. Test., ἡδονὴν ἡγούμενοι τὴν ἐν ἡμέρᾳ τρυφήν.—The n. occurs in *Titus*, i, 6, 'If any be blameless . . . not accused of riot (Vulgate, *non in accusatione luxuriæ*; Gr. Test., μὴ ἐν κατηγορίᾳ ἀσωτίας) and in 1 *Peter*, iv, 4, 'Wherein they think it strange that ye run not with them to the same excess of riot' (*in eamdem luxuriæ confusionem*, Vulgate; εἰς τὴν αὐτὴν τῆς ἀσωτίας ἀνάχυσιν, Gr. Test.).—The verbal n.: *Romans*, xiii, 13.—The adj., *Luke*, xv, 13.

The v. and the adj. derive direct from the n. The English n. *riot*, which means 'debauchery, wanton living', comes from Old Fr. *riote* (or *riotte*), 'debate; quarrel'; the Fr. word is of doubtful origin, but it may be cognate with L. *rixa*, 'contest; strife'.

Romans. The sixth book of the N.T. is *The Epistle of Paul the Apostle to the Romans*: Παύλου τοῦ ᾿Αποστόλου ἡ πρὸς ῾Ρωμαίους ἐπιστολή.

'The plural . . . suggests either the imperial people (e.g., *John*, xi, 48) or citizens of the Roman Empire (e.g., *Acts*, xvi, 21)', Souter.

Roman (in English, a n. long before it was an adj.) comes direct from L. *Romanus*, 'an inhabitant—a native—of (ancient) Rome; hence, any person belonging to either the Roman republican state or the Roman Empire': cf. It. and Sp. *Romano*. *Romanus* derives, obviously, from *Roma*, 'Rome', which may be from Gr. ῥώμη 'strength': city of strength; strong city.

room. 'Archelaus did reign in Judæa in the room of his father Herod' (*Matthew*, ii, 22).

I.e., 'in the stead (or place) of'; the phrase, *in the room of* (or *in one's room*) was current in late C. 15–mid 19, then archaic.

The word *room* belongs to the common Germanic stock; and it did not acquire its present prevailing sense (part of a house, flat, etc.) until C. 15; originally it meant 'space, dimensional extent', then 'sufficient space' (i.e., accommodation).

rudiments. 'Beware lest any man spoil you through philosophy and vain deceit, after the tradition of men, after the rudiments of the world, and not after Christ' (*Colossians*, ii, 8). Here, apparently, the meaning is 'imperfect beginnings': L. *rudimentum*, 'beginning, first principle'.

In *Galatians*, iv, 3, 'We, when we were children, were in bondage under the elements of the world', *elements of the world* renders Gr. τὰ στοιχεῖα τοῦ κόσμου, which is the phrase also in *Colossians*, ii, 8: *elements* and *rudiments*, therefore, may = 'rudimentary principles, or elementary rules'; but in *Galatians*, iv, 3, the sense may rather be 'spirits, demons' as Souter thinks.

ruler of the feast. See at **governor**, paragraph 4.

S

saint; saints.

In the N.T., *saint* has three meanings.

1. A holy or godly person: see at **Colosse**; also *Hebrews*, vi, 10, 'Your work and labour of love, which ye have shewed towards his name, in that ye have ministered to the saints'— τοῖς ἀγίοις—*sanctis* ('aux saints', Verdunoy). But the term in this sense is often rhetorical or conventional for 'a Christian', as in 1 *Corinthians*, i, 2.

2. One of 'those blessed spirits which are graciously admitted by God to partake of everlasting glory and blessedness' (Cruden), as in *Revelation*, xviii, 24, 'And in her [Babylon] was found the blood of prophets, and of saints, and of all that were slain upon the earth' (ἀγίων: *sanctorum*).

3. An angel, or rather 'a holy angel' (one not seduced by Satan), as in *Jude*, 14, 'Behold, the Lord cometh with ten thousands of his saints': 'Ιδού, ἦλθε Κύριος ἐν ἁγίαις μυριάσιν αὐτοῦ, 'Lo! the Lord has come [armed] with his sacred myriads': *Ecce venit Dominus in sanctis millibus suis*, 'Voici que le Seigneur est venu, avec ses saintes myriades', Verdunoy.

Cf. Milton's 'Gabriel, lead forth my armied saints' (*Paradise Lost, VI*, 46).

Saint comes, via Old Fr. *saint* or *seint*, from L. *sanctus* ('holy'), originally the passive participle of *sancire*, 'to enact or ratify; hence, to consecrate'.

Samaritan and **good Samaritan.** The latter, which has become a cliché, does not occur in the text of the N.T.; not even in the parable of the priest, the Levite, and the Samaritan (*Luke*, x, 30–5). The former occurs in ten places, e.g., *John*, iv, 9, 'The Jews have no dealings with the Samaritans'.

From L. *Samaritanus*, an inhabitant of *Samaria* (Heb. *Shomeron*, 'his lees, his prison, his guard, his throne, or his diamond', Cruden).

sapphire. See the quotation at **chrysolite.**

'A precious stone of a beautiful transparent blue' (O.E.D.).

Via Old Fr. *safir* (Modern Fr. *saphir*) from L. *sapphirus*, which represents Gr. σάπφειρος, cognate with Heb. *sappir*.

sardius; sardonyx. See quotation at **chrysolite.**

The *sardius* (Anglicized as *sard*), Gr. σάρδιον (from Σάρδεις, Sardis, an ancient Lydian city in the Roman province Asia), is a quartz 'varying in colour from pale golden yellow to reddish orange' (O.E.D.).—The *sardonyx*, in L. the same, from Gr. σαρδόνυξ (apparently σάρδιον + ὄνυξ, 'onyx'), is 'a variety of onyx or stratified chalcedony having white layers alternating with one or more strata of sard' (O.E.D.).

Satan. The name occurs more than thirty times in the N.T., e.g. in 'Get thee behind me, Satan' (*Matthew*, xvi, 23); ὕπαγε ὀπίσω μου, Σατανά; *vade post me, Satana* (*vade retro me* in *Mark*, viii, 33).

English *Satan* is L. *Satan* (in the O.T. only, the N.T. having *Satanas* or *Diabolus*), which transliterates Gr. Σατάν or Σατᾶν (although Σατανᾶς is the usual form); the shorter Gr. word is the nearer to the Aramaic *satan*, 'an adversary, an enemy'. The L. *Diabolus* transliterates the frequent Gr. synonym Διάβολος, 'the Slanderer' (διαβάλλειν, 'to slander'): διάβολος is the origin, or at lowest, a cognate of our *devil*; Fr. *diable* comes straight from *diabolus*.

savour, n. and v. 'If the salt have lost his savour, wherewith shall it be salted?' (*Matthew*, v, 13).—'But he [Christ] turned, and said unto Peter, Get thee behind me, Satan: thou art an offence unto me: for thou savourest not the things that be of God, but those that be of men' (*ibid.*, xvi, 23; so too in *Mark*, viii, 33).

The Gr. original of 'have lost his savour' is μωρανθῇ, 'become tainted, hence useless', and the Vulgate has *evanuerit* ('s'affadit', Verdunoy); 'thou savourest not the things that be of God' renders οὐ φρονεῖς τὰ τοῦ Θεοῦ, 'thou settest not thy mind (or heart) on the things of God' (Divine matters), and corresponds very closely to the Vulgate *non sapis ea quæ Dei sunt*.

Savour here = its essential property or character (i.e., its bitterness), its taste; ultimately from L. *sapor*, 'taste'. The v. goes, via Old Fr. *savo(u)rer*, back to L. *sapere*, 'to taste'—or rather to Late L. *saporare*.

say true. See **true, say.**

scarce adv. 'With these sayings scarce restrained they the people' (*Acts*, xiv, 18); 'When we had sailed slowly many days, and scarce were come over against Cnidus, the wind not suffering'—allowing—'us, we sailed under Crete' (*ibid.*, xxvii, 7).

Now an archaism, *scarce*, 'scarcely', arose early in C. 15, the earliest sense of adverbial *scarce* being 'scantily or sparsely' (late C. 13).

scourge, in its lit. sense 'a whip, a lash', occurs in *John*, ii, 15; in this sense, it is extant only in reference to ascetic discipline. Now used of a thing or person instrumental in divine chastisement (Attila, the C. 5 leader of the Huns, was called 'the Scourge of God', L. *flagellum Dei*), hence of 'a cause of (usually, widespread) calamity' (O.E.D.).

From Old Fr. *escorge* (or *escurge*), which is ultimately related to Late L. *excoriare*, 'to strip off the hide' (hence, 'to flay').

scribe. 'He taught them as one having authority, and not as the scribes' (*Matthew*, vii, 29); cf. *Luke*, v, 30, 'Their scribes and Pharisees murmured against his disciples', and *Acts*, iv, 5, and 1 *Corinthians*, i, 20, 'Where is the wise? where is the scribe? where is the disputer of this world?'

'A member of the class of professional interpreters of the Law after the return from the Captivity; in the Gospels often coupled with the Pharisees as upholders of ceremonial tradition' (O.E.D.). The Gr. word is γραμματεύς; the Vulgate, *scriba*, lit., 'a writer, an amanuensis' (*scribere*, to write).

scrip. 'Provide neither gold, nor silver, nor brass in your purses, | Nor scrip for your journey' (*Matthew*, x, 9–10; cf. *Mark*, vi, 8; *Luke*, ix, 3, and x, 4); 'He that hath a purse, let him take it, and likewise his scrip' (*Luke*, xxii, 36).

In the two quoted passages, the Gr. term is πήρα, 'a food-bag, a wallet' or, as Souter suggests, 'perhaps especially *a collecting bag* (such as beggar-priests of pagan cults carried)'.

Probably from Old Fr. *escrep*(*p*)*e*, 'a wallet; a purse; a bag for alms' (O.E.D.). The word is now archaic.

sear. 'Speaking lies in hypocrisy; having their conscience seared with a hot iron' (1 *Timothy*, iv, 2) : κεκαυτηριασμένων τὴν ἰδίαν συνείδησιν, 'having been cauterized'—hence, 'seared'—'as to the private consciousness': *cauteriatam habentium suam conscientiam*, 'qui ont une conscience brûlée au fer rouge', Verdunoy, who pertinently glosses thus, 'Ils portent dès ici-bas dans leur conscience une marque infamante, comme les esclaves fugitifs et les criminels portaient sur leur front une lettre gravée au fer rouge'. The O.E.D.'s definition of this sense of *sear* as 'to render (the conscience) incapable of feeling' is valid for those passages in English literature which are reminiscent of the Biblical passage, but it is not quite correct for the original passage itself: the Gr., the lit. rendering of the Gr., and Verdunoy give, or imply, a much more precise nuance.

Sear, 'to wither; to cause to wither', is of West Germanic stock.

season, in the N.T. (as also in the O.T.), means 'any period of time', including—but not restricted to—the four seasons of the year; cf. Shakespeare's 'Sorrow breaks seasons and repos-ing hours, | Makes the night morning, and the moontide night' (*Richard III*, I, iv, 76–7).

Immediately from Old Fr. *se*(*i*)*son*; ultimately from L. *satio*, 'an act of sowing', or rather from Low L. *satio*, 'a time of sowing', i.e. 'seed-time'.

secondarily, where we should say *secondly*: see the quotation at **helps.**

Latimer in his *Sermons* has this:—'When we consider that, first, who he is that commandeth it unto us; secondarily, what he hath done for us that biddeth us to obey, no doubt we shall be well content withal' (cited by Wright).

This sense, which has long passed out of use, would now be condemned as a misuse.

secure, v. 'If this come to the governor's ears, we will persuade him, and secure you' (*Matthew*, xxviii, 14): καὶ ἐὰν ἀκουσθῇ τοῦτο ἐπὶ τοῦ ἡγεμόνος, ἡμεῖς πείσομεν αὐτόν, καὶ ὑμᾶς ἀμερίμνους ποιήσομεν, '. . . and we shall make you free from care': *et securos vos faciemus*, 'et nous vous mettrons à couvert' (Verdunoy).

This sense, 'to free from care', seems to have been current only in C. 17; it occurs at least once in Shakespeare: 'Our means secure us, and our mere defects | Prove our commodities' (*Lear*, IV, i, 22).

Immediately from the adj. The adj. comes from L. *securus*, 'without care or anxiety', being the privative *se + cura*, 'solicitude, care, anxiety'.

selfsame. 'Jesus said unto the centurion, Go thy way; and as thou hast believed, so be it done unto thee. And his servant was healed in the selfsame hour' (*Matthew*, viii, 13); 'All these worketh that one and the selfsame spirit, dividing to every man severally as he will' (1 *Corinthians*, xii, 11), where *spirit* is the subject of the sentence, *all these* being the object after *worketh* (Vulgate, 'Hæc autem omnia operatur unus atque idem Spiritus, dividens singulis prout vult').

Cf. 'The selfsame heaven | That frowns on me looks sadly upon him' (Shakespeare, *Richard III*, v, iii, 286–7).

Selfsame, 'very same', is an intensified form of *same*; it arose late in C. 14; since ca. 1840 it has been literary; in C. 20, it is regarded as either archaic or affected.

Originally *self same* (L. *ipse idem*).

sentence. In *Luke*, xxiii, 24 ('Pilate gave sentence'), and 2 *Corinthians*, i, 9 ('we had the sentence of death in ourselves'), the sense is 'legal judgement' (e.g., *sentence of death*), the Gr. being Πιλάτος ἐπέκρινε, 'Pilate gave his decision', and αὐτοὶ ἐν ἑαυτοῖς τὸ ἀπόκριμα [answer] τοῦ θανάτου ἐσχήκαμεν, and the Vulgate having *Pilatus judicavit* ('Pilate ordonna', Verdunoy) and *ipsi in nobismetipsis responsum mortis habuimus* ('nous avions en nous-mêmes l'arrêt de notre mort', id.). But in *Acts*, xv, 19, 'My sentence is, that we trouble not them, which from among the Gentiles are turned to God', the meaning is '(one's) deliberate opinion, (non-legal) judgement', the Gr. Test. having διὸ ἐγὼ κρίνω, 'wherefore I decide—think it good—that . . .', and the Vulgate having *propter quod ego judico*, 'c'est pourquoi je suis d'avis que . . .' (Verdunoy).

Via Old Fr. from L. *sententia*, 'an opinion' (*sentire*, 'to feel', hence 'to be of opinion').

seraph, seraphim, seraphims; cherub, cherubim, cherubims.

The N.T. has only the latter, and even that only in the form *cherubims*, which is to be seen in the quotation at **shadow**. But as they generally go together, we can hardly ignore the seraphs.

The correct singular is *cherub*, *seraph*; the correct learned plural is *cherubim*, *seraphim*, the *-ims* form being a double plural; the unlearned, or rather the native, plural is *cherubs*, *seraphs*; the forms *cherubin(s)* and *seraphin(s)* have long been obsolete. For the exact relations and interrelations of these various forms, see esp. the O.E.D. More interesting are the etymology and semantics of the two words.

1. *Seraph*, which apparently occurs first in Milton, is a back-formation from the plural *seraphim* or *seraphin*; *seraphim*, the living six-winged creatures hovering above the throne of God (*Isaiah*, vi), is adopted *literatim* from the Vulgate; Gr. σεραφίμ (a transliteration of a Heb. word that may come from Heb. *saraph*, 'to burn').

2. *Cherub* is the Vulgate *Cherub*, the Gr. χερούβ, Heb.
k'rub (further etymology, dubious), the L., Gr. and Heb.
plurals being *Cherubim* (or *-in*), χερουβίμ (or *-ιν*), *k'rubim*.
The Cherubim guarded the ark of the covenant.

In the hierarchy of angels posited by the Pseudo-Dionysius,
the seraphim constituted the first, the cherubim the second
order: the former excel in love, the latter in knowledge: their
roles in Christian art.

serve unto. '(Priests) who serve unto the example and
shadow of heavenly things, as Moses was admonished of God
when he was about to make the tabernacle' (*Hebrews*, viii, 5).

Serve to, for *serve*, was not uncommon in C. 16–17 ('Serve
by indenture to the common hangman', Shakespeare,
Pericles, iv, vi, 187); cf. Fr. *servir à*, which, like the English
serve to, imitates L. *servire* + dative, the Vulgate having 'qui
exemplari et umbræ deserviunt cælestium' and the Gr. Test.
likewise a datival construction, οἵτινες ὑποδείγματι καὶ σκιᾷ
λατρεύουσι τῶν ἐπουρανίων.

set. 1. 'Upon a set day Herod . . . sat upon his throne, and
made an oration unto them' (*Acts*, xii, 21): where *set* is 'fixed'
or 'appointed'.

2. 'Seeing the multitudes, he went up into a mountain: and
when he was set, his disciples came unto him', (*Matthew*, v, 1;
cf. *ibid*., xxvii, 19, 'When he was set down on the judgment
seat'): where *set* is 'seated'. *Set*, 'to sit', is now dialectal and
illiterate.

The v. *set* is of common Germanic stock.

set to. 'He that hath received his testimony hath set to his
seal that God is true' (*John*, iii, 33).

'To affix as a seal. . . . Hence "to *set to* his seal" is "to
attest", as a document is attested by affixing a seal. The
expression is retained from Coverdale's version' (Wright).
The Vulgate has 'Qui accepit ejus testimonium signavit quia
Deus verax est', which Verdunoy translates, 'Celui qui a reçu

son attestation a certifié qui Dieu est vrai.'—This sense of *set to* was current in C. 14–mid. 19.

setter forth. 'He seemeth to be a setter forth of strange gods: because he preached unto them Jesus, and the resurrection' (*Acts*, xvii, 18).

A *setter forth* is 'one who publishes, promulgates, or propounds'—a sense that, arising ca. 1550, is slightly archaic.

This passage runs thus in the Gr. Test.: ξένων δαιμονίων δοκεῖ καταγγελεὺς εἶναι (where the operative word is rendered by Souter as 'a reporter, announcer, proclaimer, herald, setter forth'). In the Vulgate: 'novorum dæmoniorum videtur annuntiator esse', rendered by Verdunoy as '« il semble qu'il annonce des divinités étrangères »', parce qu'il annonçait Jésus et la Résurrection',—which affords a useful gloss on *strange* ('foreign').

several; severally. 'Unto one he gave five talents, to another two, and to another one; to every man according to his several ability' (*Matthew*, xxv, 15); 'The twelve gates were twelve pearls; every several gate was of one pearl' (*Revelation*, xxi, 21).—For *severally*, see the second passage quoted at **selfsame.**

In *his several ability*, *several* = 'particular, distinctive; hence, personal'; *every several gate* = 'each separate gate', tautological for 'each gate'. *Dividing to every man severally* = 'apportioning to every man individually'.

In brief, *several(ly)* in these passages = *separate(ly)* or *individual(ly)* as opposed to *collective(ly)*. This sense of *several* is obsolescent. The word comes immediately from Anglo-Fr.; the Anglo-Fr. from Medieval L. *separalis*, itself from Classical L. *separ,* 'separate, distinct' (O.E.D.).

shadow, v. 'And over it the cherubims of glory shadowing the mercyseat' (*Hebrews*, ix, 5): ὑπεράνω δὲ αὐτῆς Χερουβὶμ δόξης κατασκιάζοντα τὸ ἱλαστήριον, 'and far above it, Cherubim of glory'—i.e., glorious Cherubim (a Hebraistic genitive)—'overshadowing the covering of the ark': *superque* *eam erant cherubim gloriæ, obumbrantia propitiatorium*, 'audessus de l'arche, les chérubins de la gloire couvrant de leurs ailes le propitiatoire' (Verdunoy).

Shadow, 'to cast a shadow upon, to cover with a shadow', was introduced by Wyclif in 1382; the earliest sense is 'to shelter—hence, to protect—as with enfolding wings', which often occurs in *The Bible*.

Perhaps immediately from the n. The word is of the common West Germanic stock.

shambles. 'Whatsoever is sold in the shambles, that eat, asking no question for conscience sake' (1 *Corinthians*, x, 25): πᾶν τὸ ἐν μακέλλῳ πωλούμενον ἐσθίετε, 'eat everything put up for sale in the meat-market': *omne quod in macello venit manducate*, 'tout ce qui se vend à la boucherie, mangez-en' (Verdunoy).

Shambles, 'a butcher's stall': C. 15–18, then archaic except dialectally. From *shamble*, 'a table or stall for the sale of meat' (C. 14–16), a sense derivative from *shamble*, 'a table, a counter, for exposing goods for sale' (mid C. 10–13). The word is 'a common West Germanic adoption of L. *scamellum*, dimunutive of *scammum*, bench' (O.E.D.).

shamefastness. 'In like manner also, that women adorn themselves in modest apparel, with shamefastnesse' (edition of 1611; in modern editions, 'shamefacedness') 'and sobriety; not with broided hair, or gold, or pearls, or costly array' (1 *Timothy*, ii, 9).

'Modesty', esp. such modesty as is visible—nay, obvious—to every eye.

Shamefacedness is formed on *shamefaced*, which is folk etymology for *shamefast*; *shamefastness* arose ca. 1200, but has been archaic since C. 18; *shamefacedness* did not arise until ca. 1550.

shew, n. and v. '(Scribes) which devour widows' houses, and for a shew make long prayers' (*Luke*, xx, 47); 'As many as desire to make a fair shew in the flesh . . .' (*Galatians*, vi, 12); 'Which things have indeed a shew of wisdom' (*Colos-*

sians, ii, 23): here, *shew* = 'appearance', *for a shew* being 'ostentatiously'. In *Colossians*, ii, 15, 'And having spoiled'— despoiled—'principalities and powers, he made a shew of them openly, triumphing over them in it', *shew* = 'display' or 'public show'.—The v. has, in 1 *Corinthians*, xi, 26, 'For as often as ye eat this bread, and drink this cup, ye do shew the Lord's death till he come' (the institution of the Eucharist), the sense 'to represent, to figure forth, to symbolize'.

Except in *shew-bread*, the spelling *shew* is archaic.

ship, go to; shipmaster; shipmen; shipping, take; shipwrack.

Respectively 'to take ship, go on board ship' (*Acts*, xx, 13); 'a ship's captain' (*Revelation*, xviii, 17); 'sailors' (*Acts*, xxvii, 30); 'to go on board ship, to embark' (*John*, vi, 24), therefore synonymous with *go to ship*; 'shipwreck' (2 *Corinthians*, xi, 25, and 1 *Timothy*, i, 19)—only in the early editions, the actual spelling being *shipwracke*.

Go to ship belongs to C. 16–17; *take shipping* to C. 15–mid. 19.

Shipmaster has been current since C. 14, but in the simple sense, 'ship's captain', it has been archaic since ca. 1850, since when the prevailing sense has been 'a man that owns the ship he commands'. *Shipman* has been in use for rather more than a thousand years, but in C. 19–20 it has been superseded and rendered archaic by *sailor*.

shut up.
'He exhorteth them . . ., commendeth Timothy, and after friendly admonitions, shutteth up his epistle with divers salutations' (Paul's *First Epistle to the Corinthians*, heading of Chapter xvi).

I.e., concludes, winds up.

This sense of *shut up* belongs to the two hundred years beginning ca. 1550.

sick,
'ill', occurs some thirty times in the N.T. In England, it is, except in dialect, confined virtually to nausea, but in the generic sense 'ill', it is still current in the U.S.A. In *Matthew*, ix, 12, 'Jesus . . . said unto them, They that be whole need

not a physician, but they that are sick' (Gr. Test., οἱ κακῶς
ἔχοντες; Vulgate, 'male habentibus'), the word is used of
such persons 'as are sensible of the burden of their sins, and
earnestly desire to be delivered from them by Christ the
great physician' (Cruden).

sight. 'And he that sat was to look upon like a jasper and a
sardine stone: and there was a rainbow round about the
throne, in sight like unto an emerald' (*Revelation*, iv, 3):
Gr. Test., καὶ ἶρις κυκλόθεν τοῦ θρόνου ὅμοιος ὁράσει
σμαραγδίνῳ: Vulgate, 'iris erat in circuitu sedis, similis
visioni smaragdinæ': Verdunoy, 'et autour du Trône un arc-
en-ciel qui avait l'aspect de l'émeraude'. The A.V. 'to look
upon like' and 'in sight like unto' both render the Gr. ὅμοιος
ὁράσει, lit., 'in appearance, like . . .'; *in sight*, therefore, =
'in appearance; or, in aspect'. In this sense, *sight* hardly sur-
vived the 17th Century; it originated, ca. 1200.

silence, keep. See **keep silence.**

silly and **simple.** 'Of this sort'—'lovers of pleasures more
than lovers of God'—'are they which creep into houses, and
lead captive silly women laden with sins, led away with divers
lusts' (2 *Timothy*, iii, 6), where *lead captive* corresponds to the
Gr. αἰχμαλωτίζοντες, 'subduing' or 'ensnaring', and where
'silly women' corresponds to γυναικάρια, 'poor weak
women' (Souter), and the Vulgate's *mulierculas* (rendered
'femmelettes' by Verdunoy). *Silly*, here, is 'simple, guileless';
and 'guileless' (or 'artless') is the sense of *simple* in *Romans*, xvi,
19, 'I would have you wise unto that which is good, and
simple concerning evil' (Gr. Test., ἀκεραίους δὲ εἰς τὸ κακὸν;
Vulgate, 'simplices in malo'), where the precise nuance is that
of 'unsophisticated'.

   Silly, as used above, belongs to the period ca. 1540–1680,
though it lingered on to ca. 1800. It is the modern form of
seely, 'simple, foolish' (C. 16–early 17), from the same word
in the sense 'harmless' or 'innocent'; *seely* belongs to the com-

mon West Germanic stock, the adj. being the derivative of a
n. that means either 'luck' or 'happiness' or both.

similitude. 'Them that had not sinned after the similitude
of Adam's transgression' (*Romans*, v, 14); 'After the similitude
of Melchisedec there ariseth another priest' (*Hebrews*, vii, 15);
'Men . . . made after the similitude of God' (*James*, iii, 9).

In the first passage, read 'in the same way as Adam did'; in
the second and third, the sense is 'in the actual or the imagined
likeness of'. The Gr. Test. has, for the respective passages,
ἐπὶ τῷ ὁμοιώτατι, κατὰ τὴν ὁμοιότητα, and καθ᾽ ὁμοίωσιν:
now, ὁμοιότης, ὁμοίωμα, and ὁμοίωσις all = 'likeness',
but ὁμοίωμα has the nuance 'form': 'in fact ὁμοίωμα (concrete) differs from ὁμοιότης (abstract) much as simulacrum
differs from similitudo' (Souter). What, then, are the Vulgate
synonyms? They are: *in similitudinem, secundum similitudinem*,
and *ad similitudinem*: which synonymy does not wholly bear
out Souter's distinction.

In present usage, *similitude* is a literary word. It derives,
via Fr., from the L. *similitudo* (itself an abstract n. formed
from *similis*, 'like').

simple. See **silly.**

sincere. '(I pray, that) ye may be sincere and without offence
till the day of Christ' (*Philippians*, i, 10); 'As newborn babes,
desire the sincere milk of the word, that ye may grow thereby'
(1 *Peter*, ii, 2).

The Gr. Test. originals are εἰλικρινής, lit. 'unmixed',
hence 'pure, uncontaminated', and ἄδολος, 'unadulterated',
hence 'pure'.

Sincere, 'unadulterad, pure', is of mid C. 16–20; archaic
since mid C. 19. In Holland's *Pliny* we find 'the good, syncere, and true nard', and Browning, in *The Ring*, 1868, says
'Wood is cheap | And wine sincere outside the city gate'
(O.E.D.).

L. *sincerus*, 'clean; pure'.

Sion. See **Zion.**

sirs. 'He . . . would have set them at one again, saying, Sirs, ye are brethren' (*Acts*, vii, 26); cf. *ibid.*, xiv, 15,—xvi, 30,—xix, 25,—xxvii, 10, 21, 25. The singular occurs eleven times in the N.T.

In the quoted passage, the Gr. Test. reads: *Ἄνδρες, ἀδελφοί ἐστε*; the Vulgate, *Viri, fratres estis* ('Hommes, vous êtes frères', Verdunoy). Latimer, *Sermons*, ca. 1550, 'Sirs, I will tell ye what ye shall do: consider every one with himself, what Christ hath done for us'; Shakespeare, 'Sirs, strive no more' (*Titus Andronicus*, III, i, 178). 'A common form of appeal to an audience' (Wright): C. 15–20. Originally apprehended as a reduced form of *sire*, via Old Fr. from a Low L. form of Classical L. *senior* (O.E.D.).

sit at meat. 'And it came to pass, as Jesus sat at meat in the house . . .' (*Matthew*, ix, 10; cf. xiv, 9).

To be at table; i.e., to be eating a meal.

The phrase, dating from C. 14, was common in C. 16–18, then archaic. The elaboration, *at meat and meal*, has long been obsolete. (See **meat**.)

sith. 'Sith we were reconciled by his blood, when we were enemies, we shall much more be saved being reconciled' (*Romans*, v, heading).

Sith here = 'seeing that'; 'since' in the sense 'because'. 'Very common from ca. 1520 to ca. 1670, being frequently used to express cause, while *since* was restricted to time. After 1700 apparently obsolete, but revived by early C. 19 writers' (O.E.D.). Its earliest sense was 'then' or 'afterwards' (a narrative adv.); it is a reduced form of O.E. *sithan*, 'then' or 'afterwards'.

sleep, on. Asleep: as in *Acts*, xiii, 36. A C. 9–17 phrase.

sleight. 'That we henceforth be no more children, tossed to and fro, and carried about with every wind of doctrine, by the sleight of men, and cunning craftiness, whereby they lie in wait to deceive' (*Ephesians*, iv, 14): *ἐν τῇ κυβείᾳ τῶν* ἀνθρωπών, 'in men's playing with dice, i.e. trickery': *in nequitia hominum*, 'par la tromperie des hommes' (Verdunoy). 'Cunning' is the earliest sense (mid C. 13–mid 19, then archaic): cf. Shakespeare's 'As Ulysses and stout Diomede | With sleight and manhood stole to Rhesus' tents, | And brought from thence the Thracian fatal steeds' (3 *Henry VI*, IV, ii, 20–2). Of Scandinavian origin: Old Norse *slægth*, 'slyness' (O.E.D.).

smitten. = 'affected grievously, damaged; blasted, blighted' in the passage quoted in:—

so as. 'The fourth angel sounded, and the third part of the sun was smitten, and the third part of the moon, and the third part of the stars; so as the third part of them was darkened, and the day shone not for a third part of it, and the night likewise' (*Revelation*, viii, 12).

So that. *So as* is now, to convey effect or result, used only with the infinitive ('so as to darken a third part of them').

so many is 'as many' in *Hebrews*, xi, 12, 'Therefore sprang there even of one, and him as good as dead, so many as the stars of the sky in multitude, and as the sand which is by the sea shore innumerable'. An obsolete use.

sober; soberly. 'Whether we be beside ourselves, it is to God; or whether we be sober [σωφρονοῦμεν, are sober-minded], it is for your cause' (2 *Corinthians*, v, 13); 'A bishop then must be blameless, the husband of one wife, vigilant, sober [σώφρονα], of good behaviour, given to hospitality, apt to teach' (1 *Timothy*, iii, 2).—'I say . . . to every man . . ., not to think of himself more highly than he ought to think; but to think soberly' (*Romans*, xii, 3); 'Denying ungodliness and worldly lusts, we should live soberly, righteously, and godly [adv. = *godlily*]' (*Titus*, ii, 12).

Serious(ly) and/or staid(ly) in bearing, conduct, character: mid C. 14–20; slightly archaic. Via Old Fr. from L. *sobrius*, the opposite of *ebrius*, 'drunk', hence 'temperate in behaviour and character'.

sojourn. 'And God spake on this wise, That his seed should sojourn in a strange land; and that they [the foreigners] should bring them into bondage, and entreat them evil four hundred years' (*Acts*, vii, 6); 'By faith he [Abraham] sojourned in the land of promise, as in a strange country' (*Hebrews*, xi, 9).

To stay or reside for a time (at a place away from home, or in a country not one's own): from late C. 13. Shakespeare, 'The advantage of his absence took the king, | And in the meantime sojourn'd at my father's' (*King John*, I, i, 103–4).

From Old Fr., ultimately from L. *diurnus*, 'daily' (*dies*, a day), the original sense probably being 'to stay away for a *day*'.

some, 'someone' or 'one' (a usage obsolete since ca. 1760), occurs in *Romans*, v, 7, 'Scarcely for a righteous man will one die: yet peradventure for a good man some would even dare to die'; the Gr. Test. has, ὑπὲρ γὰρ τον ἀγαθοῦ τάχα τις τολμᾷ ἀποθανεῖν; the Vulgate, 'nam pro bono forsitan quis audeat mori'.

sometime (or **some time**) and **sometimes.** 'In the which [viz., certain sins] ye also walked some time' (*Colossians*, iii, 7); 'Which [viz., 'the spirits in prison'] sometime were disobedient' (I *Peter*, iii, 20); 'And you, that were sometime alienated and enemies in your mind by wicked works' (*ibid.*, i, 21).—'Now in Jesus Christ ye who were sometimes far off are made nigh by the blood of Christ' (*Ephesians*, ii, 13).

The reference in every instance is to the past; the sense is 'once (upon a time); formerly'. Hooker, in *Ecclesiastical Polity* (late C. 16) writes, 'As "By the sword of God and Gideon" was sometime the cry of the people of Israel, so it might deservedly be at this day the joyful song of innumerable multitudes.'

Sometime, 'at a certain time (in the past)', is of late C. 13–17; *sometimes*, 'at certain times (in the past')', had a much shorter life—ca. 1560–1660.

soothsaying. 'And it came to pass, as we went to prayer, a certain damsel possessed with a spirit of divination met us,

which [= who] brought her masters much gain by soothsaying' (*Acts*, xvi, 16): μαντευομένη, 'by practising soothsaying' (with a connotation of fraud): *divinando* ('en devin-
ant', Verdunoy, who adds the gloss, 'Quelques hommes
s'étaient associés pour exploiter le don de la démoniaque').

Soothsaying, 'prognostication of future events', is lit.
'truth-saying (or telling)'; with *soothsayer*, 'truth (fore)teller',
cf. German *Wahrsager*. Since mid C. 19, the word has been
archaic.

sorcerer and **sorcery**. 'When they had gone through the
isle unto Paphos, they found a certain sorcerer, a false prophet,
a Jew' (*Acts*, xiii, 6); 'But Elymas the sorcerer . . . withstood
them' (*ibid.*, xiii, 8); 'Murderers, and whoremongers, and
sorcerers, and idolaters' (*Revelation*, xxi, 8); 'Without [outside
the gates of the city of God] are dogs, and sorcerers, and
whoremongers, and . . .' (*ibid.*, xxii, 15).—'There was a certain man, called Simon, which beforetime in the same city
used sorcery, and bewitched the people of Samaria' (*Acts*, viii,
9; cf. verse 11, 'He had bewitched them with sorceries');
Revelation, ix, 21, and xviii, 23.

Sorcerer, which arose ca. 1500, is an extended form of
C. 14–16 *sorcer* (a sorcerer), itself from Old Fr. *Sorcery* arose
ca. 1300, and it comes either from Old Fr. *sorcerie* or from
Medieval L. *sorceria*, which ultimately derives from Classical
L. *sors*, 'a (person's) lot, share, fortune; a lot in divination':
cf. the learned and literary English word *sortilege*, 'divination
practised by casting lots'.

sore, adv. *Sore* = 'sorely', i.e. 'grievously' or 'severely' or
merely 'extremely'; obsolete, except in the cliché *sore afraid*.
The N.T. has 'sore vexed' (*Matthew*, xvii, 15), 'sore dis-
pleased' (*ibid.*, xxi, 15), 'sore amazed' (*Mark*, vi, 51, and xiv,
33), 'rent him sore' (*ibid.*, ix, 26), and 'They all wept sore'
(*Acts*, xx, 37).

sort. 'Brethren, I have written the more boldly unto you in
some sort' (*Romans*, xv, 15); 'Ye sorrowed after a godly sort'

(2 *Corinthians*, vii, 11; so too in 3 John, 6); in the other N.T. passages, *sort* is used precisely as it is used to-day.

In the two quoted passages, the Gr. Test. and Vulgate correspondencies are, respectively, ἀπὸ μέρους, 'in part; partly' and *ex parte*, 'par endroits' (here and there), Verdunoy; κατὰ Θεόν, 'in a manner acceptable to God', and *secundum Deum*, 'selon Dieu' (Verdunoy). In the *Romans* passage, *sort* = 'extent, degree', a sense current ca. 1570–1770; in the other, *sort* = 'way, manner', a sense current in mid C. 15–mid 19, then archaic.

Via Old Fr. from a Low L. alteration of Classical L. *sors*, 'a lot or share; hence, condition' (O.E.D.).

space. 'Then stood up ... Gamaliel ... and commanded to put the apostles forth a little space' (*Acts*, v, 34); 'I gave her space to repent of her fornication: and she repented not' (*Revelation*, ii, 21); 'There are seven kings: five are fallen, and one is, and the other is not yet come; and when he cometh, he must continue a short space' (*ibid.*, xvii, 10).

In these passages, *space* means 'an interval of time', as does L. *spatium* (the origin of Fr. *espace*, whence the English word immediately derives). In English, the time-sense precedes the space-sense: and indeed the history of *space* bears semantically on Einstein's space-time continuum theory of Relativity.

speed, v. See **God speed**.

spent. 'I will very gladly spend and be spent for you; though the more abundantly I love you, the less I be loved' (2 *Corinthians*, xii, 15): ἐγὼ δὲ ἥδιστα δαπανήσω καὶ ἐκδαπανηθήσομαι ὑπὲρ τῶν ψυχῶν ὑμῶν· εἰ περισσοτερῶς ὑμᾶς ἀγαπῶ, ἧττον ἀγαπῶμαι, 'I shall most gladly spend and be spent for the sake of your souls [intensive for "you": "for *your* sakes"] ...': *ego autem libentissime impendam, et superimpendar ipse pro animabus vestris*, 'Pour moi, je dépenserai volontiers, bien plus je me dépenserai moi-même par surcroît pour vos ames' (Verdunoy).

Here, *spend* has, basically, the sense, 'to incur expenditure', which dates from late C. 13. From L. *expendere*, which was early adopted by (Old) English, Ger., Dutch, Norse.

spikenard. 'An alabaster box of ointment of spikenard very precious' (*Mark*, xiv, 3); cf. *John*, xii, 3, 'A pound of ointment of spikenard, very costly'.—See also **nard.**

Ἀλάβαστρον μύρου νάρδου πιστικῆς πολυτελοῦς, 'an alabaster phial of ointment of (spike)nard, pure, precious': *alabastrum unguenti nardi spicati pretiosi*, 'un vase d'albâtre plein d'un parfum de nard pur, de grand prix', Verdunoy, who notes that *spicati* does not correspond to πιστικῆς, *nardi spicati* being 'de nard d'épi, nard extrait de l'épi [ear] de la plante, par opposition au parfum moins délicat extrait des feuilles'. Spikenard is 'an aromatic substance obtained from an Eastern plant, now identified as the *Nardostachys Jatamansi*' growing on the Himalayas. From Late L. *spica* (an ear) *nardi* (of nard), which renders Gr. νάρδου στάχυς, perhaps via Old Fr. *spicanarde* (O.E.D.).

spirit occurs very frequently in the N.T., e.g. in *Matthew*, iii, 16, 'And Jesus, when he was baptized, . . . saw the Spirit of God descending like a dove': τὸ Πνεῦμα τοῦ Θεοῦ: *Spiritum Dei* ('l'Esprit de Dieu', Verdunoy); and *Luke*, xi, 13, 'Your heavenly Father [shall] give the Holy Spirit to them that ask him': Πνεῦμα Ἅγιον: *spiritum bonum* ('le Saint-Esprit', Verdunoy); and 1 *Thessalonians*, iv, 8, 'God, who hath also given us his holy Spirit': τὸ Πνεῦμα αὐτοῦ τὸ Ἅγιον: *Spiritum suum sanctum* ('son Esprit-Saint', Verdunoy).

Spirit, as used in *The Bible*, has, according to Cruden, nineteen different senses; for the relation of *spirit* to πνεῦμα, see Souter at πνεῦμα and ψυχή; cf. *Holy Ghost*, q.v. at **Ghost, the Holy.** The word itself comes, via Anglo-Fr. (*e*)*spirit*, from Old Fr. *esperit*(*e*), or else directly from L. *spiritus*, 'a breathing, a breath; breath' (*spirare*, to breathe). 'The earlier English usages of the word are mainly derived from passages in the Vulgate, in which *spiritus* is employed to render Gr. πνεῦμα and Heb. *ruach*' (O.E.D.).

The semantic development is this: the breathing of God, 'the *holy* breathing', is pervasive and omnipresent, God's intangible power breathing over the Universe; that outbreathèd power is personified, invested with an ethereal (and spiritual) body, and gradually transformed into the Third *Person* of the *Trinity*.

spitefully. 'The remnant took his servants, and entreated them'—treated them—'spitefully, and slew them' (*Matthew*, xxii, 6); 'He shall be delivered unto the Gentiles, and shall be mocked, and spitefully entreated, and spitted on', i.e., spat upon (*Luke*, xviii, 32).

'Entreated spitefully' renders ὕβρισαν, 'treat outrageously or insolently'; '(be) spitefully entreated' renders the same v. (ὑβρίζω). This *spitefully* = 'contemptuously, opprobriously, virulently': mid C. 15–mid 18. *Spite* is an aphetic (foreshortened) form of *despite* (Old Fr. *despit*).

spitted, 'spat', is archaic for the preterite and past participle of *spit*.

spoil, v. 'Else how can one enter into a strong man's house, and spoil his goods, except he first bind the strong man?' (*Matthew*, xii, 29); 'Beware lest any man spoil you through philosophy and vain deceit, after the tradition of men, after the rudiments of the world, and not after Christ' (*Colossians*, ii, 8); 'Having spoiled principalities and powers, he made a shew of them openly, triumphing over them' (*ibid.*, verse 15); 'Ye . . . took joyfully the spoiling of your goods, knowing in yourselves that ye have in heaven a better and an enduring substance' (*Hebrews*, x, 34).

To plunder, whether lit. or fig.: from ca. 1340; in C. 20, archaic and rare. In *Colossians*, ii, 8, the sense is rather 'to injure (a person's) character; to affect injuriously'. Via Old Fr. *espo(i)llier* from L. *spoliare*, 'to take the possessions (armour, equipment, etc.) of (a conquered foe)'.

sport. '[These] shall receive the reward of unrighteousness, as they that count it pleasure to riot in the day time. Spots they are and blemishes, sporting themselves with their own deceivings while they feast with you' (2 *Peter*, ii, 13).

I.e., disporting themselves: ἐντρυφῶντες, 'revelling (in)', cf. 'So many hours must I sport myself', Shakespeare, 3 *Henry VI*, II, v, 34. A sense current in C. 15–18.

Either from *sport*, 'pleasant pastime', or more probably an aphetic (foreshortened) form of 'to *disport*' (to carry—L. *portare*—hence, to bear oneself in a certain way).

spue. 'So then because thou art lukewarm, and neither cold nor hot, I will spue thee out of my mouth' (*Revelation*, iii, 16): μέλλω σε ἐμέσαι ἐκ τοῦ στόματός μου, 'I intend to vomit thee from my mouth'; *incipiam te vomere ex ore meo*, 'j'en arriverai à te vomir de ma bouche' (Verdunoy).

Not, as is often stated, the early form of *spew*: *spew* occurs in C. 13, *spue* not until C. 14; *spue*, which is not even now incorrect, has, since C. 18, been considered archaic. *Spew* is the Germanic shaping of L. *spuere*, with which Gr. πτύειν is cognate. The O.E.D., in 1909, remarked, 'Not now in polite use'; but since ca. 1920, it has to some extent regained favour.

stagger. 'He staggered not at the promise of God through unbelief; but was strong in faith, giving glory to God' (*Romans*, iv, 20).

He did not flinch; did not hesitate. Lit., did not reel or totter or stumble; cf. J. Field, 1579, 'For without this, man cannot come directly to God: but they stagger and reel, not knowing which way to turn themselves'.

A variant of the synonymous *stacker* (since C. 16, obsolete except in dialect), which comes from Old Norse *stakra* (same sense): cf. early Modern Flemish *staggeren* (O.E.D.).

stanch. 'Immediately her issue'—flow, leakage—'of blood stanched' (*Luke*, viii, 44), i.e., was stanched; it ceased to flow. This intransitive use arose at the end of the 14th Century; in C. 19, it was archaic; now it is virtually obsolete.

Stanch comes from Old Fr. *estanchier*, 'to stop the flow of (blood, water, etc.); perhaps ultimately connected with L. *stagnum*, 'a pool, a pond'.

stand. In 1 *Corinthians*, ii, 5, 'Your faith should not stand in the wisdom of men, but in the power of God', the sense is 'consist'.

But in *Ephesians*, vi, 13, 'Wherefore take unto you the whole armour of God, that ye may be able to withstand'—to resist—'in the evil day, and having done all, to stand', it is 'stand firm'.

Stand is of common Germanic stock and cognate with L. *stare*.

stony. 'Some [seeds] fell upon stony places, where they had not much earth', 'But he that received the seed into stony places, the same is he that heareth the word, and anon with joy receiveth it; | Yet hath he not root in himself . . . : for when tribulation or persecution ariseth . . . , by and by he is offended' (*Matthew*, xiii, 5 and 20–1).

Here, *stony* is 'rocky': cf. 'He was driven to disperse his army into divers companies, in a stony and ill-favoured country, ill for horsemen to travell' (North's *Plutarch*, 1579: cited by Wright).

strain at, in *Matthew*, xxiii, 24, 'Ye blind guides, which strain at a gnat, and swallow a camel', is simply 'a misprint for "strain out", which is the rendering in Tyndale, Coverdale, the Great Bible, the Geneva, and the Bishops'; and is quoted in [Thomas] Lever's *Sermons* [1550] (ed. Arber), p. 85, "Wo, wo, wo unto you hipocrites that stumble at a strawe, and leape over a blocke, that strayne out a gnat, and swalowe up a camell" ' (Wright).

The Gr. Test. has οἱ διϋλίζοντες τὸν κώνωπα : κώνωψ, 'a gnat, mosquito, referred to proverbially as something small'; διϋλίζω, 'I strain, put through a sieve' (Souter). The Vulgate reads, 'excolantes culicem, camelum autem glutientes', which Verdunoy renders as 'qui filtrez le moucheron et qui avalez le chameau'.

strait. 'Enter ye in at the strait gate [*Εἰσέλθετε διὰ τῆς στενῆς πύλης*, "go in through the narrow gate"]: for wide is the gate, and broad is the way, that leadeth to destruction, and many there be which go in thereat: | Because strait is the gate, and narrow is the way, which leadeth unto life, and few there be that find it' (*Matthew*, vii, 13–14; cf. *Luke*, xiii, 24).

From Old Fr. *estreit* (from L. *strictus*, itself from *stringere*, 'to tighten, to bind tightly').

strake (*Acts*, xxvii, 17) is the past tense (preterite) of *strike*.

strange. See last sentence of the entry at **setter forth** and cf. 'His seed should sojourn in a strange land' (*Acts*, vii, 6), 'I persecuted them even unto strange cities' (*ibid.*, xxvi, 11), 'He sojourned . . . as in a strange country' (*Hebrews*, xi, 9).

'Foreign' is the sense of *strange* in these passages: the word comes from Old Fr. *estrange* (L. *extraneus*, 'external', hence 'foreign'): and 'foreign' is the earliest sense in English; it arose in late C. 13.

strangers, in 1 *Peter*, i, 1, 'Peter, an apostle of Jesus Christ, to the strangers scattered throughout Pontus, Galatia, Cappadocia, Asia, and Bithynia', = 'foreigners'. Like *space* from Fr. *espace*, it is aphetic (foreshortened) from Old Fr. *estrangier*; cf. **strange.**

strangled, in *Acts*, xxi, 25, 'They [the Gentiles] keep themselves from things offered to idols, and from blood, and from strangled, and from fornication', obviously means 'things strangled'; contrast *ibid.*, xv, 20, '. . . from pollutions of idols, and from fornication, and from things strangled, and from blood'. An inconsistency, for the Gr. Test. has *ἀπὸ . . . τοῦ πνικτοῦ* in both of these passages, and the Vulgate, 'abstineant se a . . . suffocatis' and 'abstineant se ab . . . suffocato'; *strangulation* was the obvious word to have used.

strawed. 'A very great multitude spread their garments in the way; others cut down branches from the trees, and strawed them in the way' (*Matthew*, xxi, 8); 'Reaping where thou hast not sown, and gathering where thou hast not strawed', 'I reap where I sowed not, and gather where I have not strawed' (*ibid.*, xxv, 24 and 26).

Straw is the old form of 'to *strew*', and *strawed* is the preterite (for *strewed*) and past participle (for *strewn*); the old past participle *strawn* is rare. The word is of the common Germanic stock.

stricken in years, 'advanced in years', occurs in *Luke*, i, 7, 'Both were now well stricken in years'. The phrase is now archaic, whereas *stricken in age* (which occurs in the O.T.) has been obsolete since ca. 1660.

This past participle belongs to v.i. *strike*, 'to go', i.e. 'gone in years (or, age)', which easily carries the connotation 'far gone in years'. The v.t. *strike*, 'to smite (a person or a thing)', comes from the same Germanic radical.

Stroke, in *Matthew*, xxvi, 51, version of 1611, is an old form of the preterite (*struck*).

striker. See the first quotation at **lucre.**

In this passage Wyclif has *smiter*, other versions *fighter*; the Vulgate word is *percussor*, the N.T. Gr. is πλήκτης. The O.E.D. notes it as a nonce-use, the sense being 'a person (over-)ready to resort to blows'; Souter's translation of the Gr. word is 'a pugnacious person'.

study, v. 'We beseech you, brethren, . . . that ye study to be quiet, and to do your own business' (1 *Thessalonians*, iv, 10–11); 'Study to shew thyself approved unto God' (2 *Timothy*, ii, 15).

Study = 'to endeavour earnestly' (a sense that has long been archaic). It derives immediately from Old Fr. *estudier* (from Medieval L. *studiare*, from Classical L. *studium*, 'zeal', itself from *studere*, 'to be careful, to be zealous'.

stuff. 'In that day [the second coming of Christ], he which shall be upon the housetop, and his stuff in the house, let him not come down to take it away' (*Luke*, xvii, 31).

I.e., movables, furniture; short for *stuff of household*, where *of household* is either actual or understood; cf. *household-stuff*.

From Old Fr. *estoffe*.

substance. 'Ye . . . took joyfully the spoiling of your goods, knowing . . . that ye have in heaven a better and an enduring substance' (*Hebrews*, x, 34): Gr. Test., κρείττονα ὕπαρξιν καὶ μένουσαν : Vulgate, 'meliorem et manentem substantiam', which Verdunoy renders as 'une fortune meilleure et stable'.

Here, *substance* = 'possessions, property': cf. the cliché, *a man of substance*, apart from which, by the way, this sense has been archaic since ca. 1860.

Via Old Fr., it comes from L. *substantia* ('adopted as the representative of Gr. οὐσία in its various senses', O.E.D.), which derives from *substare* (in its transferred sense, 'to be present').

succour and **succourer.** 'In the day of salvation have I succoured thee' (2 *Corinthians*, vi, 2); 'In that he himself hath suffered being tempted, he is able to succour them that are tempted' (*Hebrews*, ii, 18).—'I commend unto you Phebe our sister. . . . That ye receive her in the Lord . . . and that ye assist her in whatsoever business she hath of you: for she hath been a succourer of many, and of myself also' (*Romans*, xvi, 2).

Succourer (mid C. 15–17) comes either direct from 'to *succour*' or from Old Fr. *secourere*; *succour*, 'to help or assist; to relieve the want or distress, physical or mental, of (a person)', via Old Fr. *socorre* or *secourre* from L. *succurrere*, 'to run up to (a person)' and thus to bring assistance to him. (O.E.D.)

suddenly. 'Lay hands suddenly on no man, neither be partaker of other men's sins: keep thyself pure' (1 *Timothy*, v, 22): χεῖρας ταχέως μηδενὶ ἐπιτίθει, 'lay hands quickly on no one': *manus cito nemini imposueris*, 'n'impose les mains à personne trop vite' (Verdunoy).

The nuance is 'all at once'; the connotation is 'unthinkingly'. The adverbial *-ly* affixed to *sudden*, which comes, via Anglo-

Fr. and Old Fr., from a Low L. variant of Classical L. *subitaneus*, itself from *subitus*, 'quick, sudden' (*subire*, to come—or go—stealthily). (O.E.D.)

sufficiency. 'Our sufficiency is of God' (2 *Corinthians*, iii, 5); 'God is able to make all grace abound toward you; that ye, always having all sufficiency in all things, may abound to every good work' (*ibid.*, ix, 8).

The corresponding Gr. Test. passages are: 1. ἡ ἱκανότης ἡμῶν ἐκ τοῦ Θεοῦ, 'our ability or power [is] from God' (Vulgate, *sufficientia nostra ex Deo est*, 'notre aptitude vient de Dieu', Verdunoy);

2. ἐν παντὶ πάντοτε πᾶσαν αὐτάρκειαν ἔχοντες, 'having in everything, at all times, entire independence or self-sufficiency' (Vulgate, *in omnibus semper omnem sufficientiam habentes*, 'ayant toujours et en tout ce qu'il vous faut', Verdunoy).

In 1. *sufficiency* = 'power; capacity' (mid C. 16–mid 19, then archaic); in 2. it = 'enough' (from ca. 1530; now the predominant sense).

From L. *sufficientia*, 'a being adequate or sufficient': *sufficere*, 'to suffice'.

sunder, in. This adv. is an old form (C. 14–19) of the now usual *asunder*. 'The lord of that servant will come in a day when he looketh not for him . . . , and will cut him in sunder, and will appoint him his portion with the unbelievers' (*Luke*, xii, 46): Gr. Test., διχοτομήσει αὐτόν (will cut him in two); Vulgate, 'dividet eum partemque ejus cum fidelibus ponet'; Verdunoy, 'le mettra en pièces et lui infligera le sort réservé aux (esclaves) infidèles'.

sundry. 'God, who at sundry times and in divers manners spake in time past unto the fathers by the prophets' (*Hebrews*, i, 1): πολυμερῶς καὶ πολυτρόπως, 'to one at one time, to another at another, and in many ways': *multifariam multisque modis*, 'a plusieurs reprises et de diverses manières' (Verdunoy).

'At various times and in various manners' would probably be the modern form of the adverbial phrases.

From an O.E. word meaning 'separate, private': cf. Dryden, 'Experience finds | That sundry women are of sundry minds' (O.E.D.).

surety, of a. 'Now I know of a surety, that the Lord hath sent his angel' (*Acts*, xii, 11), i.e. for certain: Gr. Test., Νῦν οἶδα ἀληθῶς; Vulgate, 'Nunc scio vere'. The phrase arose in C. 16 and is archaic.

surfeiting. 'And take heed to yourselves, lest at any time your hearts be overcharged with surfeiting, and drunkenness, and cares of this life' (*Luke*, xxi, 34).

Surfeiting renders the Gr. Test. κραιπάλη; the Vulgate has *crapula*, 'les excès du manger' (Verdunoy); the sense is 'gluttony and the resultant loathing for food'. (It is now rare for *surfeit*.)

Surfeiting is the vbl. n. from 'to *surfeit*', which derives immediately from the n., which comes, via Old Fr. *sorfait* or *surfait* or *sorfet* or *surfet*, from L. *super*, 'over', 'excessively', + *facere*, 'to do' (O.E.D.).

swallow up. See at **contrariwise**.

swelling, adj. and n. 'Great swelling words of vanity' (2 *Peter*, ii, 18); 'Their mouth speaketh great swelling words, having men's persons in admiration because of advantage' (*Jude*, 16).—'Debates, envyings, wraths, strifes, backbitings, whisperings, swellings, tumults' (2 *Corinthians*, xii, 20).

Respectively 'inflated (by pride)' and 'inflation (by pride)': cf. Shakespeare's 'swelling port' (prideful bearing), 'swelling heart' (a heart too proud), 'swelling spirits' (proud, haughty spirits): the n. occurs in Chaucer, ca. 1386; the adj. not until two centuries later. Both come from 'to *swell*', which is of the common West Germanic stock.

synagogue occurs perhaps fifty times in the N.T.; both lit. and, as in 'the synagogue of Satan' (*Revelation*, ii, 9), fig.

The Gr. Test. word is συναγωγή ('in origin abstract, *a leading* [*bringing*] *together*, *convening* an assembly': from συνάγω, 'I gather together, collect, assemble'), 'a meeting, an assembly' (or 'a place of assembly'), esp. of Jews for scripture-reading and worship; hence applied to communities of Jewish Christians (Souter).

See esp. Hastings and Leclercq.

T

tabernacle, which occurs frequently in the N.T. as in the O.T., comes via Old Fr. from L. *tabernaculum*, 'a tent; a booth; a shed', the diminutive of *taberna*, 'a hut; a booth, a shop' (see **taverns**). Its earliest sense, both in L. and in English, is 'tent'. 'Tabernacula dicuntur a similitudine tabernarum, quæ ipsæ, quod ex tabulis olim fiebant, dictæ sunt', Festus: 'They are called tabernacles from their likeness to shops, which are so called [*tabernæ*] because they used to be made of planks'. In Irwin's recension of Cruden, we read that 'This word literally means *tent*, and is used of any sort of temporary tent or booth, as well as for the *tabernacle* erected for the worship of God. Where the word is plural, except in *feast of tabernacles* (*Leviticus*, xxiii, 34], it has the meaning of *dwelling*, or *dwelling-place*. . . . The Revised Versions mostly use the word *tent*, in place of *tabernacle*.'

Hebrews, viii, 2, 'A minister of the sanctuary, and of the true tabernacle', represents the Gr. τῶν ἁγίων λειτουργὸς καὶ τῆς σκηνῆς ῖῆς ἀληθινῆς, 'a servant of the temple and of the genuine tent', σκηνή being used of the whole tent and also of each part; *Acts*, vii, 44, 'Our fathers had the tabernacle of witness in the wilderness', renders Gr. ἡ σκηνὴ τοῦ μαρτυρίου ἦν τοῖς πατράσιν ἡμῶν ἐν τῇ ἐρήμῳ, 'the tent of witness was for our forefathers in the wilderness', where we have 'the tent as a witness between God and his people' (Souter).

The *Tabernacle* (called also *tabernacle of witness*, as above, and in the O.T., *tabernacle of the congregation*) is the curtained tent, consisting of two parts—the outer or Holy Place; the inner or

Most Holy Place—and, in the inner, containing the Ark of the Covenant (a symbol of God's presence among the Jews), and, as a whole, serving as the Jews' portable sanctuary during their years in the wilderness and until the erection of the Temple.

table. 'He asked for a writing table, and wrote, saying, His name is John' (*Luke*, i, 63); 'Ye are manifestly declared to be the epistle of Christ ministered by us, written not with ink, but with the Spirit of the living God; not in tables of stone, but in fleshy tables of the heart' (2 *Corinthians*, iii, 3).

    Gr. Test.: αἰτήσας πινακίδιον ἔγραψε λέγων, Ἰωάννης ἐστὶ τὸ ὄνομα αὐτοῦ (a πινακίδιον being '*a little* waxed *tablet*, on which to write with an iron pen', Souter); οὐκ ἐν πλαξὶ λιθίναις ἀλλ᾽ ἐν πλαξὶ καρδίαις σαρκίναις, 'not in tablets of stone, but in . . .'

    The sense 'writing tablet' has been archaic since C. 17; that of 'stone tablet for inscriptions' has survived, since C. 18 mostly with Biblical reference. From L. *tabula*, 'a flat board; a writing tablet'.

take wrong. 'There is utterly a fault among you, because ye go to law one with another. Why do ye not rather take wrong? why do ye not rather suffer yourselves be defrauded?' (1 *Corinthians*, vi, 7).

    'Take wrong' renders ἀδικεῖσθε, 'be injured, treated unjustly' (ἀδικία, (an) injustice'); it is a C. 16–17 form of *to suffer wrong*, 'to accept it patiently without resentment'; cf. the C. 20 American *take it*, 'to endure pain, distress, misfortune without groaning or moaning, recrimination or complaint'.

tare. 'Straightway the spirit tare him', i.e. tore him, i.e. rended him (*Mark*, ix, 20). Archaic preterite.

taste. 'There be some standing here, which shall not taste of death, till they see the Son of man coming in his kingdom' (*Matthew*, xvi, 28); 'If a man keep my saying, he shall never taste of death' (*John*, viii, 52); '[Jesus] by the grace of God should taste death for every man' (*Hebrews*, ii, 9); 'Those who

. . . have tasted of the heavenly gift' (*ibid.*, vi, 4); 'Have tasted the good word of God' (next verse).

Taste, transitive, as in the third and fifth quotations, is two centuries earlier (cf. Wyclif, 'He shall not taste the long death') than *taste of* (Tyndale). In the first and third quotation, the Gr. is γεύσωνται θανάτου,, 'shall experience death', and γεύσηται θανάτου. Lit., γεύομαι is 'I taste'. Shakespeare's use of *taste* in 'You have tasted her in bed' (*Cymbeline*, II, iv, 57) is merely a special application of the sense 'to experience': cf. *know*, 'to have sexual intercourse with' (a woman) and Fr. *tâter* (Old Fr. *taxer*). Via Old Fr. from Silver L. *taxare*, 'to feel, to handle', a frequentative of Classical L. *tangere*, 'to touch' (*virgo intacta*).

taverns. 'When the brethren heard of us, they came to meet us as far as Appii forum, and the three taverns' (*Acts*, xxviii, 15): Vulgate, *tres tabernas*: the Gr. Test. having ἀκούσαντες τὰ περὶ ἡμῶν, ἦλθον εἰς ἀπάντησιν ἡμῖν ἄχρις 'Αππίου καὶ Τριῶν Ταβερνῶν, 'having heard things concerning us, they came to a meeting with us—to meet us—up to—as far as—[the township of] Appi Forum and [the village of] Three Shops', a town and village on the Appian Way, the relevant name being Tres Tabernæ (or Τρεῖς Ταβέρναι, as the Gr. renders it). The L. *taberna* here means not a wine-shop but any shop—cf. the obsolete *tabern*.

temper, v. 'Our comely parts have no need: but God hath tempered the body together' (I *Corinthians*, xii, 24): ὁ Θεὸς συνεκέρασε τὸ σῶμα, 'God compounded the human body'.

From L. *temperare*, 'to mix in due proportion'; the Vulgate has *Deus temperavit corpus*. This sense has been archaic since C. 18; cf. Shakespeare, 'The queen, sir, very oft importuned me | To temper poisons for her' (*Cymbeline*, v, v, 250–1).

temperance. 'As he reasoned of righteousness, temperance, and judgment to come, Felix trembled' (*Acts*, xxiv, 25); 'Meekness, temperance: against such there is no law' (*Galatians*, v, 23); 'And [add] to knowledge temperance; and to temperance patience; and to patience godliness' (2 *Peter*, i, 6).

Temperance renders the Gr. ἐγκράτεια, 'self-control, restraint, continence', a sense dating from mid C. 14, and often (as in *meekness*) with the connotation 'forbearance' in the face of provocation to anger. Latimer, ca. 1550, 'Doctor Barnes ... preached ... a very good sermon, with great moderation and temperance of himself' (quoted by Wright). Via Old Fr. *temperaunce* from L. *temperantia*, 'moderation' (*temperare*, 'to temper or moderate').

temple. Examples are unnecessary, but there is religious, there is spiritual significance in 'The most High dwelleth not in temples made with hands' (*Acts*, vii, 48). In the N.T., all references to an actual temple are to that temple which was 'built by Herod the Great to win the allegiance of the Jews' (Irwin's Cruden); there are metaphorical references to the temple of Christ's body and of human nature at its best, these being the dwelling-places of the Godhead (*John*, ii, 19 and 21; *Colossians*, ii, 19); and in 1 *Corinthians*, iii, 16, 'Know ye not that ye are the temple of God ... ?' (ναὸς Θεοῦ, the shrine —'that part of the temple where the god himself resides', as opposed to ἱερόν, 'the whole building', as Souter points out), the human body is designated (cf. the metaphorical phrase, *to defile the temple of God*, 'to use one's body disgracefully, immorally').

From L. *templum*, 'the dwelling-place of a deity; hence, a place of divine worship; hence, esp., the house of God'.

testify. See at **persuade** (second quotation).

tetrarch. 'At that time Herod the tetrarch heard of the fame of Jesus' (*Matthew*, xiv, 1); 'Now in the fifteenth year of the reign of Tiberius Cæsar, Pontius Pilate being governor of Judæa, and Herod being tetrarch of Galilee, and his brother Philip tetrarch of Ituræa and of the region of Trachonitis, and Lysanias the tetrarch of Abilene' (*Luke*, iii, 1; cf. verse 19); *Acts*, xiii, 1.

In the gloss to *Matthew*, xiv, 1, Wyclif, in his translation (1382), writes against 'Eroude tetrarcha' (Herod, tetrarch) the words 'that is, prince of the fourthe part': the Vulgate *tetrarcha* (Ecclesiastical L. *tetrarches*) transliterates Gr. τετράρχης (τετρα, 'four', + – αρχης, 'a ruler'), 'a ruler of one of four divisions of a political territory, a province, a country'; this is a political division, made for efficient government and 'sometimes found in the Roman East' (Souter).

thank, n., singular for *thanks*, occurs in *Luke*, vi, 32, 'If ye love them which love you, what thank have ye? for sinners also love those that love them' (and in the next two verses). *To have thank* belongs to C. 10–17.

thankworthy. 'This is thankworthy, if a man for conscience toward God endure grief, suffering wrongfully' (1 *Peter*, ii, 19).
    Meriting thanks, worthy of thanks; cf. *praiseworthy*.
    For the element *thank*, see preceding entry. *Thankworthy* (in C. 16–17 also *thanksworthy*) was current in C. 14–17, then archaic.

that, for *that which*, occurs in *Matthew*, xx, 14, 'Take that thine is, and go thy way': Gr. Test., ἆρον τὸ σὸν καὶ ὕπαγε; Vulgate, 'Tolle quod tuum est, et vade' ('Prends ce qui te revient et va-t-en', Verdunoy).

there. 'The numerous combinations of *there* with a preposition are almost all antiquated; most of them, however, are to be found in our A.V. "Thereabout" (*Luke*, xxiv, 4), "thereat" (. . . *Matthew*, vii, 13), "thereby" (*John*, xi, 4; etc.), . . . "thereinto" (*Luke*, xxi, 21), . . . "thereupon" (. . . 1 *Corinthians*, iii, 10, 14), are instances, besides "therefore", "therein", "thereof", "thereon", "thereto", "thereunto", "therewith", which are of frequent occurrence' (Wright). *Thereabout* ('much perplexed thereabout') = 'about that, concerning that matter'; *thereunto* = 'to that end' (with that in view).

Thessalonians; Thessalonica. 'The First'—and 'the Second'—'Epistle of Paul to the Thessalonians' (πρὸς Θεσσαλονικεῖς); 'They come to Thessalonica, where was a synagogue of the Jews', *Acts*, xvii, 1, ἦλθον εἰς Θεσσαλονίκην . . .

The Thessalonians were of Thessalonica (modern Saloniki), an important city of Macedonia, on the Gulf of Saloniki (or Salonica); Macedonia was a Roman province.

Thomas. See *Matthew*, x, 3 (cf. *Mark*, iii, 18; *Luke*, vi, 15; *Acts*, i, 13)—*John*, xi, 16—xx, 24, 26—xxi, 2, 27; in the Vulgate, *Thomas*; in the Gr. Test., Θωμᾶς (also called Δίδυμος, Didymus, lit. 'the Twin'), a Grecization of an Aramaic word meaning 'a twin'. This apostle (whence the allusive *doubting Thomas*) gave his name to many saints; the saints to many persons less saintly; in England the given name *Thomas* ranks next to *John* and *William*.

thought. 'Take no thought for your life, what ye shall eat, or what ye shall drink; nor yet for your body, what ye shall put on? Is not the life'—*the* is here tautological—'more than meat [q.v.], and the body than raiment?' (*Matthew*, vi, 25).
   Be not anxious, suffer not melancholy, take not excessive care, be not distressed, be not grieved: *thought*, 'anxiety; distress of mind', was current in C. 13–mid 17.

throughly, 'thoroughly', occurs in *Matthew*, iii, 12 (cf. *Luke*, iii, 17), 2 *Corinthians*, xi, 6 ('throughly made manifest'), and 2 *Timothy*, iii, 17. Arising ca. 1430, *throughly* became archaic ca. 1740; in C. 20, it has been obsolete.

thyine wood (*Revelation*, xviii, 12) is 'supposed to be the African coniferous tree *Callitris quadrivalvis*, which yields gum sandarac' (O.E.D.). Apart from translations of *The Bible*, and commentaries thereon, the word occurs only in Christopher Smart's *David*.

Timothy, 'one who honours God', is L. *Timotheus*, Gr. Τιμόθεος ('A certain disciple was there, named Timotheus', *Acts*, xvi, 1: μαθητής τις ἦν ἐκεῖ, ὀνόματι Τιμόθεος): τιμάω, 'I give honour to', + Θεός, 'God'. 'Like other Providential pre-Christian names (e.g., *Theophilus*) it was welcomed by the Church, especially when Timotheos, "the beloved disciple of the Apostle St Paul", . . . was, ca. 97, stoned to death by "the infuriated worshippers of the great idol, 'Diana of the Ephesians'" (Benedictines [*The Book of Saints*])' (Partridge).

tinkling cymbal, a. See the quotation at **charity.**

The corresponding Gr. is κύμβαλον ἀλαλάζον, 'a clanging (or clashing) cymbal': *clanging* is much more apposite than *tinkling*, for a cymbal is a pair (properly, one of the pair) of concave plates (brass or bronze) struck together to produce a clangor or sharp, ringing sound.

The English word comes, in O.E. direct from L. *cymbalum*, in M.E. from L. via Old Fr. *cymble*; the L. word transliterates the Gr. κύμβαλον, which is formed on κύμβη, '(the) hollow of a vessel' (O.E.D.).

tithe, v. 'But woe unto ye, Pharisees! for ye tithe mint and rue and all manner of herbs, and pass over judgment and the love of God' (*Luke*, xi, 42); in *Matthew*, xxiii, 23, it is 'pay tithe of mint and anise and cummin'.

Tithe renders ἀποδεκατοῦτε, 'you take a tenth part of, and give it away': ἀπό, 'away', and δέκα, 'ten'. Used as early as King Alfred's time, *tithe* is an ecclesiastical term, often in reference to these two passages and in the sense, 'to be extremely and manifestly scrupulous in small matters while ignoring or neglecting important duties'.

Tithe comes from an O.E. v. formed on *teotha*, 'a tenth'.

tittle. 'One jot or one tittle' (*Matthew*, v, 18); 'It is easier for heaven and earth to pass, than one tittle of the law to fail' (*Luke*, xvi, 17).

Tittle is used to render κεραία, which is used to designate 'the little points or corners by which some of the Hebrew letters are distinguished from each other' (Wright). Etymologically, *tittle* is a doublet of *title*: both come from L. *titulus*, 'a superscription'; in Late L., *titulus* came to be used as a near-synonym of *apex* (the accent over a long vowel). O.E.D.

Titus. 'I ... took Titus with me also' (*Galatians*, ii, 1): συμπαραλαβὼν καὶ Τίτον: *assumpto et Tito*.—'Titus [is departed] unto Dalmatia' (2 *Timothy*, iv, 10): *Τίτος εἰς Δαλματίαν: Titus in Dalmatiam.*

The name means either 'honourable' (*τίω*, 'I honour') or 'safe, protected' (L. *tutus*).

'The Puritans shunned the great New Testament names, which, belonging to saints, were regarded as unclean. Timothy, first bishop of Ephesus, was naturally suspect, and Titus, destroyer of Jerusalem, would be repugnant to enthusiasts for the Hebrew tradition. The most notorious Titus in our annals'—Titus Oates, flagitious fabricator of a Popish plot (1678–80)—'has not helped to popularize the name' (*Jack and Jill*).

to, in *Matthew*, iii, 9, 'We have Abraham to our father'—cf. *Luke*, iii, 8—and elsewhere, represents an O.E. construction and is equivalent to *for*. (This construction, as Wright points out, occurs in Act. IV, sc. i, v. 308, of Shakespeare's *Richard* II, 'I have a king here to my flatterer'.) The Gr. Test. reads, *Πατέρα ἔχομεν τὸν ᾽Αβραάμ;* the Vulgate, 'Patrem habemus Abraham'.

to you-ward is 'towards you' in 2 *Corinthians*, i, 12. Similarly *to us-ward* is 'towards us'. The construction was common in C. 16–17.

tongue. See at **peoples** (first quotation).

topaz. See the quotation at **chrysolite.**

Probably the *yellow* (or *oriental*) *topaz*, which is either a yellow sapphire or a corundum; in modern use, the topaz is the *true* (or *occidental*) *topaz*, 'a fluo-silicate of aluminium . . . transparent and lustrous' (O.E.D.).

Via Old Fr. from L. *topazus* (Vulgate *topazius*), which merely transliterates Gr. *τόπαζος* (N.T. *τοπάζιον*); the Gr. word either comes from the name of an island in the Red Sea (Pliny's opinion) or is cognate with Sanskrit *tapas*, 'heat, fire' (a modern view: O.E.D.).

tormentor. 'This lord was wroth, and delivered him to the tormentors, till he should pay all that was due unto him'

(*Matthew*, xviii, 34): παρέδωκεν αὐτὸν τοῖς βασανισταῖς, 'handed him over to the torturers' (βασανιστής: from βασάνιζω, 'I torture').

Here, *tormentor* = 'an official torturer', a sense that, arising in late C. 13, was common ca. 1480–1620, then literary, and in mid C. 19–20 archaic. Via Anglo-Fr. (and Old Fr.) from Medieval L. *tormentare*, 'to inflict torture upon': cf. the next.

torments, n. 'All sick people that were taken with divers diseases and torments' (*Matthew*, iv, 24): πάντας τοὺς κακῶς ἔχοντας, ποικίλαις νόσοις καὶ βασάνοις συνεχομένους, 'all the ill (persons), afflicted with various maladies and severe pains'.

In late C. 13–mid 18, *torment* was used mostly of physical suffering; since ca. 1750, mostly of mental or spiritual suffering.

Ultimately from L. *torquere*, 'to twist'.

touching and **as touching** are archaic for 'concerning' or 'with regard to'; e.g., 'We have confidence in the Lord touching you' (2 *Thessalonians*, iii, 4); *as touching* occurs, e.g., in *Matthew*, xviii, 19, and xxii, 31.

Originally a present participle, as also was *concerning*, it is often short for 'that touches—refers—relates—to': 'We have, in the Lord, confidence that (or which) relates to you'. But in due and rapid course, *touching* (like *concerning*) becomes entirely prepositional.

toward. See **ward.**

translate and **translation.** 'By faith Enoch was translated that he should not see death' (*Hebrews*, xi, 5); cf. *Colossians*, i, 13.—'Before his translation he had this testimony, that he pleased God' (*Hebrews*, xi, 5).

The Gr. Test. reads: πίστει Ἐνὼχ μετετέθη, lit. 'was removed or transferred'; πρὸ γὰρ τῆς μεταθέσεως, 'removal'.

Ecclesiastical terms (both were introduced by Wyclif in 1382) for the conveyance of a person to heaven without his first dying. Perhaps via Old Fr., but probably direct from L. *transferre* ('to transfer, carry across'), passive participle *translatus*.

travail, n. and v. 'Sudden destruction cometh upon them, as travail upon a woman with child' (1 *Thessalonians*, v, 3); 'My little children, of whom I travail in birth again until Christ be formed in you' (*Galatians*, iv, 19).

To *travail* occurs earliest (ca. 1250) in the sense, 'to exert oneself, to work hard', and was soon (by 1300 at latest) applied to a woman 'in *labour*' (suffering the pangs of childbirth); the n. follows the same development. Via Old Fr. from C. 6 L. *trepalium*, an instrument of torture.—*Travel* is a doublet: to travel was, in medieval England, much more arduous than it is in C. 20.

treatise. 'The former treatise have I made, O Theophilus, of all that Jesus began to do and teach' (*Acts*, i, 1): Τὸν μὲν πρῶτον λόγον ἐποιησάμην περὶ πάντων, 'I made the first account (or narrative) concerning everything', the sense 'account' deriving from the primary sense 'a word, an utterance'.

Tyndale used 'treatise' in *Luke*, i, 1, where the R.V. has 'declaration'; in C. 14–mid 17, *treatise* signified any writing; in mid C. 17–20 uses it connotes a methodical or formal discussion or exposition of a subject and would not be applied to a narrative or predominantly descriptive work.

Via Old Fr. from L. *tractare*, 'to handle'; L. *tractatus*, 'a handling; a discussion', has given us the doublet *tractate*.

trow. 'Doth he thank that servant because he did the things that were commanded him? I trow not' (*Luke*, xvii, 9): οὐ δοκῶ, 'I think not': *non puto*.

Trow, 'to believe, think, suppose', is of C. 11–20, but archaic since ca. 1850. Of the West Germanic stock, it is O.E. *truwian*, from O.E. *truwa*, 'belief, faith'.

true, say. 'He knoweth that he saith true, that ye might believe' (*John*, xix, 35).

I.e., 'speaks the truth'—lit., 'speaks truly'. This phrase was current in C. 15–17 and is synonymous with the obsolete *tell true*.

trump. 'We shall all be changed, | In a moment, in the twinkling of an eye, at the last trump: for the trumpet shall sound, and the dead shall be raised incorruptible, and we shall be changed' (1 *Corinthians*, xv, 51–2); 'The Lord himself shall descend from heaven with a shout, with the voice of the archangel, and with the trump of God: and the dead in Christ shall rise first (1 *Thessalonians*, iv, 16).

The Gr. Test. word is σάλπιγξ, 'a bugle, a war trumpet'; the Vulgate, *tuba*.

From the Fr. *trompe* (of uncertain etymology), *trump*, 'a trumpet', arose in late C. 13; since C. 18, it has been literary; since late C. 19, archaic too.

try. See at **catholic.**

tutor. 'But [the heir] is under tutors and governors until the time appointed of the father' (*Galatians*, iv, 2): ἀλλὰ ὑπὸ ἐπιτρόπους ἐστὶ καὶ οἰκονόμους, 'but he is under legal guardians and stewards': *sub tutoribus et actoribus est*, 'il dépend de tuteurs et d'administrateurs' (Verdunoy).

As 'a legal guardian', *tutor* was brought in by Wyclif (1382) and was very common in C. 16–17; by 1750, it was obsolete.

Either directly, or indirectly via Old Fr. *tutour* (Modern Fr. *tuteur*), from L. *tutor*, 'one who watches; a protector' (*tueri*, 'to watch, guard, protect'): O.E.D.

U

uncomely. 'If any man think that he behaveth himself uncomely towards his virgin, if she pass the flower of her age, and need so require, let him do what he will, he sinneth not: let them marry' (1 *Corinthians*, vii, 36).

In an unbecoming or unseemly manner. (Adj. used as adv.: mid C. 14–mid C. 17.)

uncorruptible. See at **corrupt.**

uncorruptness, which generally means 'the quality of being uncorrupt', has in *Titus*, ii, 7, 'In all things shewing thyself a pattern of good works: in doctrine shewing uncorruptness, gravity, sincerity', the specific sense, 'purity', the Gr. being ἀφθορία, 'purity, freedom from taint' (Souter).

unction. 'Ye have an unction from the Holy One, and ye know all things' (1 *John*, ii, 20): ὑμεῖς χρίσμα ἔχετε ἀπὸ τοῦ ἁγίου, 'you have an anointing from the Messiah': *vos unctionem habetis a Sancto*, 'vous avez une onction de la part du Saint', Verdunoy, who glosses thus, ' "Une onction": le Saint-Esprit (cf. 27), qui donne une science religieuse complète et par là immunise contre les erreurs'.

'Literally, "anointing", as the word is rendered in 1 John, ii, 27. It is applied to the spiritual influence of the Holy Ghost. The word still exists in its literal sense in . . . "extreme *unction*", the ceremony of anointing with oil in cases of extreme sickness, reckoned among the seven sacraments of the Roman Catholic Church' (Wright).

Direct from *unctio* (genitive *unctionis*), action-noun from L. *unguere*, 'to smear'.

unjust. 'The lord commended the unjust steward, because he had done wisely: for the children of this world are in their generation wiser than the children of light' (*Luke*, xvi, 8): ἐπῄνεσεν ὁ κύριος τὸν οἰκονόμον τῆς ἀδικίας, 'the master praised the steward of injustice'—'a Hebraistic genitive, equivalent to the adj. ἄδικος [unjust, unrighteous]', Souter: *laudavit dominus villicum iniquitatis*, 'le maître loua l'intendant infidèle' (Verdunoy).

Unjust here = 'dishonest', a sense it carried in C. 16–18, after which it has been archaic and usually reminiscent of the Biblical passage.

English *un* + *just*, which, perhaps via Fr., comes from L. *justus*, 'equitable' (*jus*, 'right or law').

unlearned, in 2 *Timothy*, ii, 23: see at **gender.**

unprofitable. 'Cast ye the unprofitable servant into outer darkness' (*Matthew*, xxv, 30); 'We are unprofitable servants: we have done that which was our duty to do' and no more (*Luke*, xvii, 10).

The corresponding Gr. Test. and Vulgate original and rendering are τὸν ἀχρεῖον δοῦλον, 'the useless (or unworthy) slave (or servant)', and *inutilem servum*, 'l'esclave inutile' (Verdunoy); δοῦλοι ἀχρεῖοι and *servi inutiles*.

The word dates from 1325 and is formed of the English prefix *un*, 'not' + *profitable*, which comes, via Fr., from L. *profectus*, 'an advance; profit' (*proficere*, 'to make progress'). O.E.D.

unrebukeable; unreproveable. 'I give thee charge . . . | That thou keep this commandment without spot, unrebukeable, until the appearing of our Lord Jesus Christ' (1 *Timothy*, vi, 13–14).—'To present you holy and unblameable and unreproveable in his sight' (*Colossians*, i, 22).

Both words mean 'blameless'—offering no grounds for rebuke or reproof. The former appears in Tyndale (1530); the latter in Wyclif (1382). *Unreprov(e)able*, which was common ca. 1550–1680 (O.E.D.), is now preferred in the form *irreprovable*, although *irreproachable* is much more usual.

unrepentance. 'Christ upbraideth the unthankfulness and unrepentance of Chorazin, Bethsaida, and Capernaum' (*Matthew*, xi, heading).

Impenitence: C. 16–17; then archaic; in C. 20, virtually obsolete. *Unrepentance* is the English *un*, 'not' + *repentance*, which, via Old Fr., comes from L. *pænitere* or *pœnitere*, 'to cause to repent'.

unsearchable. 'How unsearchable are his [—God's—] judgments, and his ways past finding out!' (*Romans*, xii, 33); 'Unto me . . . is this grace given, that I should preach among the Gentiles the unsearchable riches of Christ' (*Ephesians*, iii, 8).

Not 'that cannot be sought' (a rare sense, unrecorded before C. 19) but 'that cannot be searched·into, so as to be exactly estimated' (O.E.D.); hence 'inscrutable', as in 'The unsearchable and secret ways | Of nature' (Robert Bridges); the word occurs earliest in Wyclif (1382).

unseemly, adv. '(Charity) doth not behave itself unseemly' (1 *Corinthians*, xiii, 5).

The use of the adj. as adv. (cf. **uncomely**) belongs to the approximate period 1370–1750, after which it is literary and archaic, as in Bayard Taylor's translation of Goethe's *Faust*, 'Something'—somewhat—'immodest or unseemly free?' (O.E.D.).

untoward. 'Save yourselves from this untoward generation' (*Acts*, ii, 40): Σώθητε ἀπὸ τῆς γενεᾶς τῆς σκολιᾶς ταύτης, 'be saved from this perverse generation' (σκολιός, lit. 'crooked', becomes metaphorically so—'crooked in nature', Souter): *Salvamini a generatione ista prava*, 'Sauvez-vous de cette génération perverse' (Verdunoy).

Un, 'not' + *toward*, 'docile'; *untoward*, introduced by Tyndale in 1526, was 'in frequent use from ca. 1580 to ca. 1700' (O.E.D.); in C. 18–19, literary; in C. 20, archaic—almost obsolete.

unwashen, 'unwashed', in *Matthew*, xv, 20, and *Mark*, vii, 2 and 5, belongs to late C. 10–17, after which it is archaic in England though common in U.S.A. in C. 18–19. *Unwashed* is not found before the 14th Century.

use, in the A.V., frequently = 'to practise; to observe', as in 'We know that the law is good, if a man use it lawfully' (1 *Timothy*, i, 8); this sense fell into disuse in the late 18th Century.

usury. 'Thou oughtest therefore to have put my money to the exchangers [q.v.], and then at my coming I should have received mine own with usury' (*Matthew*, xxv, 27; cf. *Luke*, xix, 23): ἐκομισάμην ἄν τὸ ἐμὸν σὺν τόκῳ, 'I should have recovered that which is mine, with interest [added]': *ego recepissem utique quod meum est cum usura*, 'j'aurais retiré ce qui est à moi avec un intérêt' (Verdunoy).

In this sense, *usury* was current in mid C. 15–18, then archaic. (Prob. via Old Fr.) from Medieval L. *usuria* = Classical L. *usus*, 'interest' (*uti*, 'to use').

uttermost. 'Verily I say unto thee, Thou shalt by no means come out thence, till thou hast paid the uttermost farthing' (*Matthew*, v, 26): ἕως ἂν ἀποδῷς τὸν ἔσχατον κοδϱάντην: *donec reddas novissimum quadrantem*, '. . . que tu n'aies payé la dernière pièce' (Verdunoy).

Uttermost, 'last' (of a series, store, supply, etc.), was introduced by Latimer in 1553; after C. 17, archaic and nearly always in allusion to the Biblical passage. *Uttermost* = *most utter* = *most out* = 'furthest out, most remote; last'. Both elements belong to the West Germanic stock.

V

vagabond, adj. 'Certain of the vagabond Jews, exorcists, took upon them to . . .' (*Acts*, xix, 13): Gr. Test., τινες καὶ τῶν περιερχομένων Ἰουδαίων ἐξορκιστῶν, where περιερχόμενοι is rendered by Souter as 'strolling': Vulgate, 'quidam et de circumeuntibus Judæis exorcistis', compactly translated by Verdunoy as 'quelques exorcistes juifs ambulants'.

Vagabond = 'nomadic' (C. 15–20, though slightly archaic since C. 19). Perhaps via Old Fr., but certainly from L. *vagabundus*, 'wandering' (*vagari*, 'to wander').

vain, in the sense 'empty, worthless', is frequent in the A.V.: e.g., in *Matthew*, vi, 7, 'When ye pray, use not vain repetitions, as the heathen do'. Except in *vain regrets* (a cliché), this sense of *vain* has been archaic since C. 18. From Old Fr. *vein* or, as also in Modern Fr., *vain*, which comes from L. *vanus*, 'empty, void'. Cf.:—

vanity (L. *vanitas*, via Old Fr.) corresponds to **vain**. In the A.V. it has six main senses: see Cruden. Note that in *Romans*, viii, 20 ('The creature was made subject to vanity'), the sense is 'disorders and destruction'; in 2 *Peter*, ii, 18 ('great swelling words of vanity'), it is 'emptiness'; and in *Acts*, xiv, 15 ('Ye should turn from these vanities'), it = 'ignorant folly.'

variance. See quotation at **emulation.**

In C. 15–17, *variance* was common for 'discord' or 'dissension'. Bunyan, 1684, 'She makes variance betwixt rulers and subjects, betwixt parents and children'; Beveridge, 1711, 'What is variance? A sin opposed to amity' (O.E.D.).

Via Old Fr., from L. *variantia*—itself from *variare*, 'to vary'.

vaunt. 'Charity vaunteth not itself, is not puffed up' (1 *Corinthians*, xii, 4).

Vaunt, 'to boast', is archaic except in poetry and in very rhetorical speech. Here, the nuance is 'does not extol itself, does not glorify itself, is not loud in its own praise', which has been obsolete since ca. 1850. From Fr. *vanter* (cf. Medieval L. *vantare*): ultimately cognate with L. *vanus*, 'empty'.

very, adj. 'Do the rulers know indeed that this is the very Christ?' (*John*, vii, 26).

Very is 'true', 'the very Christ' is the true Christ, Christ himself, the veritable Christ. This sense, now archaic except as an echo of the Biblical phrases 'very God of very God', 'very and eternal God', 'the very Christ', was 'very common from ca. 1300 to ca. 1600' (O.E.D.). From Old Fr. *ver(r)ai* (Modern Fr. *vrai*), which is from the stem of L. *verus*, 'true'.

vex. 'My daughter is grievously vexed with a devil' (*Matthew*, xv, 22); 'He is lunatick, and sore vexed' (*ibid.*, xvii, 15); 'Herod the king stretched forth his hands to vex certain of the church' (*Acts*, xii, 1), where *certain* = 'certain persons (i.e., members)', a usage that, corresponding to Gr. Test. τινας τῶν ἀπὸ τῆς ἐκκλησίας and the Vulgate 'quosdam de ecclesia', belongs to ca. 1400–1630; Wyclif, here, renders the Gr. as 'sum men'.

Vex used to be a much stronger word than it is now: in the first two passages it = 'tormented'; in the third, 'harass' or 'oppress'.

Via Fr., from L. *vexare*, 'to harass, maltreat, abuse'—transferred senses of the original meaning, 'to move violently, to shake', the v. being a frequentative of *vehere*, 'to carry'.

vile. In *Romays*, i, 26, 'God gave them up unto vile affections' (sodomy and lesbianism), we have the modern sense; but in *Philippians*, iii, 21, 'Who shall change our vile body that it may be fashioned like unto his glorious body', the sense is 'contemptible', and in *James*, ii, 2, 'A poor man in vile raiment', the sense is 'cheap' or 'worthless', which = Fr. *vil* (cf. *à vil prix*, 'cheaply'), itself from L. *vilis*, 'of little value or low price; cheap'—hence 'common, base' and (of clothes) 'mean, wretched'.

virtue. 'Jesus, immediately knowing in himself that virtue had gone out of him, . . . said, Who touched my clothes?' (*Mark*, v, 30); 'The whole multitude sought to touch him; for there went virtue out of him, and healed them all' (*Luke*, vi, 19).

Here, *virtue* = 'power, potency, strength, force', all in the physical sense. The Gr. Test. has δύναμις ('physical power') in both passages; the Vulgate has *virtus*. This sense survives in the medical nuance 'efficacy' ('All virtue goes out of a medicine if the container is left unstoppered').

The L. *virtus* is lit. 'manliness' (male physical excellence), from *vir*, 'a man; hence, a husband'. In Classical L., the dominant sense is 'courage'; in English, the 'courage' sense of *virtue* has been obsolete since mid C. 19.

vocation. 'The vocation of the Gentiles' (*Matthew*, xxii, heading); 'I . . . beseech you that ye walk worthy of the vocation wherewith ye are called' (*Ephesians*, iv, 1).

The Gr. Test. has κλῆσις, 'a calling, invitation, summons of [i.e., by] God to the religious life' (Souter); the Vulgate, 'Obsecro itaque vos . . . ut digne ambuletis vocatione qua vocati estis' ('Je vous exhorte donc . . . à marcher d'une manière digne de l'appel dont vous avez été appelés', Verdunoy). Whence we see that *vocation* is used 'in its original sense of "calling" . . ., i.e. to the knowledge of salvation' (Wright).

volume. 'Then said I, Lo, I come (in the volume of the book it is written of me,) to do thy will, O God' (*Hebrews*, x, 7).

The sense of *volume*, here, is 'a roll of parchment, papyrus, etc., containing written matter; a literary work (or part of one) recorded in this form' (O.E.D.); since C. 18, archaic except historically.

Via Old Fr. *volum(n)e*, from L. *volumen*, 'a coil; a roll' (itself from *volvere*, 'to roll').

W

wag, v. 'They that passed by reviled him, wagging their heads' (*Matthew*, xxvii, 39); Vulgate, 'moventes capita sua'.

I.e., shaking their heads: in C. 14–17, *wag*, 'to move, to stir', was dignified English, as in Shakespeare's 'You may as well forbid the mountain pines | To wag their high tops and to make no noise, | When they are fretten with the gusts of heaven' *The Merchant of Venice*, IV, i, 76); in C. 19–20, familiar English—and rather trivial. A word of Scandinavian origin.

wake. '(Our Lord Jesus Christ,) who died for us, that, whether we wake or sleep, we should live together with him' (1 *Thessalonians*, v, 10).

I.e., 'are awake' in the sense 'are alert', 'are on the watch': common in M.E. and early Modern English. *Wake* and *watch* are doublets.

The Gr. Test. has εἴτε γρηγορῶμεν εἴτε καθεύδωμεν; the Vulgate, 'sive vigilemus [keep vigil], sive dormiamus' (Verdunoy, 'dans la veille ou dans le sommeil').

want. 'The punishment of him that wanteth the wedding garment' (*Matthew*, xxii, heading).

I.e., that lacks—is without—does not, at the time, possess.

A word of Scandinavian origin, probably Old Norse *vanta* (O.E.D.).

wantonness. 'Let us walk honestly [i.e., respectably; in a seemly fashion], as in the day; not in rioting and drunkenness, not in chambering and wantonness, not in strife and envying' (*Romans*, xiii, 13); 'When they speak great swelling words of vanity, they allure through the lusts of the flesh, through much wantonness, those that were clean escaped from them who live in error' (2 *Peter*, ii, 18).

Unchastity or, more precisely and probably, lasciviousness. The Gr. Test. has, in both passages, the plural of ἀσέλγεια, 'lewdness'; the sense, therefore, is 'acts of lewdness' (i.e., sexual caresses and intercourse). The Vulgate uses the plural of *impudicitia* in the former; *luxuria* in the latter.—Etymologically, *wantonness* = 'want or lack of disciple'; cf. preceding entry.

ward, adv. 'Used as a termination to denote motion towards a place; "to-*ward*", signifying "with regard to", when used of an action, and "towards" when actual direction is indicated. Thus "to us-ward" (. . . *Ephesians*, i, 19; 2 *Peter*, iii, 9), . . . "to you-ward" (2 *Corinthians*, xiii, 3; *Ephesians*, iii, 2)', Wright.

A construction that was very common in C. 16–17.

ward, n. 'When they were past the first and the second ward, they came unto the iron gate that leadeth unto the city' (*Acts*, xii, 10).

A guard, i.e. a body or company of guards or watchmen; not, as Wright admits as an alternative, a prison. The Gr. Test. has φυλακή, to which corresponds the *custodia* of the Vulgate (with Verdunoy's *garde*). *Ward* and *guard* are doublets of a Germanic original: the difference coming down to us, through M.E., from Old Fr. regional differentiation.

ware, adj. *Matthew*, xxiv, 50—in the edition of 1611; *Acts*, xiv, 6, 'They were ware of it, and fled unto Lystra and Derbe, cities of Lycaonia'; 2 *Timothy*, iv, 16, 'Of him be thou ware also; for he hath greatly withstood our words'.

In 'They were ware of it', *ware* = 'aware' or, more precisely, 'cognizant' or 'informed'; in 'Of him be thou ware', the meaning is rather 'Be cautious—on your guard—in respect to him'. Both nuances are obsolete; and had, since C. 18, been archaic. From O.E. *wær*, the word is of the common Germanic stock; *aware* is a derivative—at least in the sense that the O.E. original of *aware* is formed on O.E. *wær*.

ware, in *Luke*, viii, 27, = 'wore', the preterite of 'to *wear*' (clothes): this was the prevalent form in C. 15–17, being followed by *wore* in C. 16; the earliest form was *werede*.

warfare, go a; war a warfare. 'Who goeth a warfare anytime at his own charges?' (1 *Corinthians*, ix, 7): goes to war.— 'This charge I commit unto thee, son Timothy, . . . that thou . . . mightest war a good warfare' (1 *Timothy*, i, 18): wage war efficiently and effectually.

To *go a warfare* = *go a-warfare*, i.e. 'to go on or in warfare', *a* being the obsolescent preposition that we see in 'The church is a-building'. The phrase is of C. 15–mid 17.

To *war warfare* is of C. 16–early 17.—*Warfare* = *war-fare*; i.e., war-going.

watch; watching. Before the Captivity, there were three night-watches, whereas in *Matthew*, xiv, 25 (cf. *Mark*, xiii, 35) a fourth watch is mentioned, 'having been introduced among the Jews by the Romans. *Watch* and *wake* are the same word', i.e., they are doublets formed, by substantivization, from an O.E. verb that belongs to the common Germanic stock; 'hence a *watch* is the portion of time during which one watches or remains awake' (Wright). So in *Luke*, xii, 37, *watching* is a participle, meaning 'being on the watch, awake', and in 2 *Corinthians*, vi, 5, and xi, 27, *watching* is a n., meaning 'wakefulness' or 'sleeplessness'.

way. In the N.T., as in the O.T., *way* should be understood to signify 'road' wherever the interpretation 'road' indubitably yields the better sense, as Sir George Grove pointed out in Smith's *Dictionary of the Bible*. Usually the corresponding Gr. term is ὁδός; the corresponding Vulgate term, *via*: the primary sense of both the Gr. and the L. word is ('path' or) 'road'.

To *go one's way* (*Mark*, x, 52), like *go one's ways* (*Luke*, x, 3; *John*, xi, 46), is to depart: the former is archaic, the latter only dialectal now.

In *Mark*, viii, 3 and 27, and ix, 33 and 34—*Luke*, x, 4 and xxiv, 32—and 1 *Corinthians*, xvi, 7, *by the way* = 'on the road' (or, by implication, 'on the journey').

Way, the. 'He went into the synagogue, and spake boldly . . ., disputing and persuading the things concerning the kingdom of God. | But when divers were hardened, and believed not, but spake evil of that way before the multitude, he departed from them, and separated the disciples, disputing daily in the school of one Tyrannus' (*Acts*, xix, 8–9); cf. 'There arose no small stir about that way' (verse 23): briefly, *that way* = 'that course of life'.—'Jesus saith unto him [Thomas], I am the way, the truth, and the life' (*John*, xiv, 6): briefly, 'that course of life which leadeth to heaven—to eternal life'.

Cf. Massinger's *The Virgin Martyr* (1622), I, i, 'Have these my daughters reconciled themselves, | Abandoning for ever the Christian way, | To your opinion?', which illuminates the fact that, in the *Acts* passages, *way* = 'the Christian religion', for which it is usual to write, *the Way*. In Hastings, it is suggested that 'the way' and 'that way', in the three passages quoted above, might well be rendered 'the (or that) way of salvation', i.e., the way to salvation: cf. Cruden's 'the method of salvation, or doctrine of the gospel', which is a shade too narrow. In the Gr. Test., the term is ἡ ὁδός, glossed by Souter as '*the* way of life', i.e., Christianity. The Vulgate has *via Domini* in *Acts*, xix, 9 and 23, and simply *via* in *John*, xiv, 6 ('Ego sum via, et veritas, et vita'), Verdunoy's renderings being 'la voie (du Seigneur)' for the two passages from *Acts*, and 'le chemin' for the other. In Oriental religions, *way* stands rather for 'a set of rules concerning conduct'—ethical rather than religious.

well. 'Christ answered . . ., Whosoever drinketh of this water shall thirst again: | But whosoever drinketh of the water that I shall give him shall never thirst; but the water that I shall give him shall be in him a well of water springing up into everlasting life' (*John*, iv, 13–14).

'The force of [this passage] is greatly increased by remembering that "well" . . . originally signified a spring or fountain and not merely a pit containing water.

> 'It springeth up as doth a welle,
> Which may none of his stremes hide,
> But renneth out on every side.
>   Gower, *Confessio Amantis*, 1, 293',

as Wright says. This sense has, except in Scottish, been archaic since late C. 17 and obsolete since late C. 18. Ultimately from a Germanic verb meaning 'to bubble up' (cf. Swinburne's 'welling water's winsome word').

what. 'And they said, What need we any further witnesses? for we ourselves have heard of'—from—'his own mouth' (*Luke*, xxii, 71).

Here, *what* = 'why?'—'for what end? what purpose?'

In the Translators' Preface, 1611, we come upon the sentence, 'But what mention we three or four uses of the Scripture, whereas whatsoever is to be believed or practised, or hoped for, is contained in them?'—Cf. ' "But since he hath | Served well for Rome—" | "What do you prate of service?" ' (Shakespeare, *Coriolanus*, III, iii, 83).—'What sit we then projecting peace and war?' (Milton, *Paradise Lost*, II, 329).— (Wright; O.E.D.)

A mid C. 9–17 usage.

when as. 'Now the birth of Jesus Christ was on this wise: When as his mother Mary was espoused to Joseph, . . . she was found with child' (*Matthew*, i, 18).

I.e., when.

When as (in C. 17–20, also *whenas*) belongs to C. 15– mid 18, then it became archaic: its use in Scott and Maurice Hewlett is archaistic.

whereunto. See at **resemble.**

whether, conjunction. 'Whether it is easier to say to the sick of the palsy, Thy sins be forgiven thee; or to say, Arise, and take up thy bed and walk?' (*Mark*, ii, 9).

This use of *whether*, as an interrogative particle introducing a direct question expressive of a doubt between alternatives, has been archaic since ca. 1740 and virtually obsolete since ca. 1830. The Vulgate reads, 'Quid est facilius dicere paralytico: Dimittuntur tibi peccata; an dicere: Surge...' ('Lequel est le plus aisé, de dire...: Tes péchés sont pardonnés, ou de dire: Lève-toi...', Verdunoy).

whether, pronoun. 'Whether of them twain did the will of his father?' (*Matthew*, xxi, 31).

I.e., which of the two ...

Obsolete since ca. 1860, and archaic since C. 18. The word, which is of the common Germanic stock, derives direct from *whether* as an adjective = 'which' (C. 9–early 18).

while as. 'The way into the holiest of all was not yet made manifest, while as the first tabernacle was yet standing' (*Hebrews*, ix, 8).

The conjunction *while as*, 'while', flourished ca. 1560–1700; since ca. 1790, it has been archaic and, since ca. 1830, virtually obsolete. Often written as one word: cf. *whenas* and *whereas*.

whiles. 'Agree with thine adversary quickly, whiles thou art in the way with him' (*Matthew*, v, 25).

I.e., while. *Whiles*, the genitive of *while*, 'a portion of time', appeared first only in combination (*sumehwiles*, later *somewhiles*; *otherhwiles*, 'at other times'); it was current in late C. 15–mid 18, then it became archaic; moreover, it is mainly Scottish.

whisperer and **whispering,** n. The former occurs in *Romans*, i, 29; the latter in 2 *Corinthians*, xii, 20, 'Envyings, wraths, strifes, backbitings, whisperings'.

Whispering is 'secret and malicious information' (Wright);

a *whisperer* is 'a malicious tale-bearer; a secret informer (though not to the police); esp., a secret slanderer'. Both terms, in these senses, arose in C. 16 and became archaic ca. 1850.

In *Romans*, i, 29, the Vulgate has *susurrones*; in 2 *Corinthians*, xii, 20, *susurrationes*.

whit. 'Are ye angry at me, because I have made a man every whit whole on the sabbath day?' (*John*, vii, 23); 'He that is washed . . . is clean every whit' (*ibid.*, xiii, 10); 'I suppose I was not a whit behind the very chiefest apostles' (2 *Corinthians*, xi, 5).

Every whit (cf. the colloquial *every bit*: 'He's every bit as good as you are') = 'wholly' or 'entirely' and is obsolete; *not a whit* = 'not at all' (colloquially 'not a bit') and is merely an obsolescent cliché. Unrecorded before early C. 16, *whit* derives from O.E. *wight*, which in adverbial phrases bears the meaning 'amount' or 'degree'.

white, v. 'Ye are like unto whited sepulchres' (*Matthew*, xxiii, 27); 'His raiment became shining, exceeding white as snow; so as no fuller on earth can white them' (*Mark*, ix, 3).

White, 'to whiten' (make white), is archaic; the specific sense, 'to bleach' (as in the *Mark* passage), has been obsolete since ca. 1750. It comes from the O.E. *hwitian*, 'to whiten' (itself from adj. *hwit*, 'white').

whole and **wholesome.** 'They that be whole need not a physician, but they that are sick' (*Matthew*, ix, 12); 'And they . . . found the servant whole that had been sick' (*Luke*, vii, 10).—'Wholesome words, even the words of our Lord Jesus Christ' (1 *Timothy*, vi, 3).

Whole is 'in good health' (L. *integer vitæ*), 'healthy', 'hale' (a doublet of *whole*), a sense that has been archaic since C. 18; cognate is the archaic sense, 'unhurt, uninjured, unwounded', i.e., with skin, organs, body *entire* (unbroken).

Wholesome words are beneficial or salutary words: words conducive to spiritual well-being.

whore occurs four times in the N.T.—but only in *Revelation*; in reference to *the Whore of Babylon*, i.e. figuratively. The corresponding Gr. Test. word is πόρνη (a prostitute), which is used in all four passages (*Revelation*, xvii, 1, 15, 16, and xix, 2); the Vulgate has *meretrix* (except in xvii, 16, where *fornicaria* is preferred). '*Whore* is now confined to coarse and abusive speech, except in occasional echoes of historical expressions, as *the whore of Babylon*' (O.E.D.). Origin: Old Norse *hora*. The spelling in *wh* arose in C. 16.
    Cf. **harlot**.

whoremonger. (Five times in the N.T.: not at all in the O.T.) A lecher or fornicator; esp. (and originally) a fornicator that frequents whores. The term came into English in 1526, with Tyndale's rendering of *Ephesians*, v, 5, which passage is, in the A.V., 'No whoremonger, nor unclean person, . . . hath any inheritance in the kingdom of Christ': Gr. Test., πόρνος; Vulgate, 'fornicator'.

wicked, n. 'And then shall that Wicked be revealed, whom the Lord shall consume with the spirit of his mouth'—with his breath—'and shall destroy with the brightness of his coming' (2 *Thessalonians*, ii, 8).
    Gr. Test., Καὶ τότε ἀποκαλυφθήσεται ὁ ἄνομος (lit., the lawless one; hence, the sinful one); Vulgate, 'Et tunc revelabitur ille iniquus' ('et alors se manifestera l'impie', Verdunoy). And cf. *Ephesians*, vi, 16, 'Above all, taking the shield of faith, wherewith ye shall be able to quench all the fiery darts of the wicked' (Gr. Test., τοῦ πονηροῦ: Vulgate, 'nequissimi': Verdunoy, 'du Mauvais': R.V., 'of the evil one'.

will, v. 'She came in straightway with haste unto the king, and asked, saying, I will that thou give me by and by in a charger the head of John the Baptist' (*Mark*, vi, 25); 'It is not of him that willeth, nor of him that runneth, but of God that sheweth mercy' (*Romans*, ix, 16); 'These things I will that thou affirm constantly' (*Titus*, iii, 8).
    This sense of *will*—'to desire, to wish'—has been obsolete

since ca. 1860; during the preceding hundred years, it was archaic. (But the past tense, *would*, survives in literary English, 'I would that he were here'.) The verb *will* is of common Germanic stock.

will-worship. 'Which things have indeed a shew of wisdom in will worship, and humility, and neglecting of the body' (*Colossians*, ii, 23).

The Gr. Test. has ἅτινά ἐστι λόγον μὲν ἔχοντα σοφίας ἐν ἐθελοθρησκείᾳ, 'which are things corresponding to—having an analogy to—wisdom in service (or worship) of the will', i.e. 'in worship of self', but probably, as Souter suggests, the context favours 'in worship of the angels'; the Vulgate has 'Quæ sunt rationem quidem habentia sapientiæ in superstitione', but *in superstitione* is too strong; Verdunoy renders it as 'culte spontané' and in the gloss renders it more precise as 'culte exagéré des anges'.

In post-A.V. writers (mostly theologians) there has been a tendency to restore the term *will-worship* to the sense suggested by the Gr. compound and to make it mean 'worship according to one's own will; or worship imposed by human will; but, in either case, without divine authority', as the O.E.D. shows.

wine; wine-bibber. A *wine-bibber*, 'a continual drinker of wine', is a drunkard (see also **bibber**), as in 'The Son of man came eating and drinking, and they say, Behold a man gluttonous, and a winebibber, a friend of publicans and sinners' (*Matthew*, xi, 19).

'One of the words which seem open to a good deal of misuse is "wine"; and it might be worth your while to go into the differences (if any) between the original Greek words, oinos [οἶνος, L. *vinum*], etc. The rabid prohibitionist is apt to suppose that the Cana miracle resulted in nothing better than unfermented grape juice, which seems a poor kind of drink for a wedding' (a University friend, in a letter—June 30, 1939—to the writer). To suppose that *to turn water into wine = to turn water not into wine but into a grape-juice cordial* is gratuitous wrong-headedness; Christ was no pussy-footing prohibitionist, but an unsnobbish mingler with men. He was, however, abstemious.

winefat. 'A certain man planted a vineyard, and set an hedge about it, and digged a place for the winefat' (*Mark*, xii, 1).

I.e. 'wine-vat': 'the vessel into which the liquor flows from the wine-press', says Wright; but this is incorrect, for, properly, the wine-vat is that vat in which grapes are pressed in the process of wine-making, hence the wine-press itself.

Winefat (or *wine-fat*) is a C. 16–17 form.

wise. 'Now the birth of Jesus Christ was on this wise' (*Matthew*, i, 18) *wise*, used thus, occurs in three other N.T. passages; *in no wise*, 'in no fashion', i.e. 'not at all', occurs in seven.

Wise, 'way, manner', is archaic, but it was common in C. 15–17. The O.E. *wise* (of common Germanic stock: cf. the cognate Gr. εἶδος, 'form, shape') signified 'manner, mode, condition', also 'thing, affair; cause, reason' (O.E.D.).

wise, on this. See **on this wise.**

wish, v. 'Fearing lest we should have fallen upon rocks, they cast four anchors out of the stern, and wished for the day' (*Acts*, xxvii, 29).

I.e., longed for. *Wish*, 'to long, to yearn', was current in C. 13–mid 17; since C. 17, it has become much less intense.

wist, 'knew', occurs in *Mark*, ix, 6, 'He wist not what to say' (cf. xiv, 40); *Luke*, ii, 49, 'Wist ye not that I must be about my Father's business?'; *John*, v, 13; *Acts*, xii, 9, and xxiii, 5.

Wist is the preterite of the archaic *wit*, 'to know', which comes from O.E. *witan* (of the common Germanic stock: cf. Ger. *wissen*).

wit, v. 'Moreover, brethren, we do you to wit of the grace of God bestowed on the churches of Macedonia' (2 *Corinthians*, viii, 1).

To *wit* is to know (see *wist*); 'we do you to wit' means 'we cause you to know': cf. ' "Now go thou, sir Lucan," said the king, "and doe me to wite what betokeneth that noise in the field" ' (Malory, quoted by Wright).

withal. 'It seemeth to me unreasonable to send a prisoner, and not withal to signify the crimes laid'—charged—'against him' (*Acts*, xxv, 27).

Lit., *with all*, it means primarily 'along with the rest'; here, 'at the same time' (late C. 16–20; now archaic).

without = 'beyond' in 'We will not boast of things without our measure' (2 *Corinthians*, x, 13—cf. verse 15).

This sense of *without* belongs to C. 15–mid 17. With *without measure*, cf. Fr. *outre mesure*. The Gr. Test. has εἰς τὰ ἄμετρα ('to a limitless degree', Souter); the Vulgate, 'in immensum'.

witness, n. and v. *Witness*, applied to a person, is frequent in the N.T.; as 'evidence, testimony', it is no less frequent; in *John*, i, 7, both senses occur within the compass of one short sentence, 'The same came for a witness'—i.e., as a witness— 'to bear witness of the Light'.—The v. is both transitive and intransitive: 'to attest' or 'to testify'; 'to give evidence' or 'to give evidence against'; as, e.g., in 'The Holy Ghost witnesseth in every city, saying that bonds and afflictions abide me' (*Acts*, xx, 23) and 'There he receiveth them, of [= by] whom it is witnessed that he liveth' (*Hebrews*, vii, 8). The phrase, 'to witness witness' (*John*, v, 32) = 'to bear witness'.

Witness, v., which derives directly from the n., is apparently unrecorded before ca. 1300, whereas the n. occurs at least as early as 950 in writing and prob. as early as C. 8 in speech. *Witness*, n., is, in O.E., *witnes*, i.e. *wit*, 'knowledge', + the prefix *-nes* (our *-ness*). Originally an abstract n., it very early became concrete and agential: cf. the sense-development of Fr. *témoin* (L. *testimonium*).

The Gr. Test. for 'a witness' (person) or 'witness' (evidence) has respectively μάρτυς (in *Acts*, xxii, 20, and *Revelation*, ii, 13, the sense approximates to that of the derivative *martyr*, 'one who bears witness to his faith by dying for it'), accusative μάρτυρα, and μαρτύριον.

wont, adj. (originally participial), 'accustomed'—now archaic—is to be found in four N.T. passages:—*Matthew*, xxvii, 15, 'Now at that feast the governor was wont to release unto the people a prisoner'; *Mark*, x, 1, 'As he was wont, he taught them again'; *Luke*, xxii, 39, 'He came out, and went, as he was wont, to the mount of olives'; *Acts*, xvi, 13, 'A river side, where prayer was wont to be made'.

   Wont is the past participle of the obsolete *won*, 'to be accustomed or used (to do something)', a sense deriving from the primary one, 'to stay habitually, to dwell (with a person or in a place)'; this *won* represents O.E. *wunian*, which is of the common Germanic stock.

Word, the. Passages bearing upon the theological and philosophical use of *word* are these:—'The sower soweth the word' (*Mark*, iv, 14, in reference to the Parable of the Sower); above all, 'In the beginning was the Word, and the Word was with God, and the Word was God' (*Iohn*, i, 1), the Gr. Test. having Ἐν ἀρχῇ ἦν ὁ λόγος, καὶ ὁ λόγος ἦν πρὸς τὸν Θεόν, καὶ Θεὸς ἦν ὁ λόγος, and the Vulgate, 'In principio erat Verbum, et Verbum erat apud Deum, et Deus erat Verbum', rendered by Verdunoy as 'Au commencement était le Verbe, et le Verbe était auprès de Dieu, et le Verbe était Dieu' or, in the Introduction to the Gospel, 'Dans le principe était le Verbe, et le Verbe était auprès de l'être divin, et être divin était le Verbe',—from which passages one notes that the A.V., the Vulgate (*verbum*'s emphatic position at end of sentence), and Verdunoy make *word* the subject of the last part of the triad ('the Word was God'), whereas the Gr. Test. apparently makes God (Θεός: *Deus*) the subject; 'When ye received the word of God which ye heard of us, ye received it not as the word of men, but as it is in truth, the word of God, which effectually worketh also in you that believe' (1 *Thessalonians*, ii, 13), Gr. Test. ἀλλὰ . . . λόγον Θεοῦ, ὅς καὶ ἐνεργεῖται (is operative) ἐν ὑμῖν τοῖς πιστεύουσιν, Vulgate 'Sed . . . verbum Dei, qui [not *quod*] operatur in vobis qui credistis'; 'Upholding all things by the word of his power' (*Hebrews*, i, 3: in reference to Christ), Gr. Test. φέρων τε τὰ πάντα τῷ ῥήματι (utterance) τῆς δυνάμεως αὐτοῦ, Vulgate 'portansque omnia verbo virtutis suæ'; 'There are three that bear record in heaven, the Father, the Word, and the Holy Ghost: and these three are one' (1 *John*, v, 7), the Vulgate reading 'Tres sunt qui testimonium dant in cælo: Pater, Verbum, et Spiritus sanctus; et hi tres unum sunt', this passage being absent from the Gr. Test. and Christ being here equated with *the word incarnate* (made flesh) —*le verbe incarné*.

Into the theology, it is not my business to go; for a comment on the philosophy, see Partridge, p. 2, footnote 2; for the etymology of *word*, see the O.E.D.—for λόγος, and ῥῆμα, see Souter—for λόγος, see also R. C. Trench, *Synonyms of the New Testament*, 7th ed., 1871, at pp. 272, 315–20—for *verbum*, see Lewis & Short; for the semantics of *le Verbe*, see Littré. But theological and philosophical students will, in general, consult Hastings at *word* and, in particular, Archbishop J. H. Bernard's *Commentary on the Gospel of St. John*, for *John*, i, 1.

work, v. 'The law worketh wrath' (*Romans*, iv, 15); 'Tribulation worketh patience' (*ibid.*, v, 3); 'The sorrow of the world worketh death' (2 *Corinthians*, vii, 10).

I.e., 'to produce' (prob. via the old sense, 'to create'), a sense that has been obsolete since ca. 1850. The modern verb is the result of a merging of two O.E. verbs, *wyrcan* and *wircan*.

The Gr. Test. and Vulgate readings help to render the meaning clearer: ὁ γὰρ νόμος ὀργὴν κατεργάζεται (accomplishes) and 'Lex enim iram operatur' ('Car la Loi a produit la colère', Verdunoy); κατεργάζεται recurs in *Romans*, v, 3, and 2 *Corinthians*, vii, 10, and so does *operatur*.

work-fellow. 'Timotheus my workfellow, and Lucius, and Jason, and Sosipater, my kinmen, salute you' (*Romans*, xvi, 21): Gr. Test. ὁ συνεϱγός μου.

Introduced by Tyndale, *work-fellow* has, since ca. 1850, given way to *work-mate*. Lit., a work-companion.

works, good. See **good works.**

worship. 'He may say unto thee, Friend, go up higher [at table]: then shalt thou have worship in the presence of them that sit at meat with thee' (*Luke*, xiv, 10).

I.e., respect or honour—a sense current ca. 1000–1630. *Worship* is O.E. *weorthscipe*, lit., *worth* (value) + *ship*, a prefix denoting state or condition; cf. *hardship*.

worthy. 'He that knew not, and did commit things worthy of stripes, shall be beaten with few stripes' (*Luke*, xii, 48); 'They which commit such things are worthy of death' (*Romans*, i, 32).

In early Modern English, *worthy* was a neutral word: 'deserving' (of good, of ill, of either good or ill); lit., 'of precisely a *worth* or value to . . .'. With the passages above, cf. 'He that steleth any part of a man's substaunce, is worthy to lose his lyfe', Sir John Cheke, *The Hurt of Sedicion*, 1549. This construction is slightly archaic.

wrest. '. . . Things hard to be understood, which they that are unlearned and unstable wrest, as they do also the other scriptures, unto their own destruction' (*2 Peter*, iii, 16).

From O.E. *wræstan*, of common Germanic stock. The sense here, 'to overstrain the meaning or the bearing of (a passage or a word)', was very common, the O.E.D. tells us, ca. 1575–1700; 'He can . . . wrest the obvious meaning of a passage to perfection', T. R. Glover, 1909. The corresponding verb in the N.T. is στϱεβλόω, lit., 'I twist, . . . stretch on the rack', hence 'strain'; the Vulgate has 'depravant' (they debase).

writing table. See **table.**

Y

yoke-fellow. 'And I entreat thee also, true yokefellow, help those women which laboured with me in the gospel' (*Philippians*, iv, 3).

I.e., fellow-worker; lit., a person 'yoked' with another, i.e. associated with him in work or in other occupation; the derivative sense, 'a husband, a wife' (generically, 'a spouse'), has fallen into disuse. It is Tyndale's rendering (1526) of σύζυγος, in the Gr. Test. γνήσιε σύζυγε (Vulgate, 'germane compar'), σύζυγος being a shortened form of σύνζυγος, which Souter renders as 'yoke-fellow, companion, colleague'; but there is reason for thinking that it is a proper name: 'Perhaps a proper name', says Souter; 'Littéralement "véritable Synzygos" (collaborateur). La Vulgate a pris le nom propre pour un nom commun ("compar")', says Verdunoy—without a precautionary 'perhaps'.

you-ward. See **to you-ward.**

yourselves is nominative (subject of the sentence) in 'Yourselves know that we are appointed thereunto' (1 *Thessalonians*, iii, 3); 'Yourselves know perfectly that the day of the Lord so cometh as a thief in the night' (*ibid.*, v, 2: where *so* is tautological).

Ourselves and *themselves*—*myself, yourself, himself,* and *herself*: all these were used in this way in the 16th and 17th Centuries; since then, their employment in the role of self-contained nominatives has been archaic and, since ca. 1850, somewhat affected—except in verse, where they subserve the poet in overcoming some metrical difficulty.

Z

zeal; zealous, zealously. 'I bear them [the Israelites] record that they have a zeal of God, but not according to knowledge' (*Romans*, x, 2); 'Ye sorrowed after a godly sort, what care-

fulness [anxiety] it wrought in you, yea, what clearing
[excusing] of yourselves, yea, what indignation, yea, what
fear, yea, what vehement desire, yea, what zeal, yea, what
revenge', i.e., desire for revenge (2 *Corinthians*, vii, 11); 'I
know the forwardness [eagerness] of your mind ... ; and
your zeal hath provoked [incited] many' (*ibid.*, ix, 2); 'Concerning zeal, persecuting the church' (*Philippians*, iii, 6)—Vulgate, 'secundum æmulationem, persequens ecclesiam Dei', the
subject being *ego*; 'I bear him record, that he hath a great zeal
for you' (*Colossians*, iv, 13).—'Zealous of the law' (*Acts*, xxi,
20); 'zealous toward God' (*ibid.*, xxii, 3); and in four other
N.T. passages.—'They zealously affect you' (*Galatians*, iv,
17); 'It is good to be zealously affected always in a good
thing' (*ibid.*, verse 18).

Zeal (in C. 14, *zeel* or *zele*) was used by translators of *The
Bible* to render both L. *zelus* (or its synonym *æmulatio*) and its
original, the Gr. ζῆλος, which signifies 'fervour', hence
'ardent love' or 'righteous indignation', according to the context; generally there is a connotation either of rivalry or of
partisanship.

In *Romans*, x, 2, the Gr. Test. reads, ζῆλον Θεοῦ (enthu-
siasm for God) ἔχουσι; the Vulgate, 'æmulationem Dei
habent, sed non secundum scientiam'. In 2 *Corinthians*, vii, 2,
the L. word is *æmulatio*, the Gr. is ζῆλος; in 2 *Corinthians*,
ix, 2, the same; in *Colossians*, iv, 13, the Gr. word is πόνος
(labour; trouble), the L. is *labor*.

Zion or **Sion.** 'Behold, I lay in Sion a stumbling-stone and
a rock of offence' (*Romans*, ix, 33: Vulgate, 'Ecce pono in
Sion lapidem offensionis, et petram scandali'); 'And so all
Israel shall be saved: as it is written, There shall come out of
Sion the Deliverer' (*ibid.*, xi, 26: Vulgate, 'Veniet ex Sion qui
eripiat').

The N.T. Gr. form is Σιών; the ordinary Gr. form is Σεῖον
or Σειών, on Heb. tsīyōn. *Sion* or *Zion*, or, in full, *Mount
Zion* (lit., 'the lofty mount'), is that mountain 'on which the
Davidic citadel of Jerusalem was built, and thus the centre

of the life of the people Israel' (Souter). Among Jews, the word abounds in religious, theological, and historical overtones and connotations: to them it is no mere *nomen*; it is almost *numen*.

Sion is the earliest English form; *Zion* did not arise until C. 17; an intermediate form was Syon (C. 15).

THE CHRISTIAN LIBRARY

Classics of the Christian faith in deluxe, hardcover, gold stamped, gift editions. These beautifully crafted volumes are in matching burgundy leatherette bindings so you can purchase a complete set or pick and choose. All books are complete and unabridged and are printed in good readable print. **Only $6.95 each!**

ABIDE IN CHRIST, Andrew Murray
BEN-HUR: A TALE OF THE CHRIST, Lew Wallace
CHRISTIAN'S SECRET OF A HAPPY LIFE,
Hannah Whitall Smith
CONFESSIONS OF ST. AUGUSTINE
DAILY LIGHT, Samuel Bagster
EACH NEW DAY, Corrie ten Boom
FOXE'S CHRISTIAN MARTYRS OF THE WORLD,
John Foxe
GOD AT EVENTIDE, A.J. Russell
GOD CALLING, A.J. Russell
GOD OF ALL COMFORT, Hannah Whitall Smith
GOD'S SMUGGLER, Brother Andrew
HIDING PLACE, THE, Corrie ten Boom
HIND'S FEET ON HIGH PLACES, Hannah Hurnard
IMITATION OF CHRIST, THE, Thomas A. Kempis
IN HIS STEPS, Charles M. Sheldon
MERE CHRISTIANITY, C.S. Lewis
MY UTMOST FOR HIS HIGHEST, Oswald Chambers
PILGRIM'S PROGRESS, John Bunyan
POWER THROUGH PRAYER / PURPOSE IN PRAYER,
E.M. Bounds
QUIET TALKS ON PRAYER, S.D. Gordon
SCREWTAPE LETTERS, C.S. Lewis
WHO'S WHO IN THE BIBLE, Frank S. Mead

Available wherever books are sold.

or order from:

Barbour and Company, Inc.
164 Mill Street   Box 1219
Westwood, New Jersey   07675

If you order by mail add $2.00 to your order for shipping.

INSPIRATIONAL LIBRARY

Beautiful purse / pocket size editions of Christian Classics bound in flexible leatherette or genuine Bonded Leather. The Bonded Leather editions have gold edges and make beautiful gifts.

THE BIBLE PROMISE BOOK   Over 1000 promises from God's Word arranged by topic. What does the Bible promise about matters like: Anger, Illness, Jealousy, Sex, Money, Old Age, et cetera, et cetera.

> *Flexible Leatherette* . . . . **$ 3.95**
> *Genuine Bonded Leather* **$10.95**

DAILY LIGHT   One of the most popular daily devotionals with readings for both morning and evening. One page for each day of the year.

> *Flexible Leatherette* . . . . **$ 3.95**
> *Genuine Bonded Leather* **$10.95**

WISDOM FROM THE BIBLE   Daily thoughts from the Proverbs which communicate truth about ourselves and the world around us. One page for each day in the year.

> *Flexible Leatherette* . . . . **$ 3.95**
> *Genuine Bonded Leather* **$10.95**

MY DAILY PRAYER JOURNAL   Each page is dated a has a Scripture verse and ample room for you to record you thoughts, prayers and praises. One page for each day of the year.

> *Flexible Leatherette* . . . . **$ 3.95**
> *Genuine Bonded Leather* **$10.95**

Available wherever books are sold.

or order from:
Barbour and Company, Inc.
164 Mill Street   Box 1219
Westwood, New Jersey   07675

If you order by mail add $1.00 to your order for shipping.